FOR THE SAKE
OF EXAMPLE

ALSO BY ANTHONY BABINGTON

Autobiographical:

No Memorial

Historical:

The Power to Silence
A History of Punishment in Britain

A House in Bow Street
Crime and the Magistracy, London 1740–1881

The English Bastille
A History of Newgate Gaol and Prison Conditions
in Britain 1188–1902

The Rule of Law in Britain
From the Roman Occupation to the present day

FOR THE SAKE OF EXAMPLE

CAPITAL COURTS-MARTIAL
1914–1920

BY

ANTHONY BABINGTON

WITH A POSTSCRIPT BY
MAJOR-GENERAL FRANK RICHARDSON
CB, DSO, OBE, MD

LEO COOPER
IN ASSOCIATION WITH
SECKER & WARBURG

First published by Leo Cooper in association with
Secker & Warburg Ltd,
54 Poland Street, London W1V 3DF

ISBN 0-436-03050-0

Photoset in Great Britain by
Rowland Phototypesetting Ltd, Bury St Edmunds, Suffolk
and printed in Great Britain by Billing & Sons Ltd, Worcester

CONTENTS

*I consider all punishment to be
for the sake of example and the
punishment of military men in
particular is expedient only in
cases where the prevalence of
any crime, or the evils resulting
from it, are likely to be
injurious to the public interest.*

THE DUKE OF WELLINGTON

ACKNOWLEDGEMENTS

I should like to express my deepest gratitude to Mr J. C. Andrews, FLA, the Chief Librarian, Mr Charles Potts, MBE, MA, ALA, the Head of the Military Section and Miss Stephanie Glover, ALA, at the Ministry of Defence Library, Whitehall, for their constant help and advice with regard to published material during the preparation of this book. Also to Miss Erica Watson, lately on the staff of the Library, who always gave me such invaluable assistance.

I am particularly grateful for the judgment, guidance, and encouragement of my literary agent, David Fletcher, who read successive sections of the book whilst I was writing it and whose comments were invariably both cogent and constructive.

I want to thank Reginald Pound, biographer of A. P. Herbert, for certain details of A.P.H.'s service with the Royal Naval Division in the First World War, and to Brigadier B. B. Rackham, CBE, MC, who actually served with him in France and who has supplied me with much useful and interesting information. In my efforts to find out the facts regarding capital courts martial in the armies of other nations involved in the fighting on the Western Front I have been greatly assisted by the Army Attaché at the French Embassy in London and by the Defence Attachés at the Embassies of the United States of America and the Federal Republic of Germany. I have also received help in this matter from the Military History Research Department at Freiburg. I am indebted to the Commonwealth War Graves Commission for information about the instructions issued on the Western Front for the burial of executed men and to the Public Information Office at the House of Commons for certain details concerning Ernest Thurtle's career. I am also indebted to Mr Julian Sykes for his valuable help particularly in relation to the footnotes on pp. 94 and 106.

I am grateful to the Department of Sound Records at the Imperial War Museum for permission to quote from their recorded interviews with men who had served on the Western Front.

Lastly, I wish to express my most sincere gratitude to Miss Margaret Waldron who has typed the book for me.

PREFACE

THE NUMBER OF soldiers in the British Army who were executed by firing squads during the First World War is utterly insignificant compared with the massive carnage at the front. They are the unremembered. At the time of their condemnation they were branded as 'shirkers', 'funks' and 'degenerates', whose very existence was best forgotten. Yet, ever since, the manner in which they were tried and their subsequent treatment have given rise to a profound uneasiness in the national conscience. Death did not come to them, random and abrupt, on the field of battle; it came with measured tread as the calculated climax of an archaic and macabre ritual carried out, supposedly, in the interests of discipline and morale.

The files relating to the courts martial of these men have been closed to the public ever since. For more than sixty years they have lain in the archives as a missing chapter from the history of the war – a chapter without which it would be difficult to form a definitive evaluation of the attitude of the government ministers and the senior commanders to the troops who were fighting in the line.

It can now be revealed that the general disquiet about these events has been more than justified. Viewed by the standards of today few of the executed men received the most elemental form of justice. They were tried and sentenced by courts which often regarded themselves as mere components of the penal process and which, until the final year of the war, were asked to perform a complex judicial function without any sort of legal guidance. The cases for the accused were seldom presented adequately and sometimes were never presented at all. If crucial matters were raised which might have established their innocence they were rarely investigated by members of the court. Capital sentences were passed, and were later sanctioned by senior officers, with no proper enquiries being made into the backgrounds of those who were being condemned or into other factors which might have served to mitigate their punishment. And at the end, they were only told of their impending executions a matter of hours before being taken out and shot, usually in front of an audience of enforced spectators. What made it even worse was the fact that the decision of a court martial was virtually unappealable.

If soldiers accused of cowardice or of desertion in the face of the enemy had looked to the medical officers for assistance or compassion then they were likely to have looked in vain. The army doctors as a whole seem to have set themselves up as an extra branch of the provost corps, intent on securing the extreme penalty for such offenders whenever possible.

Undoubtedly the ministers responsible for military affairs were in a position to ameliorate these procedures, had they wished to do so. Instead, they frequently misled Parliament when they were pressed for information concerning executions which were taking place in the field.

I am very much aware of the distress which could still be occasioned to the relations of the executed men if their names were revealed, and I have avoided giving any particulars, including the names of their units, from which they might be identified. They are the central figures in this grim story but throughout the following pages they must remain anonymous.

Lastly I would like to emphasize that any opinions expressed in this book are entirely my own and for those opinions I and my publisher, between us, take full responsibility.

I
THE TRANSITION TO WAR

B RITAIN'S INVOLVEMENT IN the struggle which had broken out on the Continent of Europe during the summer of 1914 followed with dramatic suddenness after the mighty German armies had swept across the frontiers of neutral Belgium.

When Britain declared war on Germany on 4 August 1914, she could with difficulty muster an expeditionary force of some 160,000 officers and men, comprising six infantry divisions and one cavalry division together with supporting arms. Although these troops were well-disciplined and highly-trained regular soldiers, reinforced with a number of hastily-mobilized reservists, they were unprepared and ill-equipped for the conditions of warfare which they were about to encounter.

The British Expeditionary Force, thereafter known as the BEF, began to embark from Southampton on 9 August. Having arrived at ports on the north coast of France they were taken by train to a concentration area between Maubeuge and Le Câteau. Their tactical role had neither been planned nor prepared. Lord Kitchener, the Secretary of State for War, had issued a somewhat vague directive to General Sir John French, the British Commander-in-Chief, stating:

> The special motive of the Force under your control is to support and co-operate with the French Army against our common enemies. The peculiar task laid upon you is to assist the French Government in preventing or repelling the invasion by Germany of French and Belgian territory, and eventually to restore the neutrality of Belgium, on behalf of which, as guaranteed by treaty, Belgium has appealed to the French and to ourselves.

For centuries the British Army had been governed by a system of control which was once referred to as the 'discipline of fear'. Until 1881 the principal instrument of punishment was the cat-o'-nine-tails. Flogging parades were a habitual occurrence, the miscreant being stripped to the waist and pinioned to a triangle of halberds, with the rest of his regiment or brigade watching as enforced spectators while the thongs descended on his blotched and bleeding flesh.

A Royal Commission which issued its Report in 1836[1] had heard evidence from numerous witnesses that young soldiers frequently fainted on flogging parades. A sergeant in the Foot Guards had said that the fainting was caused both by the sight of the victim's back and by his cries. 'The cries,' he added, 'are as distressing as the sight.' The Commissioners reported their unanimous opinion that the infliction of corporal punishment in the Army was essential for the maintenance of proper discipline; the fact of its being carried out in public provided a beneficial example which served to prevent 'the spreading of a disorderly or mutinous spirit'. They compared the system of punishment in the French Army where there was no flogging, but where, in consequence, no less than 45 offences were punishable with death. A military execution in the British Army was unknown in peacetime, said the Commissioners. 'On active service,' they continued, 'although sometimes resorted to, it is less common than in the French service in which it is the basis of discipline.'

By then an execution in the British Army for a military offence had indeed become a rarity even when regiments were campaigning overseas. The records of courts martial held throughout the world were listed in a central register in London, and a cursory search through the volumes for the period from 1853 to 1856 has not revealed a single death sentence imposed during the Crimean War. There were many trials for such offences as desertion, absence without leave, disobedience, sleeping on post, quitting post, insubordination, and striking a superior officer. The usual punishment awarded was 25 or 50 lashes or, more infrequently, a period of detention with hard labour. Two private soldiers who deserted during the siege of Sebastopol were sentenced to penal servitude for life.

In his authoritative study of the discipline and constitution of the British Army which was published in 1869,[2] Charles M. Clode assumed that capital punishment for desertion was a thing of the past. Clode had made a detailed study of the War Office records and the most recent case he mentioned of a death sentence for desertion occurred as far back as 1803.

Flogging was finally abolished in the British Army in 1881. Eighteen years later when Britain became involved in her next major military conflict it might have been imagined that an increased reliance would be placed on the death penalty, but this was not the case. The War Office court martial returns for the years 1899 to 1902, the period of the Boer War, show that very few executions were carried out in South Africa. The usual sentences for the offences of desertion and sleeping on post varied between a few months' imprisonment with hard labour and ten years' penal servitude; those for quitting post and shamefully delivering up a position ranged to a maximum of 15 years' penal servitude; for striking a superior officer a soldier might be sentenced to as little as 28 days' Field Punishment or as much as ten years' penal servitude. The customary sentence for cowardice seems to have been ten years' penal servitude, but this was frequently commuted to a considerably shorter period.

The court martial returns for the South African campaign show that no executions took place in 1899 and 1900 while Lord Roberts was Commander-in-Chief. Nor did the policy in regard to capital punishment become appreciably harsher when Roberts was succeeded by Kitchener. This is a little surprising as Kitchener had a reputation for brutality and was, said his biographer, 'filled with a ruthlessness which took no account of personal feelings'.[3] Although he confirmed two death sentences in 1901, one for desertion and one for murder, he commuted several others, imposed for cowardice, desertion, sleeping on post, and murder, to terms of imprisonment or penal servitude. In 1902 two Australian officers were executed for the reprisal killing of Boer prisoners during the bitter guerrilla warfare which ensued before the signing of the peace treaty in May 1902.

When the British Army went into action in the summer of 1914, a number of offences were still punishable with death or with such a lesser penalty as the court martial thought fit to impose. These included mutiny, cowardice before the enemy, disobedience of a lawful order, desertion or attempted desertion, sleeping or being drunk on post, striking a superior officer, casting away arms or ammunition in the presence of the enemy, leaving a post without orders, abandoning a position, and treacherously communicating with or in any way assisting the enemy. A soldier was guilty of desertion if he went absent with the intention of never returning to the Army or with the intention of avoiding 'some particular important service'.

By 20 August 1914 the concentration of the BEF was virtually complete and on the following day five British divisions began their advance into Belgium, co-ordinating their progress with that of the two French armies moving to their right. The Belgian defence forces, crushed by sheer weight of numbers and of firepower, were falling back on Antwerp and the invading Germans were poised for the continuation of their march towards the French frontier. Captain Walter Bloem, a novelist and playwright serving as a reserve officer in the Brandenburg Grenadiers, commented joyfully, 'It was fabulous, surely a dream. Was the whole war just a game, a kind of sport? Was the Belgian Army just a pack of hares?'[4] The knowledge that the BEF were moving into position to engage them did not cause Bloem any undue concern. He wrote:[5]

English soldiers? We knew what they looked like by the comic papers; short scarlet tunics with small caps set at an angle on their heads, or bearskins with the chin-strap under the lip instead of under the chin. There was much joking about this, and also about Bismarck's remark of sending the police to arrest the English Army.

On 22 August the BEF made their first contact with the leading German units in the vicinity of Mons and on 23 August they were involved in severe fighting for most of the day. It was not an easy baptism of fire for the untried British troops. The weather was oppressively hot and sultry and many of them were still suffering from the after-effects of their recent inoculations. In addition, the uneven surfaces of the rough cobbled Belgian roads had increased the strain and fatigue of their long forced march.

After his initial engagement with the BEF Walter Bloem was to change his opinion about them. Bloem's regiment, so proud and confident in its martial tradition, had been decisively repulsed and reduced to little more than company strength. 'Wherever I looked, right or left,' he said, 'were dead and wounded, quivering in convulsions, groaning terribly, blood oozing from fresh wounds.' He added bitterly, 'They apparently knew something about war, these cursed English, a fact soon confirmed on all sides.'[6]

On 24 August the British Commander-in-Chief received information that the French armies on his immediate right were in process of withdrawing, leaving exposed the whole of his southern flank. There followed the BEF's retreat from Mons which continued with scarcely a pause until 5 September when they drew up in a defensive line to the south-east of Paris. During this time they covered a distance of about 200 miles and in the constant fighting suffered casualties of almost 20,000 in killed, wounded and missing. According to the British Official History of the campaign, they had been:

> confronted with greatly superior numbers by the most renowned army in Europe, and condemned at the very outset to undergo the severest ordeal which can be imposed upon an army. They were short of food and sleep when they began their retreat; they continued it, always short of food and sleep, for thirteen days; and at the end of the retreat they were still an army, and a formidable army.

It has been estimated that during the retreat the men in the infantry only managed to obtain an average of four hours' rest a day. The Official History quotes one of the officers as saying, 'I would never have believed that men could have been so tired and so hungry and yet live.'

To the pursuing Germans, said Bloem, the retreat of the BEF resembled a hasty departure rather than a disorderly rout. They left behind them 'broken-down cars, burnt supplies, and so on, but no rifles or equipment'.[7] The British prisoners seen by Bloem were 'fine, smart young fellows', but were 'almost insolent in their cool off-handedness'.[8] He tells of one incident which characterized the savage nature of the hand-to-hand combat throughout this phase of the campaign. Two officers and 25 men from a British infantry battalion had penetrated a wood occupied by the Germans. The British party was isolated and surrounded but decided to fight it out. In the end 23 of them, including both the officers, were killed and the four survivors were taken prisoner. Walter Bloem walked past the scene of their last stand a short while later. 'On the way', he said, 'we stumbled on a dead English soldier in the undergrowth with his skull split open: then another with a bent bayonet in his breast.'[9]

The first British soldier to be executed during the war was court-martialled on 6 September, the day after the Mons retreat had ended. Private H, a member of a Home Counties regiment, was 19 at the time. He had enlisted in Dublin in February 1913 at the age of 17. In the early hours of the morning on 6 September H had been discovered by a gamekeeper hiding in a barn on Baron Edouard de Rothschild's estate at Tournan, just to the south of the River Marne. H was dressed in civilian clothing but his uniform was lying at his side. The gamekeeper asked him what he was doing there and H was alleged to have replied, 'I have had enough of it. I want to get out.' He was handed over to the French police who immediately delivered him into the custody of a British Provost Marshal. The same day, H was tried for desertion by a Field General Court Martial, the members of which were a colonel, a captain and a lieutenant. It is not known whether or not he had an officer to defend him. H told the court that he had inadvertently become detached from his unit and he was in the process of trying to find them again when he had gone into the barn to rest. He denied making the remark to the gamekeeper and said that he could not remember why he had changed into civilian clothes. No address in mitigation of sentence was made on his behalf and the court had sentenced him to death.

That afternoon, or in the evening, Sir John French confirmed the sentence. Two days later, on 8 September, a captain in the Provost Marshal's branch visited H in the guardroom of his battalion just before 6.30 in the morning. The captain read out the findings of the court martial to him and told him that the sentence of death had been confirmed. Within the next 45 minutes H had been taken before a firing squad and shot. Probably H had had little in the way of worldly possessions. He had made a soldier's will in the back of his army paybook leaving everything he owned to his girl-friend in Dublin.

Army Routine Orders for the BEF on 10 September contained the following austere announcement:

[H's number, rank, name, and unit] was tried by a Field General Court Martial on September 6th, 1914, for desertion. The sentence of the court was to 'suffer death by being shot'. The sentence was duly carried out at 7.7 a.m. on September 8th, 1914.

The Allied armies returned to the offensive on 6 September and during the next four days all German hopes of a quick, decisive military victory were completely shattered at the strategically far-reaching Battle of the Marne. The Germans were pushed back gradually across the River Aisne but on 14 September they turned and stood their ground. 'It was the first day', says the Official History, 'of that "stabilisation" of the battle line which was to last for so many weary months – the beginning, for the British, of trench warfare.'

Sir John French seemed determined to apply the sternest disciplinary standards to the BEF from the outset. Army Routine Orders for 14 September, in a paragraph headed 'Courts Martial', revealed that the commanding officers of two infantry battalions had been convicted of a charge of 'behaving in a scandalous manner unbecoming to the character of an officer and a gentleman'. During the retreat from Mons, it was stated, they had agreed together, without due cause, to surrender themselves and their men to the enemy. They had been sentenced to be cashiered. It was also announced that a driver in the Army Service Corps and a private in a cavalry regiment had both been sentenced to death for sleeping at their posts during the closing stages of the retreat. These sentences had been commuted by the Commander-in-Chief to two years' imprisonment with hard labour, 'in recognition of the gallantry displayed by the troops in the field and their soldierly bearing under severe hardship'. The paragraph concluded:

The Commander-in-Chief takes this opportunity of again impressing on all ranks the absolute necessity for the maintenance of the strictest discipline, without which success cannot be maintained. Failure to maintain the highest standard of discipline will result in the infliction of the most severe punishment.

About the time of this order a lieutenant in the East Surrey Regiment, who was to win a VC in 1915, wrote in his diary:

Since our fight at Mons on August 23rd we had not had a single day's rest. When we were not fighting, we were marching as hard as we could. Men were physically weak from the long marches and mentally weak from the continual strain of never being out of reach of the enemy's guns. . . . It is scarcely surprising that under these conditions traces of panic and loss of self-control occurred.[10]

On 27 September Army Routine Orders disclosed that a second execution had taken place. An infantry private had been tried and convicted by court martial on 24 September on a charge of 'misbehaviour before the enemy in such a way as to show cowardice'. The sentence of the court, 'to suffer death by being shot', had been carried out at 5.56 a.m. on 26 September.

Private W, the condemned soldier, was a member of another Home Counties regiment; neither his age nor his length of service were revealed at his court martial. On 16 September his company had been in position in the ill-defined front line, entrenched behind a farmhouse. A shell had landed near him, wounding two other men. Immediately afterwards W had left his trench and walked back towards the rear. His company sergeant-major had asked him where he was going and he replied that he too had been hit. W was not seen again for six days when he reported back to his battalion, unwounded and still in possession of his rifle and equipment. No defence was put forward on his behalf at his trial, not even the obvious one that he had been shaken or dazed by the force of the explosion and had temporarily lost control of himself. Sir Douglas Haig, his Corps Commander, in recommending that the sentence of death should be carried out, had written, 'I am of the opinion that it is necessary to make an example to prevent cowardice in the face of the enemy as far as possible.'

In the second half of September 1914, the Allied and German armies had faced each other across a static front extending for a total length of about 320 miles with none of the commanders having much idea how to break the deadlock. For the troops in the front line it was a life of incessant discomfort and danger. Shelling was almost continuous. During the hours of daylight any movement was liable to attract the attention of snipers. The nights were fully occupied with patrols, raids, working parties and the replenishment of supplies. None of the belligerents, least of all the British, had either trained or properly equipped their armies for a prolonged period of trench warfare. The strategical plan of the German High Command had been to conduct a holding operation against the Russians in the east whilst they crushed the French forces in the west in a campaign which was scheduled to last for about six weeks. For their part, the French had envisaged a short defensive campaign at the outset followed by a massive counterstroke in which the German armies would be decisively defeated. As for the British, they had never contemplated their military forces being expected to play any more than a very minor role in a European war.

Britain regarded herself first and foremost as a great naval power. She had maintained her small standing army principally to govern and protect her overseas dependencies. The British had also been thinking in terms of a very short war; in fact, even after the earlier fighting, Sir John French still persisted in the belief that it would be over within three months.

Lord Kitchener was one of the earliest leaders amongst the nations involved in the war to perceive that the estimates of its probable length by the politicians and the strategists alike had been hopelessly over-optimistic. In his own view the military struggle was going to last for a full three years and Britain would have to make a far greater contribution to it. He therefore planned to raise a vast new army of civilian volunteers and he appealed at once for the first 100,000 recruits. Thanks to the surge of patriotic fervour which was sweeping the country at that time the response was enormous and by the end of 1914 nearly a million men had enlisted.[11] In addition, over 60 per cent of the peacetime Territorial Force, whose only commitment was to serve in the United Kingdom, had volunteered for duty overseas.

It remained to be seen how rigorously the Army's stringent code of discipline would be applied to this rushed intake of temporary soldiers. Most of them had been impelled to join up through the most unselfish of motives – a resolute sense of duty or an emotional desire to serve their country in her hour of need. Many had neither the physique nor the temperament of the fighting man and still retained a visionary concept of warfare distorted by notions of chivalry and romance. Few of them at the moment of enlistment could possibly have predicted their reactions under fire or their endurance to the sights, the sounds and the strains of the battlefield.

At the beginning of October 1914 the BEF was transferred from its established positions to the east of Paris, and once again took over the left of the Allied line, stretching southward from the Channel ports. The First Battle of Ypres commenced about two weeks later with the British attacking across the Flanders plain. The circumstances were particularly difficult for the infantry. The Germans had a preponderance of heavy artillery and were amply equipped with machine guns. The terrain provided very little natural cover and, with the abnormally high water level below the surface of the soil, any trenches which were dug soon filled with water. The troops attacking the town of La Bassée were involved in the heaviest fighting of all. They were shelled and counter-attacked continuously night and day until, on 20 October, they were brought to a complete standstill. By then the men were so tired that it is said that they were even falling asleep over their rifles whilst they were still in action.

The next member of the BEF to be executed was Private T from a

West Country regiment, one of the many young soldiers who were in action for the first time. T had been detained for a few days in a field hospital in France suffering from dysentery. He was discharged on 18 October and attached to a party marching up to the line to rejoin their battalion. During the afternoon he went absent. The following morning the adjutant of another unit saw T walking through a village dressed in civilian clothes. Mistaking him for a local resident, the officer started to question him about the nearest German positions. He failed to obtain any response and then noticing that T was wearing army boots he arrested him as a suspected deserter. Four days later T was court-martialled. He stated in his defence that his nerves had been shattered by the recent fighting and especially by the incessant shellfire. Without undergoing any form of medical examination Private T was shot at dawn on 28 October.

The desperate struggle continued throughout the damp misty days of the autumn. The Germans were now attempting to break through the British lines with the object of capturing Dunkirk and Calais, the loss of which would have had devastating consequences for the Allies. At the end of October several divisions in the BEF were showing signs of complete exhaustion and Sir John French notified Lord Kitchener that unless he was sent immediate replenishments of shells his infantry would be fighting without any artillery support whatsoever. The high rate of casualties, too, was beginning to undermine the ability of the Army to maintain its fighting efficiency. One division had already lost 45 per cent of its officers and 37 per cent of its men. On 1 November Lord Kitchener met the French President and Commander-in-Chief at Dunkirk and warned them that the BEF could not be effectively reinforced before the late spring of 1915 and that British military power would not be at its full strength until the summer of 1917.

The BEF's heavy losses in those early battles had been entirely unforeseen and the new drafts from home were quite inadequate to fill the gaps. On 11 November the Germans made an all-out attack on the British positions but the attenuated line managed to hold fast. By then the onset of winter had worsened the miseries of life at the front. Towards the close of November the nights turned frosty and there were intermittent heavy falls of snow. The trenches in those days were neither elaborate nor continuous; they usually consisted of a series of shallow pits, scraped out with short-handled entrenching tools, which were often knee-deep in slush and water. The dugouts, in which the troops were supposed to seek rest and shelter, were deeper holes surmounted by a flimsy covering of wood and earth.

By the beginning of December the First Battle of Ypres had declined into stalemate and, owing to the increasingly adverse weather conditions, the season for open, mobile warfare had come to an end. Since the commencement of the campaign the BEF had suffered just under 90,000 casualties, of which approximately one in ten had been killed in action. In the period of reorganization which followed a number of courts martial took place.

Private B of an Eastern Counties regiment was sentenced to death for desertion on 9 December. In mid-November he had been sent back from the line to accompany a sick soldier to the Regimental Aid Post. Having delivered up his charge B had gone absent. A few days later, dressed in civilian clothes, he was arrested by a gendarme in Haze-brouck where he had broken into an unoccupied house. At his court martial B claimed that he had been captured by the Germans who had stripped him of his uniform and issued him with dungarees. He had managed to escape, he said, and he had still been searching for his unit at the time of his apprehension. Not surprisingly, B's story was disbelieved. He was executed on 19 December.

Soon after the outbreak of war the British government had taken steps to bring home all the regular troops who could be spared from garrison duties overseas. These were now sent, together with two divisions from the Indian Army and 22 Territorial battalions, to reinforce the depleted ranks of the BEF. The British launched an abortive attack with four divisions in mid-December which petered out with no ground being gained. The High Command were slow to realize that machine gun fire and the use of barbed wire entanglements had immeasurably increased the vulnerability of attacking infantry compared with the battles of the past. Kitchener was still opposed to any increase in the allocation of machine guns to infantry battalions. Sir Douglas Haig, the future Commander-in-Chief of the BEF, also believed that the value of the machine gun as a defensive weapon was being greatly exaggerated.

Before the end of 1914 Sir John French confirmed another two death sentences. Both soldiers had been tried and convicted together on charges of attempted desertion. Two days before Christmas a Battery Sergeant-Major in the Royal Horse Artillery had been looking around in an empty farm a few miles behind the line. He had forced his way into a barn and had discovered the two men in civilian clothes hiding in a pile of straw. At first they had pretended to be French and the sergeant-major might well have been taken in had he not found two army caps and two service rifles buried in the straw. He had arrested the men who had then admitted that they belonged to a Home Counties regiment and that they had gone absent a few days previously when their battalion was moving up to the trenches. They were court-martialled on 30 December and were shot standing side-by-side on 12 January 1915.

The war establishment of a British infantry battalion at that time was 30 officers and 990 other ranks. The Official History makes this comment on the state of BEF at the end of 1914:

> In British battalions which fought from Mons to Ypres there scarcely remained with the colours an average of one officer and thirty men who had landed in August, 1914. The old British Army was gone beyond recall.

Notes

1. Report of His Majesty's Commissioners for Inquiring into the System of Military Punishments in the Army, 1836.
2. Charles M. Clode, *Military Forces of the Crown*, Vol. 2.
3. Philip Magnus, *Kitchener. Portrait of an Imperialist*.
4. Walter Bloem, *The Advance From Mons 1914*.
5. Ib.
6. Op. cit.
7. Ib.
8. Ib.
9. Ib.
10. Lieutenant George Roupell, quoted in David Ascoli, *The Mons Star*.
11. The atmosphere was equally euphoric in Germany. Walter Bloem speaks of 'scenes so stirring and so full of intense patriotism as to be beyond belief'. It was, he says, 'the picture of a nation rising up immense in its unity, gigantic in its strength to complete its self-expression, to fulfil its destiny'. Op. cit.

2

COURTS MARTIAL IN THE FIELD

I N TIME OF peace the highest judicial tribunal in the British Army had been the General Court Martial, consisting of at least five officers who were usually advised by a legally-qualified judge-advocate. During the war, except for the trial of officers, most of the serious charges arising overseas were dealt with by Field General Courts Martial (FGCM), which were less formal[1] and were far more simple to convene.

The Rules of Procedure, set out in the *Manual of Military Law*,[2] laid down that an FGCM must ordinarily comprise not less than three officers and that whenever possible the president should hold the rank of major or above. A judge-advocate could be appointed to assist them but this very rarely happened. If the court consisted of three or more officers they had power to award any sentence which could have been awarded by a General Court Martial; however, they could only pass a sentence of death if all the members were in agreement.

The ordinary wartime FGCM was composed of either three or four officers, the senior of whom, probably a major or a lieutenant-colonel but occasionally a captain, acted as president. It was customary for the prosecution to be conducted by the accused soldier's adjutant and for a junior regimental officer, referred to as 'the prisoner's friend', to defend him. A civilian barrister or solicitor was not allowed to appear at any court martial outside the United Kingdom without the permission of the Army Council.

According to the Rules of Procedure every accused must be afforded a proper opportunity of preparing his defence, and must have the freest communication with his witnesses which was consistent with good order and military discipline and with his own safe custody. Time and again at courts martial during the war there was no real defence to the charge and the evidence or statement of the accused amounted to little more than a plea of extenuating circumstances. In those rare cases where there was a genuine defence it must be questionable how often it was adequately put forward. The defending officer was usually hampered by his inability as an advocate and his lack of knowledge of law and procedure. In addition, owing to the confusion and impermanence of conditions at the front it was often impossible to contact or to identify some essential witness.

On several occasions it was suggested in the House of Commons that soldiers on trial for their lives should be defended by professional lawyers. Early in 1916 the Under-Secretary of State for War said at Question Time, 'It is obvious that counsel cannot be employed on courts martial which take place in the field.'[3] Much later in the war, he told the Commons that if a man on a capital charge had no one to defend him 'a suitable officer would be found for the purpose whenever possible'.[4] A government minister in December 1917 refused to accept the suggestion from a backbencher that out of 25 executions confirmed by the Commander-in-Chief during the previous October only one prisoner had had any officer to defend him.[5] Even under conditions of active service it is difficult to believe that a soldier was usually condemned to death without at least being offered the assistance of a defending officer. There were occasions, no doubt, where through obstinacy or mere fatalism the offer was refused. Often when the charge was almost irrefutable the prosecution witnesses were not cross-examined at all and the soldier on trial adduced no evidence in his defence. In May 1915 the president of an FGCM in France, which had sentenced a man to be shot for desertion, put in a memo to the Commander-in-Chief, 'He was given every opportunity of giving evidence on his own behalf or making a statement. I asked him several times if he had some explanation to give for going absent and he simply replied, "No".' On at least two other occasions, one in July 1917 and the other in April 1918, men were executed for desertion who had not been represented at their trials. The Commander-in-Chief was fully cognizant of the position when he confirmed both the death sentences. In the latter case the accused soldier's division was actively engaged in operations against the enemy on the day of the court martial and he had chosen to proceed with the trial rather than having it adjourned until an officer became available to assist him with his defence. The court made it clear to the Commander-in-Chief that they had done everything within their power to elicit any facts which might help the prisoner and had warned him repeatedly of the serious position in which he stood if he refused to make a defence.

In theory all trials by court martial were open proceedings and could be attended by any members of the public or the press who chose to be present. In practice, however, courts martial in the field invariably took place in private.[6] This was partly due to the circumstances of active service and partly to the attitude of many senior officers who regarded the trials as purely domestic affairs, solely concerned with the administration of military discipline. Their approach to the matter was autocratic and stern. Lord Wavell attended his first court martial as a 19-year-old subaltern of the Black Watch in 1902. The memory remained with him all his life, says his biographer, because of the president's insensitive behaviour to the accused.[7]

In A. P. Herbert's novel *The Secret Battle*, much of which was based on his own wartime experiences, he says that courts martial in the BEF generally took place in the best bedroom at some estaminet with the members of the court seated in front of a vast white bed. Before he enlisted in 1915 Alan Herbert had graduated in jurisprudence at Oxford University and he took part, both prosecuting and defending, at a number of courts martial in France. Through the pen of the narrator in *The Secret Battle* he described the difficulties of the officer for the defence. A great many members of the court considered him superfluous to the proceedings and, if he made any attempts at any genuine advocacy, 'they could not stomach the sight of him'. Although the Rules of Procedure provided that the prisoner's friend should be granted all the rights of a professional counsel, the narrator went on:

> Many courts I have been before have never heard of the provision; many, having heard of it, refused flatly to recognize it, or insisted that all questions should be put through them. When they do recognize the right they are immediately prejudiced against the prisoner if the right is exercised. Any attempt to discredit or genuinely cross-examine a witness is regarded as a rather sinister piece of cleverness; and if the Prisoner's Friend ventures to sum up the evidence in the accused's favour at the end – it is often 'that damned lawyer-stuff'. Usually it is safer for a prisoner to abandon his rights altogether in that respect.

A further hindrance to the advocate was created by the slow pace of the evidence, as the President compiled his longhand note. Herbert's narrator explains:

> After a question was put there was a lengthy pause while the officer wrote; then there was some uncertainty and some questions about the exact form of the question. . . . Finally, all being satisfactorily settled and written down the witness was allowed to answer. But by then the shiftiest witness had had time to invent a dozen suitable answers. No liar could possibly be caught out – no deceiver ever be detected – under this system.

After the prosecution case had been completed the prisoner was entitled either to give evidence on oath or to make an unsworn statement, if he chose to do so. He could also call witnesses for the defence. The court was then closed whilst the members considered their findings.

The court re-opened when a decision had been reached. At that time, if the verdict was 'not guilty' it was disclosed forthwith: if it was 'guilty' the president simply stated the court had no findings to announce and they proceeded to hear evidence with regard to the prisoner's character. Finally, the defending officer or the prisoner himself could make a plea in mitigation of sentence, after which the president declared, 'The proceedings in open court are terminated', and the court was again closed, this time for the members to deliberate on the sentence.[8]

The reason why no announcement was made after a verdict of 'guilty' was that neither the conviction nor the sentence became official until they were confirmed by the proper confirming authority, which for capital offences was the Commander-in-Chief of the area in which the crime had been committed. When a trial was over, although the accused knew full well if he had been convicted, he remained in total ignorance of the sentence which had been passed on him until promulgation took place days or weeks later.

If an officer was detailed to sit on a court martial he had no option in the matter. Court martial duty was generally unpopular in the Army. Speaking in a debate in the House of Commons just after the war a Member who had served as an officer in France said, 'I have never yet met a lay officer who did not loathe to sit on a court martial.'[9] In the same debate another Member, who had had extensive experience of courts martial in the BEF, said, 'Sometimes I found a court martial which was all that could be desired in every way. Other times I found one which was utterly incompetent for its work. I thought it was a scandal to ask such a court to adjudicate upon any case whatever.'[10] The same speaker went on to tell the House of a major who had informed him that whenever he sat on a court martial he always imposed the maximum sentence laid down by the Army Act so that the confirming authority could reduce it if necessary. On the other hand, the speaker said, he had been informed by a confirming officer that he never reduced a sentence, because he considered that the members of the court had actually seen the witnesses and were in a far better position than he was to assess the proper punishment for the offence. It seems strangely illogical for a tribunal with a complete sentencing discretion to pass the maximum penalty coupled with a recommendation that it should be reduced. Yet a number of courts martial which imposed the death sentence added a recommendation, sometimes a strong recommendation, to mercy. The answer may lie in the fact that a number of inexperienced and comparatively junior officers were completely out of their depth when sentencing for serious offences. The official statistics show, in fact, that out of all the death sentences by courts martial during the war years only approximately 10 per cent were actually confirmed.

After a court martial had condemned a soldier to death, the papers in the case were passed up in turn to his commanding officer, his brigade, division, corps and army commanders for each of them to add their views as to whether the sentence should be commuted or confirmed. Then the file was sent to the judge-advocate's branch to ensure the proceedings had been in order; and lastly it was placed before the Commander-in-Chief for his ultimate decision. At the beginning of 1915 a circular memorandum was issued by the War Office telling commanding officers exactly what information they were required to provide on such occasions. Firstly, they were to give particulars of the soldier's character, 'from a fighting point of view as well as that of general behaviour', specifying his previous conduct in action and his period of service overseas. Secondly, they were to report on the state of discipline within their unit. And thirdly, in the case of convictions for desertion, they were to give their opinion, 'based on your personal knowledge and that of your officers on the soldier's characteristics', as to whether the crime 'had been deliberately committed with the object of avoiding the particular service involved'. If a colonel happened to express a negative view upon this last matter he was really saying that he disagreed with the verdict reached by the court, as the necessary intention was an essential element in the legal definition of desertion.

Apart from the notes of evidence recorded by the president at the trial and the commanding officer's opinions pursuant to the circular, the only additional document which had to be forwarded with the court martial papers was the condemned soldier's Army Form B.122, his conduct sheet.[11] The B.122 would show his date of enlistment and a list of his previous disciplinary offences, but it would disclose nothing more. Sometimes, of course, further details with regard to his background or his circumstances would emerge from the notes of evidence, usually from what he had said in his own defence or from his statement in mitigation of sentence. This, however, would have been merely fortuitous since in most cases neither the accused soldier nor his defending officer were fully aware of the sort of factors which might be pertinent to the application of mercy.

It is hardly conceivable that a Commander-in-Chief should have made his decision whether to confirm or commute a sentence of death on the paucity of information which was usually available to him. The personal details of the condemned man were largely ignored – his age, his domestic responsibilities, whether he was a regular, a territorial, a Kitchener volunteer, or at a later stage in the war a conscript; and if he happened to be serving only for the duration, his character as a civilian, his occupation in peacetime and his prospects. Apart from the circumstances of the offence, the issue of life or death seems to have been determined by two factors – whether it was considered that the condemned man had the makings of a good soldier; and whether his execution might be beneficial for the immediate needs of discipline.

After the finish of his trial the prisoner who had been convicted of a capital offence was removed in custody to a place of detention at his divisional or his corps headquarters. He was returned to the guard-room of his own unit just prior to the promulgation of his sentence. Early in 1918 the Under-Secretary of State for War told the House of Commons that in the BEF there was an interval of 'somewhere about fourteen days' between a soldier being sentenced to death and his execution by a firing squad.[12] Apart from the first two executions of the war the usual period actually varied between nine and sixteen days; but on occasion, when there was some reason for the delay, it could extend up to a month or more.

If the Commander-in-Chief had confirmed a death sentence the promulgation generally took place at a special parade of the conde-mned man's unit on the evening before his execution. At the parade, which was attended by the prisoner under escort, his adjutant or another officer read out extracts from the evidence at his trial, the findings and sentence of the court, and the order of confirmation by the Commander-in-Chief. Sometimes this ritual was delayed until the morning on which the prisoner was to be shot.

It might have seemed, for the sake of humanity, that the terrible news of his impending fate should have been broken to the con-demned man in the privacy of his detention room, but the agonizing ordeal of the promulgation parade remained as an authorized proce-dure throughout the war. Apparently there were senior officers who considered that it served a useful purpose, as in November 1916 a divisional directive concerning a private about to be executed ordered that promulgation was to take place in front of as many men as could be made available.

One can assume that on many occasions the instincts of compassion superseded the rigid formalities of army discipline and the condemned man was informed of his sentence as sympathetically as circumstances would permit. During the summer of 1915 the GOC of a division in France issued instructions that a death sentence, just confirmed, should be promulgated to the soldier in private by one of his battalion officers, with the chaplain and the medical officer in attendance.

Death was no stranger in the forward lines of battle, but most soldiers were sustained in action by an innate belief in their own invulnerability. The certainty of proximate death to be suffered ignominiously at the hands of his own comrades must have been a horrifying prospect for the condemned man.

On 2 January 1915, Lord Kitchener sent a letter to Sir John French at the headquarters of the BEF in which he said:

I suppose we must now recognize that the French Army cannot make a sufficient break through the German lines to bring about the retreat of the German forces from Northern Belgium. If that is so, the German lines in France may be looked upon as a fortress that cannot be carried by assault and also that cannot be completely invested, with the result that the lines may be held by an investing force whilst operations proceed elsewhere.

The months of January and February 1915 were a period of extreme privation for the troops in the front line. That winter in Flanders was said to be the worst within living memory. The incessant rain interspersed with heavy falls of snow resulted in severe flooding. The British trenches, lacking both duck-boards and drainage, were perpetually waterlogged and in constant need of maintenance and repair. And the shelling and sniping continued to take their steady toll of casualties. Owing to the absence of a proper system of communication trenches the wounded could only be evacuated under cover of darkness. George Roupell recorded in his diary:

When a man was wounded, the cry went up, 'Where's the officer? A man hit!' It was the officer's job to put on iodine and bandage up the wound. The officers were supplied with hypodermic syringes and morphia tablets to keep the men quiet till we could get them away, but on the whole the men were wonderfully good, and it was only in the more serious cases that one used drugs.[13]

A modest effort was being made to provide the troops with a primitive form of welfare. Laundry, bathing and disinfestation centres were set up in the rear areas; and a routine of reliefs and rest periods was introduced for units which were actually involved in the fighting. By the end of January the strength of the BEF had grown to just over 347,000 and it had been divided into two armies, the first commanded by Sir Douglas Haig and the second by Sir Horace Smith-Dorrien.

By this stage a substantial proportion of the BEF consisted of men who had been recalled from the reserve. They were not always the best quality of soldier for the type of fighting on the Western Front. In December 1914 Sir John French had complained to the War Office that some of the reinforcements being sent to him were over 50 years old and had not fired a rifle since the Boer War. A commanding officer in the 6th Division, reporting on the state of discipline in his unit at the end of February 1915, stated, 'There is a lot of drunkenness and absence resulting from it in a battalion which is composed of about two-thirds reservists.'

The prevalence of desertion during those winter months was causing a great deal of anxiety to the senior officers in the BEF; so much so that Sir Henry Rawlison, the GOC of IV Corps, ordered that a personal message from him should be read out to all units under his command, warning them of the dire consequences which might follow a conviction for this offence. Sir Horace Smith-Dorrien considered that the remedy must be more drastic. The only way of discouraging the men who were deserting to avoid service in the trenches, he said at the end of January, was 'to carry out some death penalties'. A brigadier in the 1st Division set out the reasons for commending such a course in a note to his divisional commander. He wrote:

> Every infantry officer of experience will confirm my opinion that there comes a point when men will risk imprisonment or penal servitude rather than carry on their ordinary duty. They know that long sentences inflicted in war are whittled down as they pass up the military hierarchy and that if a sentence is not ended before the end of the war they may look forward to an amnesty at the end of hostilities. The execution of a man has a salutary effect on the bad and weak characters (in resisting temptation). The number of men likely to desert in the face of the enemy is very small and is composed of a few bad and weak characters. But if these few are able by their crime to obtain the safety and comfort of a prison their numbers will soon be swelled by others of slightly less weak character.

It was extremely difficult for soldiers who went absent from their units to remain at liberty behind the line in France for very long, and it was even harder for them to return to England. The Military Police patrolling the roads, the villages, the towns and the railway stations in the vicinity of the battle areas were constantly checking passes and travel documents. A stringent surveillance was kept of all troops entering the Channel ports of Le Havre, Boulogne, Rouen and Dieppe, while Allied and neutral vessels using these harbours were inspected periodically to ensure that no British soldiers were illicitly on board.

During January and February 14 soldiers were condemned to death and shot on the Western Front. Thirteen of them had been convicted of desertion and one, a corporal, for the offence of 'quitting post'.

These early desertion cases conformed to the patterns which were to become all too familiar throughout the course of the war. Some men went absent after a prolonged spell in action because they were unable or unwilling to put up with any more; some could not withstand the traumatic impact of their initial experiences in battle; some who were resting or in reserve had not the willpower to face a further period in the line; and some had been unbalanced by domestic worries or by bad news from home.

Private C and Private S were members of the same battalion of the Guards. They deserted at the beginning of November during the heavy fighting near Ypres when they had been in action almost continuously since the previous August. C, the older of the two, was a reservist; he had served as a regular from 1904 until 1912 and had been recalled to the colours when the British Army had mobilized. S had enlisted in 1909 and was still serving at the outbreak of war. Their commanding officer described C as an excellent soldier, but said that S had not lived up to his peacetime reputation since he had been on active service. Both men had remained at liberty for two months, being looked after for most of that time by a French farmer's wife. They were finally arrested when the Military Police raided the farm and found them hiding in a locked barn.

A number of survivors from the original BEF went absent around Christmas and the New Year. This was attributed by the staff to the amount of hard drinking that went on in units which were temporarily relieved from service in the line. Early in January a brigadier in the 6th Division issued an instruction that in future instead of charging troops with drunkenness they should be court-martialled for the capital offence of cowardice before the enemy.

The first NCO to be executed during the war had deserted after being in action for only three days. Corporal L was a regular soldier from Lancashire. His battalion had arrived in France in the latter part of August and had immediately been thrust into the line at the battle of Le Câteau. On 27 August, whilst the fighting was still at its height, L went absent. He had then drifted around the towns and villages behind the front, and had ended up living with a French woman at Nieppe. He was arrested by the Military Police on 21 December. At his trial Corporal L did not explain his motive for deserting: perhaps it was too obvious to require an explanation. He was shot on 22 January.

Two more of the executed men were reservists who had joined their battalions in January and had deserted after a very short time in action. A private from the North Country had gone into the line on 10 January and had absented himself on 20 January. Two days later he was found in the hold of a mail boat which was about to sail from Le Havre. He put forward no defence at his court martial but stated that he had been removed from his home at the age of 15 and had never seen his parents since then. The other man, a private in a Scottish Highland regiment, had deserted at the end of his first week in action.

Three of the soldiers executed during this period had deserted from battalions which had been resting but were under immediate orders to return to the line. Private S came from Middlesex and was 19 years of age. He had enlisted in the Regular Army five days before Britain entered the war and had been sent to France as a reinforcement after the briefest possible training. He went absent on 23 January and was apprehended 24 hours later. The other two, both of whom were regulars, had also deserted in January. One of them, a lance-corporal in a Yorkshire regiment, had been recommended to mercy by the court on account of his previous good service in action and his excellent character. However, this did not save him from being shot. His army commander, Smith-Dorrien, was of the opinion that as no executions had been previously carried out in the condemned corporal's division an example was necessary to emphasize the seriousness of desertion.

A young private from an Irish regiment who had been with the BEF since the middle of September deserted from the front-line trenches two days before Christmas and remained at large until he was arrested in Armentières on 9 February. He told the court that he had gone absent on a sudden impulse after receiving a letter from home telling him that his two brothers had been killed in action. He was sentenced to death and executed.

During the first week of February a corporal and four privates, all members of the same section in an infantry battalion, were tried together on a charge of leaving their post without orders from their superior officer. The incident had occurred in the early hours of the morning on 28 January when they had been on duty in a front-line trench. A German patrol had crossed no-man's-land unnoticed and had grabbed a British soldier's rifle through a loophole in the parapet. Although the patrol had retired immediately with their souvenir a rumour had spread along the trench, fostered no doubt by the sudden outbreak of firing, the taut nerves and the darkness, that the Germans had actually occupied a portion of the line. The accused corporal, who was in charge of a section post, had panicked and, accompanied by the other four, had run back to the support trenches. Just before they had left their positions someone had been heard to shout, 'Clear out, boys! The Germans are on us! We have no chance!' An officer and a sergeant had quickly taken control of the situation in the sector and the five accused had been ordered to return to their company where they were placed under arrest.

At the court martial the corporal was condemned to death and the four private soldiers were each awarded ten years' penal servitude. These sentences were all confirmed by the Commander-in-Chief.

Soldiers were always encouraged to plead 'Not Guilty' to capital offences, however flimsy or nonexistent their defences. One of the few cases during the war where a man pleaded 'Guilty' to a charge of desertion occurred in the Second Army on 30 January 1915. Sir Horace Smith-Dorrien was obviously troubled by such an occurrence and in a memorandum to the Deputy Judge Advocate General at GHQ he pointed out that there had been no evidence on oath against the accused. 'Although this is legally correct,' he went on, 'it is a question as to whether when a death sentence is involved the court martial should not make the man plead "Not Guilty" and take sworn evidence.' Despite Sir Horace's doubts the sentence was confirmed by Sir John French and the soldier was executed.

A considerable number of the sentences of penal servitude and imprisonment imposed by courts martial during the war were suspended within a short while under the provisions of the Army (Suspensions of Sentences) Act, 1915; when this occurred the soldier concerned was returned to his unit for normal duties and a date was set, usually three months ahead, for the sentence to be brought forward for reconsideration. If his conduct was good in the meanwhile, or if he performed a deed of gallantry in the field, his sentence might be remitted when it came up for review; on the other hand, if the report on his behaviour was unsatisfactory it could be implemented right away. A third alternative open to the reviewing officer was again to postpone the decision until some time in the future.

Notes

1. At one FGCM in France in 1914 there was no Bible available and witnesses were sworn on a 'handsomely bound French cookery book'. David Ascoli, *The Mons Star*.
2. *Manual of Military Law*, 1914.
3. House of Commons, written answers, 20 January 1916.
4. House of Commons, oral answers, 6 March 1918.
5. House of Commons, written answers, 6 December 1917.
6. The *Manual of Military Law*, 1914, stated: 'The court can deliberate in private, and may either withdraw for the purpose or cause the court to be cleared; but at other times the court must be open to the public, military or otherwise, so far as the room or tent in which the court is held can receive them. It is not usual to place any restriction on the admission of reporters for the press.'
7. John Connell, *Wavell, Scholar and Soldier*. Field Marshal Earl Wavell (1883–1950) was one of the most respected military commanders of the Second World War.
8. The information in this paragraph was supplied to the author by Mr Harold Dean, CB, QC, Judge Advocate General of the Forces, 1972–9.
9. Captain Thorpe, House of Commons, Army (Annual) Bill, Committee stage, 11 April 1921.
10. Major M. Wood, House of Commons, Army (Annual) Bill, Committee stage, 11 April 1921.
11. Very often the B.122 was not available.
12. House of Commons, oral answers, 16 January 1918.
13. Quoted by David Ascoli, op. cit.

3
NEUVE CHAPELLE AND THE SECOND BATTLE OF YPRES

I T HAD BEEN hoped that Haig's First Army would be able to carry out an offensive in the area of Neuve Chapelle during February 1915, but the continuation of the bad weather made this impossible. When the attack was eventually commenced on 10 March a slight frost had temporarily hardened the muddy and waterlogged surface of the ground.

This was the first planned offensive by the BEF on the Western Front and it formed a prototype which was to be followed with minor variations for the rest of the war. During the night of 9–10 March, parties were sent out to clear away or cut passages through the British wire, and well before dawn the attacking formations were concentrated in the front-line trenches. At 7.30 a.m. an artillery barrage opened up, designed to pulverize the German positions and to destroy their wire entanglements. At zero hour, just after 8 a.m., the artillery lifted to new targets behind the enemy line and the waiting troops left the cover of their trenches, clambering up small ladders which had been placed at regular intervals along the parapet. No-man's-land at this point was about 200 yards wide and the men were supposed to cross it in close formation at a steady double, but movement was extremely difficult owing to the thick mud underfoot. If they reached the German trenches they went in with the bayonet.

Bayonet drill was regarded as particularly important by the British Army; recruits spent hours jabbing and thrusting at bags of straw and learning to swing the rifle butt as a kind of cudgel. According to the manual of training then in use, 'The bayonet is essentially an offensive weapon. In a bayonet assault all ranks go forward to kill or be killed.' A private in the 1st Lincolns described his first bayonet charge as 'a proper bloodthirsty affair'. He went on:

> I can't remember whether I got home with the point. I do know that the Germans didn't like the taste of steel and they soon made a bolt for it. I can't say I blame them. A bayonet is a wicked weapon.[1]

Although the attack on 10 March was reasonably successful and Neuve Chapelle was captured, during the next two days the British could make no progress. On 13 March Sir John French reported to Kitchener, 'Cessation of forward movement is necessitated by the fatigue of the troops, and above all by want of ammunition.' In this brief battle the First Army had suffered nearly 13,000 casualties.

General Joffre, the French Commander-in-Chief, was pressing for the BEF to launch another major assault in the latter part of March while the French Army was concentrating for its spring offensive, but Sir John French was reluctant to embroil his forces again before he had received sufficient reinforcements from home. He did agree, however, to carry out a series of small-scale attacks and to take over about five miles of the French forward line. 'It seemed to the British officers at the front', says the Official History of the campaign, 'that they were being sacrificed to gain time until the French were ready for a big spectacular effort; but this, even if ever intended, did not materialize.'

During the months of March and April nine soldiers of the BEF were condemned to death for desertion and shot. They were all regulars or reservists and eight of them had gone absent in October and November of the previous year.

The term 'shell-shock', which was later applied to a variety of conditions emanating from the traumas of the battlefield, had not then come into use. In subsequent years Lance-Sergeant W, who was court-martialled in the middle of March, might have been considered a victim of shell-shock. He was a regular soldier aged 26 and was serving in a famous Rifle regiment. His division had landed in France with the initial contingent of the BEF and had suffered severely both in the retreat from Mons and in the First Battle of Ypres. As a result of the fighting in early November W's own battalion had been reduced to little more than 150 men. About this time he went absent. Nothing more was heard of him until an evening just before Christmas when, still dressed in uniform, he called at the house of a boot-maker in Arques and begged to be given a bed for the night. The boot-maker, noticing that W looked wet through and exhausted, took pity on him and invited him in. He then saw that W appeared to have a flesh wound in one of his hands.

W had remained at the boot-maker's house until, as the result of a tip-off, he was arrested by a gendarme at the beginning of March 1915. He was handed over to the Military Police and interrogated by a major who reported that he seemed half-dazed and was either unwilling or unable to answer the simplest questions. Eventually W made a statement in writing in which he asserted that he had undergone some sort of nervous breakdown directly after being wounded in the hand. He repeated this in his defence at his subsequent trial, but the court was

unimpressed and sentenced him to death. Someone at Army Headquarters who read the papers in the case thought that an enquiry ought
to be made into W's mental state, and an instruction was issued on 19
March that he should be kept under observation by a medical officer. It
is difficult to say whether or not a thorough psychogenic investigation
was carried out on Lance-Sergeant W as he was shot at dawn four days
later.

It was most unusual in the early stages of the war for a soldier under
sentence of death to be examined by a doctor. A private in a Lancashire
regiment said at his trial that during the previous year, while he was
serving in India, he had been in hospital with nervous trouble and
heart failure. No attempt was made to check the truth of his statement.
He had taken part in the retreat from Mons and had deserted at the end
of October, at a time, he said, when terror had almost driven him out
of his mind. General Smith-Dorrien considered this to be a case which
deserved 'the most severe penalty'. The man was shot towards the end
of April.

Another soldier from the same battalion, Lance-Corporal I, had
been executed six days earlier. I was a regular who had enlisted in July
1914 at the age of 18. After only two months' training he had been sent
to France with a draft of reinforcements in the middle of September.
He had deserted during the First Battle of Ypres and was eventually
apprehended at Boulogne in February 1915. I had had his nineteenth
birthday while he was in custody awaiting court martial but even his
extreme youth at the time of his offence had not saved him from the
firing squad.

Three of the soldiers who were executed in April had been recommended to mercy by their courts of trial. Two of them had excellent
characters and one had been praised for his conduct in action. Senior
commanders not infrequently ignored such recommendations in deciding whether a death sentence should be commuted or confirmed.

Since military executions were carried out largely for their exemplary effect, it would be interesting to discover what sort of reactions
they evoked within the Army. Stephen Graham, who joined a Guards
battalion of the BEF in 1917, says[2] that a young soldier in the company
to which he was posted had been court-martialled and shot for
cowardice[3] two years previously after the battle of Neuve Chapelle.
Graham had had an opportunity of speaking to some of the men who
had been there at the time and he wrote: 'The company was mortified
at the imputation of cowardice to any of its ranks, and felt that they
were in a way disgraced by the sentence.'

Apart altogether from any affront to regimental pride there is ample
evidence that an execution for a military offence gave rise to a great
deal of revulsion and resentment in a condemned man's immediate

unit. One result of this was that it was frequently alleged that he had been wrongly convicted, sometimes on perjured evidence. A case in point was the execution referred to by Stephen Graham, the details of which he had obtained from hearsay and from battalion mythology. Graham starts from the premise that the executed soldier, to whom he refers as Private X, had been 'one of the bravest boys in his company, and at the time one of the most eager'. The conviction had been procured, he says, mainly upon the evidence of a hated sergeant-major. According to Graham's version, an enemy shell had burst very close to Private X during an attack and he had wandered away in a dazed condition. When he had turned up again his Company Sergeant-Major had accused him of cowardice and desertion and had immediately placed him under close arrest. At the court martial, Graham goes on, 'the judges were men of another regiment; they took the Sergeant-Major's word against Private X's obscurely-written, verbose defence'. Accordingly, X was found guilty and sentenced to death.

What had actually occurred was that Private X had deserted from his battalion when it was taking part in a dawn attack at Neuve Chapelle on 11 March 1915. He had last been seen advancing with his platoon at 7 a.m. and about three hours later, while the attack was still in progress, he had been found at the battalion ammunition dump in the rear. He was questioned by a sergeant-major and had said that his company commander had sent him back on an errand. Later he had changed his story and stated he had been on his way back to his billet to fetch some cognac. At his court martial he simply said that he had lost his head in the fighting and that he bitterly regretted what he had done. He made no mention of being dazed by a shell. Private X was recommended to mercy but the death sentence was confirmed.

It is noticeable how often in the mythological accounts of cases in which men were executed, a malicious officer, warrant officer or NCO has become the villain of the piece. It may be that as these tales were told and re-told they grew into allegorical condemnations, not only of the whole supposed system of military injustice, but also of the fearsome power which was wielded by those who misused their military authority.

On 22 April, a beautiful spring day, the Germans counter-attacked to the south of Ypres and introduced a new horror to the weaponry of warfare. During the afternoon the officers and men of an Algerian division of the French Army were mystified to observe a strange greenish-yellow cloud drifting towards their trenches on a light breeze. Presently they were enveloped in a choking, lethal haze of chlorine vapour. Many of those who escaped asphyxiation abandoned their positions and struggled back to the rear. For the next few hours, unknown to the Germans, a portion of the Allied line was virtually unmanned. Neither the French Army nor the British had taken any precautions against the use of gas and no protective equipment was available for their troops. Early directions to the BEF were that in the event of a gas attack they should hold wetted cloths or handkerchiefs over their mouths and noses; proper respirators were not issued until the summer of 1916.

The BEF was involved in sustained and heavy fighting for the whole of May 1915, a month which saw the conclusion of the Second Battle of Ypres, as well as the battles of Aubers Ridge and Festubert. Although they continued to suffer severe casualties they made no appreciable gains of ground and achieved no significant improvements in their tactical situation. They were still suffering from a shortage both of artillery and of shells; so much so that Sir John French had had to inform the War Office on 25 May that unless his reserves of ammunition were immediately replenished he would have to suspend all further offensive operations. A German cavalry officer's description of a sector of front around Ypres at this time is quoted in the Official History. He said:

> The whole countryside is yellow. The battlefield is fearful. A curious sour, heavy, penetrating smell of dead bodies strikes one. . . . Bodies of cows and pigs lie, half decayed; splintered trees, the stumps of avenues; shell crater after shell crater on the roads and in the fields.

For the whole of that summer the positions of the opposing armies on the Western Front remained fairly static. In the grim and sustained conditions of trench warfare the BEF was suffering casualties at an average rate of 300 a day. The shelling, bombing, patrolling and raiding were constant, and the snipers continued to take their steady toll. Roland Leighton wrote to Vera Brittain telling her about the first death in his platoon shortly after his arrival at the front.[4] The man was shot through the temple while firing over a parapet, said Leighton:

> I did not actually see it thank Heaven. I only found him lying very still at the bottom of the trench with a tiny stream of red trickling down his cheek on to his coat.

Meanwhile a new army of citizen-soldiers was being hastily trained in Britain and formations in the line were being reinforced by drafts of Kitchener volunteers, sometimes within three or four months of their enlistment. Robert Graves has said that most of the men who joined his battalion in France during May 1915 were either over-age or under-age.[5] When they had enlisted some of them had pretended to be younger than they really were and some of them had pretended to be older. Of the 40 soldiers in Graves' own platoon at the time, 14 were over 40 and five were boys of less than 18.

During the months of May, June, July and August, 18 soldiers were executed in the BEF, 14 for desertion, three for cowardice, and one for murder.

Six of the deserters who were shot in June and July might well have been suffering from some form of traumatic neurosis, but only one of them was medically examined before he was executed. A Scottish private, who was not represented by an officer at his trial, had joined his battalion in France the previous December and had gone absent five months later. His company commander said that he had been a good soldier and had borne an excellent character until just before his desertion when he suddenly seemed to have lost his nerve. The divisional commander was not impressed by this and urged that the death sentence should be carried out as there had been several other desertions from the same battalion and an example was necessary. Two regular soldiers from Worcester had deserted together at the end of June. The first, a man in his thirties, had served for 13 years and was a veteran of Mons; the second, who was 25, had been in France since November. Their commanding officer spoke well of their conduct in action but commented that both of them had appeared to be suffering from nervous strain.

Several of the executed men had pleaded for leniency at their trials on account of their mental condition at the time of their offences. Private H, a young soldier in a Kent regiment, had enlisted in the Regular Army in 1913. He deserted during the retreat from Mons and he was arrested by the Military Police in Paris the following May. His nerves had been shattered, he said, by the sights he had seen at the Battles of Mons and Le Câteau and he had reached the end of his endurance. His brigade commander considered his case a bad one deserving the extreme penalty. Another regular soldier, Private D, had enlisted in a Scottish regiment in June 1914. He had served with the BEF since the beginning of the fighting and had deserted from a front-line trench during a heavy artillery bombardment in March 1915. D, who was described by his commanding officer as being a well-behaved man but not a particularly intelligent one, claimed that he had lost his memory after a shell had exploded very close to him and he had wandered off in a daze. Although amnesia resulting from shell-burst was never accepted by the military commanders as a pretext for desertion, it sometimes received more credence from regimental officers with personal experience of the massive barrages on the Western Front. A corporal who said he had suffered loss of memory induced by hearing shellfire was sentenced to death for desertion in July 1915, by a court consisting of a major, a captain and a lieutenant, all of whom had served in the line. They recommended him to mercy on the ground that he might have been speaking the truth. Their recommendation was not followed and the corporal was shot.

The first Kitchener volunteer to be executed was sentenced to death for desertion in June 1915. Private T, a member of a Surrey regiment, was 24 at the time of his conviction. He had enlisted for the duration of the war on 9 September 1914. In April, just before the Second Battle of Ypres, he had left his battalion while it was marching up to the trenches. He told the court that he could not remember much about it. At the time, he said, he had been verminous, covered in sores and under treatment from his medical officer for dysentery. Eventually he had walked to Boulogne where a sailor had given him some civilian clothes and advised him to see the British Consul. He had reported to the consulate and had been sent back to England. He was arrested as an absentee at Dover soon after he landed. T was shot on 1 July 1915, less than nine months from the day he had volunteered to serve in the Army.

It was apparent that soldiers who had only enlisted for the duration were going to be punished with the same severity as members of the Regular Army if they committed any military offences. Two more early volunteers were executed for desertion during the summer of 1915, one at the end of July and the other at the beginning of August. Private P from Worcester, a man with a wife and children, had joined up on 29 September 1914. He was sent to a battalion in France early in 1915 and had instantly acquired a good reputation with his officers. In the middle of June, when his company were resting a few miles behind the line, they received orders to carry out an assault the following morning. At evening roll-call P was missing. He was arrested about three weeks later and having put forward no defence at his trial he was shot with two other men from his battalion on 26 July. Private P had volunteered for a Somerset regiment within a few weeks of the outbreak of war. He went with a draft to the BEF at the commencement of the Second Battle of Ypres. At the end of July while his battalion was engaged in heavy fighting he disappeared for four days. In the course of his plea in mitigation he said that he was used to hearing regularly from home but at the time of his desertion he had received no letters for several weeks and he was extremely upset about it. The court sentenced him to death with a recommendation to mercy on the ground that he had been suffering from mental worry. The sentence on P was confirmed and he was shot on 19 August.

As a matter of official policy executions were given the maximum publicity within the BEF. Not only were the particulars announced in the Commander-in-Chief's routine orders but much fuller details were often published in the routine orders for the condemned men's own divisions. When an infantry private had been executed in May 1915, the routine orders for the 8th Division included a summary of the evidence at his trial and even mentioned the name of the place where he had been shot. The divisional commander added his personal direction at the end of the announcement: 'The above is to be read out on parade to every squadron, battery and corresponding unit in the Division.'

The constant emphasis on executions for desertion gave rise to the inevitable distortions, rumours and exaggerations. An infantry lance-corporal stated at his court martial in April 1915 that having become separated from his section during an attack he had been afraid to report back as he had heard that men were being executed habitually for merely being absent without leave. At another trial during the same month a gunner in the Royal Horse Artillery said that he had been drunk in Armentières for two days without a pass and he had only deserted because his friends had warned him that if he reported back to his battery he would probably be shot.

So great was the natural dread of the firing squad that many men awaiting trial by court martial on capital charges endeavoured to escape from custody. The security arrangements at most guardrooms in the BEF were inadequate and the number of escapes was extremely high, but usually the fugitive soldiers were recaptured within a short space of time. A private in a North Country regiment managed to abscond no less than three times before being executed in the middle of April.

Three men, two regulars and a reservist, were shot for cowardice during the spring and summer of 1915. Private H was a regular soldier in a Midland regiment and had served with the BEF for five months at the time of his court martial. In the early hours of the morning on 9 May his battalion had been in the assembly trenches waiting to make a dawn attack. They had come under heavy shellfire and had suffered a number of casualties. When the order was given to start the assault H was missing. He had reported to another unit three days later saying he had had to fall out as he had sprained his ankle. He was promptly examined by a doctor who had found nothing wrong with him. His commanding officer said that he had absented himself on two previous occasions at the height of a battle without any charges being brought against him, and that he was a worthless fighting soldier, only intent on saving his own skin.

Private C, a regular in a Lancashire regiment, was another soldier with an unfortunate record in action. He had been a member of the original BEF and had deserted at the end of August 1914. He was arrested the following October but had escaped from custody and had remained at liberty until just before Christmas. C was court-martialled in January 1915 and was sentenced to three years' penal servitude. He had served about three and a half months of this term when it was suspended on 4 May and he was returned to his battalion in the line. On the evening of 23 May they were manning a support trench near Ypres and C told several men in his section that he was not feeling well. At 3 a.m. next morning they were subjected to a gas attack. When it was over C had disappeared. An hour and a half later he was found by a private in the RAMC lying at the side of a road a couple of miles behind the line in a dazed and exhausted condition. C was taken to a field ambulance dressing station where he was examined by a doctor and was found to be free from gas poisoning. After he had been convicted of cowardice and sentenced to death, his brigadier commented, 'I fear that if immediate examples are not made of the men who quit their trenches the fighting qualities of the Brigade will deteriorate.' C was executed on 12 June.

Another soldier was shot for cowardice on 16 July. Private B was a Londoner and was serving in a Rifle regiment. He was a man in the middle-thirties who had joined the Army in 1898 and had been called up from the Reserve on the outbreak of war. He had been posted to the Western Front in November 1914. On 24 June 1915, B's battalion had been in the trenches in a particularly active sector of the line. Shortly after dawn they were ordered to man the parapet and to open rapid fire after a mine had been exploded under the forward German trench directly in front of their positions. B had persistently refused to leave his dugout, telling his platoon sergeant that he felt too shaky to stand on the fire-step. He stated in his defence at his trial that on two occasions in the past he had been found to be suffering from nervous debility. After the explosion of the mine, he said, his nerves had been so upset that he had not known what he was doing. A week before his execution B was examined by a medical board which reported that he appeared to have no mental abnormality.

The first soldier in the BEF to be executed for murder was a corporal in the Royal Engineers who was tried by General Court Martial in May 1915. He had shot a lance-corporal in his own unit with his rifle after an argument in an estaminet. He was sentenced to suffer death by hanging. For the remainder of the war men who were condemned to death for murder by courts martial overseas were always sentenced to suffer death by shooting, just as if they had been condemned for purely military offences.

Notes

1. Quoted by David Ascoli, in *The Mons Star*.
2. Stephen Graham, *A Private in the Guards*.
3. He was actually shot for desertion.
4. Vera Brittain, *Chronicle of Youth, War Diary 1913–1917*.
5. Robert Graves, *Goodbye to All That*.

4
LOOS AND GALLIPOLI

THE WESTERN FRONT and the Gallipoli peninsula were still countless miles away from the everyday lives of the people at home in Britain. Their accustomed routine had scarcely been affected by the war. The civil population was encountering few shortages, few restrictions, few hardships, and few dangers. Most people had failed to appreciate as yet the barbarity of the fighting and the arid nihilism of the battlefield. 'The spirit of 1915', says the historian A. J. P. Taylor, 'was best expressed by Ian Hay, a writer of light fiction, in *The First Hundred Thousand* – a book which treated soldiering as a joke, reviving "the best days of our lives" at some imaginary public school.'[1]

Nevertheless, a profound change was taking place in the national attitude towards the war. This was brought about by several factors. There were the increasing frequency of the casualty lists in the daily newspapers and the sporadic gaps amongst the menfolk of families and personal friends. Vera Brittain recorded in her diary on 17 May 1915, 'The length of the casualty list is terrible – it again breaks the record – over 400 officers and 2,000 men.'[2] And people were becoming accustomed to the blue uniforms of the wounded in streets and public places, and to the occasional disquieting sight of the disfigured and the maimed. Above all, the idealistic concepts of the nobility of battle were being shattered by revelations from the Western Front. When Roland Leighton decided to volunteer for the infantry at the age of 19 early in 1915, Vera Brittain wrote that his dominant reason 'seems to be the vague moral sense of acting up to his faith in, his highest opinion of, himself – the worship and indefinite pursuit of heroism in the abstract'. The following September, after his first five months in action, Leighton was to tell her in a letter from the trenches:[3]

Let him who thinks that War is a glorious, golden thing . . . let him look at a little pile of sodden grey rags that cover half a skull and a shin bone and what might have been its ribs, or at this skeleton lying on its side, resting half-crouching as it fell, supported on one arm, perfect but that it is headless, and with tattered clothing draped around it; and let him realize how grand and glorious a thing it is to have distilled all Youth and Joy and Life into a foetid heap of hideous putrescence.

The highest proportion of casualties in the early encounters had been amongst the junior officers who had led their men into battle with drawn swords and wearing distinctive uniforms. The Regular Army captains, majors, colonels and above were now accorded accelerated promotion in the new divisions which were joining the BEF.

The British officer corps on the outbreak of war had belonged to an army which occupied a unique position in Europe, for unlike any of the other major powers Britain had never established a vaunted military tradition. For most of its turbulent history, since its inception soon after the Restoration, the Standing Army had been constitutionally mistrusted and socially abhorred. Service as a soldier had seldom been regarded as particularly praiseworthy or particularly noble; in fact, until well on into the nineteenth century the mass of the British people had viewed their peacetime Army with aversion and contempt. As a consequence, military recruitment had always been one of the government's most pressing problems and they had had recourse throughout the ages to a number of unsavoury devices such as bribery, deception, the enlistment of convicts from the goals, and the impressing of the homeless and the unemployed. One of the reasons for the unpopularity of the Army had been the brutality of its punishments. The branding of deserters with the letter D had only been abolished in 1871, ten years before the abolition of military flogging.

Army officers for the most part were the younger sons of aristocratic families. Under the Purchase System, which had also ended in 1871, the ordinary method of obtaining a commission, or of achieving any subsequent promotion up to and including the rank of colonel, had been by the payment of a substantial sum of money. Even after this irrational process had been abolished and officer-cadets had been made to pass through the Royal Military College at Sandhurst or the Royal Military Academy at Woolwich, the standard of professionalism did not substantially improve. A committee set up in 1902 to study the training of army officers reported that commissions were granted far too readily to cadets who had not attained a requisite degree of knowledge or skill.[4] A witness had told the committee, 'I am sorry to say that the officer wanted in the Army is only one who can command from £150 to £1,500 a year.'

The officers in the Regular Army had created their own sub-culture with an odd assortment of tenets – a reverential obsession with personal courage, an impassioned devotion to their regiments, an emotional insularity, and an arrogant elitism. As soon as the author Robert Graves arrived at his regimental depot with an emergency commission in the winter of 1914 he was reminded of his good fortune in being there at all.[5] To obtain a commission in peacetime, he was told, a candidate had not only to distinguish himself in the passing-out examination at Sandhurst and to be strongly recommended by two serving officers, but he had also to possess a guaranteed income which would enable him to play polo, hunt and to preserve the social reputation of the regiment. These requirements were waived in the case of war-emergency officers but they must understand that they did not 'belong' to the regiment in the special sense. When Graves was posted to one of the regular battalions in France, after serving in the line for three months with another unit, the colonel, the second-in-command and all the other officers immediately made him aware of his inferior status by a display of incivility which was both loutish and puerile. This behaviour might not have been typical of every regiment, nor even of the majority of regiments, but it was, perhaps, symbolic of the lack of sensitivity amongst certain prewar officers in the Regular Army.

Out of the ten senior generals who commanded formations in the field between 1914 and 1918, and who therefore had most influence over the implementation of death sentences, seven had been trained at Sandhurst and one at Woolwich. Sir John French had started his service career as a midshipman in the Navy and Sir Herbert Plumer had been commissioned directly into an infantry regiment at the age of 19. Three of the ten had been educated at Eton and two at Harrow. As regards active service, all of them had taken part in the Boer War either as regimental officers or with appointments on the staff. Prior to the Boer War they had all seen action in one or more subsidiary campaigns such as those in Egypt, the Sudan, Burma, Afghanistan and Matabeleland, or else with the various punitive expeditions which took place against the tribesmen in India. No British general, however, had personal experience of anything that had remotely resembled the carnage of the Great War battlefields, the stresses and strains of a Western Front bombardment, or the appalling discomfort and the constant danger of existence in the trenches. The châteaux in which they based their headquarters were, for the most part, secluded havens of tranquillity far removed from the bloody turmoil of the fighting line.

It was considered by the British military authorities that the BEF would not be capable of mounting a large-scale offensive before the spring of 1916 when the necessary numbers of men and munitions would have become available. General Joffre, however, had other ideas and during the summer of 1915 he was constantly urging Sir John French to launch a big attack before the close of the year. In June he proposed that the offensive should take place across what he termed 'the favourable ground' between Loos and La Bassée. Both Sir John French and Sir Douglas Haig, his senior Army Commander, were of the opinion that the particular sector of the front suggested by General Joffre would be, in reality, completely unsuitable for an attack, but Joffre refused to consider any alternative plan. Haig, who had made a personal reconnaissance of the area, reported:

> The ground, for the most part bare and open, would be swept by machine-gun and rifle fire both from the German front trenches and from the numerous fortified villages immediately behind them and a rapid advance would be impossible.

Sir Henry Rawlinson, the commander of the corps which would have to bear the brunt of the fighting, recorded his disquiet in his diary. 'It will cost us dearly,' he wrote, 'and we shall not get very far.'

In August 1915 the military situation was worsening for the Allies. The Russians were suffering a series of heavy defeats at the hands of the Germans in the east, the Austrians were overrunning the Italian Armies in northern Italy, and the British expedition was heading for failure at Gallipoli. In what seemed to be a crisis situation Kitchener came round to Joffre's view that a simultaneous offensive must be opened in the early autumn by the French in the Champagne and Artois districts and by the British in the area of Loos. And so the die was cast. The Official History states:

> Under pressure from Lord Kitchener at home due to the general position of the Allies, and from Generals Joffre and Foch in France, the British Commander-in-Chief was therefore compelled to undertake operations before he was ready, over ground that was most unfavourable, against the better judgment of himself and General Haig.

General Joffre remained confident of the success of his plans. The French Armies, he said, were approaching the summit of their strength, new British formations were arriving steadily in France, and about a third of the German military forces were engaged against the Russians on the Eastern Front. It was finally agreed that the combined Anglo-French offensive would commence on 25 September.

By that time the strength of the BEF had increased to just over 900,000 officers and men, a large proportion of whom were untried and undertrained. A total of 75,000 troops from six different divisions were to take part in the first attack. There would be a preliminary bombardment of the German positions lasting for 96 hours, followed by a short, intensive concentration of high explosive and chlorine gas on their front-line trenches just before the assault took place. Then the massed formations would move across a no-man's-land, which was in places as little as 100 yards wide.

The story of the Battle of Loos has often been told. It is a story of courage and confusion, of faulty planning and pointless sacrifice of life. In some places the British captured the forward German trenches but elsewhere they were mown down by machine-gun fire and could make no headway at all. The gas had been released from cylinders just before the attack went in and only part of it had drifted across to the German lines; the remainder had either lingered motionless on the British side of no-man's-land or had blown back into the faces of the advancing troops causing heavy casualties among them. Unfortunately, many of the men had abandoned the primitive, early-style gas helmets which were cumbersome and suffocating, severely restricting the hearing and vision of the wearer. By nightfall on the first day of the offensive the battle positions of the British were scattered and disorganized. About one in every six of the men who had taken part in the fighting had been either killed, wounded, gassed or taken prisoner.

The following day two of the newly-arrived British divisions, neither of which had ever been in the front line before, were thrown into the attack. Before they went over the top, an observer commented, 'The men appeared to be very tired, and many complained that they were dead beat owing to the succession of night marches from St. Omer.' They assaulted through a blinding rainstorm and were beaten back in disorder with heavy losses.

The Battle of Loos dragged on until early in November with the Allies making no substantial progress. Eventually the onset of wintry conditions and the exhaustion of the troops compelled the BEF to abandon the offensive. In any event, Loos had been intended as a diversion to the great French attack, and this had been brought to a halt in the middle of October. The total British casualties at Loos were not far short of 60,000.

The BEF then prepared itself for another arduous and immobile winter in the trenches. Raymond Asquith, the son of the British Prime Minister, had joined a battalion in the line as a junior subaltern in November 1915. He described his first reactions to the conditions in a letter home.[6] The trenches, he said, were far more uncomfortable but less dangerous than he had been led to expect. They were so filthy that there was a temptation to walk about on top of them rather than at the bottom. The wearing of waders was essential 'as mud and water are well above the knee and the cold intense'. An unpleasant feature, he added, was the vast number of rats, 'which gnaw the dead bodies and then run about on one's face making obscene noises and gestures'. Recently in his battalion's sector a number of cats had taken to nesting in the corpses. Towards the end of his first tour of duty in the trenches Asquith wrote, 'I shall be glad of a rest. The cold and mud and the interminable nights when one tramps through the frozen slush visiting sentries and either may not or cannot sleep are very wearisome – more to the spirit, oddly enough, than to the body.'

The execution rate in the BEF fell slightly during the closing months of 1915. From the beginning of September until the end of the year eight soldiers were sentenced to death and shot, seven of them for desertion and one for murder. The number of Kitchener volunteers who were serving in France by then exceeded the number of regulars and reservists and it was becoming possible for men to be facing a firing squad within a comparatively short time after their day of enlistment. A 21-year-old London youth who joined up in a Cornish regiment on 24 February 1915 was posted to a battalion in France as an officer's servant three weeks later. At the end of July his division went into the line, and he and a number of other servants were left behind at a camp near Armentières. He then formed the idea that he could get home for a few days and slip back again unnoticed before the battalion returned to the camp. He stole an officer's uniform, a cheque-book and some money and walked to Boulogne where he was arrested dressed as a lieutenant. He was executed on 29 September about seven months after he had enlisted, without ever having been in action.

A deserter was not always granted clemency just because he had surrendered himself voluntarily to the authorities. Privates S and L, who were court-martialled on 21 September, had enlisted together in a Rifle regiment the previous April. They were both in the upper thirties and were old soldiers who had already finished their time on the Reserve. S was a veteran of the Boer War and L had served for 12 years in another regiment. They went absent on 22 August while their battalion was resting in billets behind the line. On 28 August they surrendered to the British Consul at Dunkirk declaring themselves to be deserters. L said in his defence that he was the only support of his widowed mother. S stated that he had been very drunk at the time he went absent. Both men were sentenced to death but were recommended to mercy on account of their previous good work in the trenches. General French considered that in spite of the mitigating factors the sentences should be confirmed, and the two men were shot together on 3 October.

A deserter's former bravery in action usually stood him in good stead after he had been sentenced to death. Sometimes, however, it was nullified by his motives – or the motives attributed to him – at the moment he had committed his offence. Driver J had joined a field battery in BEF in April 1915. It was said that from the start of his service in France he had behaved with ability and courage. On 12 June he deserted from a forward firing position about a mile away from the German lines, and he remained absent until he was arrested in a nearby village on 4 August. In his comments on the case Driver J's brigade commander came out with the information that J was suspected of having stolen a large sum of money from a ruined house in Ypres, and that his commanding officer believed he had absented himself with the intention of spending it on women and drink. That being so, the brigadier declared, he was a deliberate skulker who should be executed. J was shot on 15 September.

There were certain soldiers in the BEF who seemed determined to avoid serving in the line. Private D, a member of a Northumberland regiment, was an example. He was a single man aged about 40 who had been a regular soldier for 13 years before the war and had re-enlisted as a volunteer in August 1914. He joined a division in France in September 1914 and deserted the following December. He was returned to his battalion under a suspended sentence of imprisonment and had continually absented himself from the trenches without any further serious charges being brought against him. Eventually he deserted again during September 1915 and remained away for over three weeks. At his court martial in December D pleaded for leniency, saying that his sister and her two children were entirely dependent on him. He was sentenced to death and was executed early in 1916.

A soldier who was awaiting trial by court martial was usually handed over to his company by the provost sergeant when his battalion was going into the trenches. He then served in the ordinary way until his unit had completed its duty in the line, whereupon he would be returned to the custody of the provost sergeant, to be detained under close arrest in the battalion guardroom or guard-tent. When a man was about to be tried for a capital offence he had a great inducement to redeem his reputation, and it was frequently mentioned in the course of a statement in mitigation that immediately prior to his court martial the accused soldier had volunteered for a dangerous bombing party or for a fighting patrol into no-man's-land.

The second soldier in the BEF to be executed for murder was a Welshman who was tried by FGCM in November 1915. While his division was in reserve he had entered his billet in a drunken condition and fired his rifle indiscriminately at other members of his platoon, one of whom had been killed. In all the circumstances a civilian jury might well have found him guilty of manslaughter rather than of murder.

An Allied invasion of the Gallipoli peninsula with the object of capturing the Dardanelles had first been discussed by the British War Council at the end of 1914. The actual landing took place on 25 April 1915, and the operation was a disaster from the start. The Turkish divisions in Gallipoli, trained by a German military mission and led by a German general, had spent six months improving their defensive positions. They fought everywhere with the same pertinacity and courage. By 8 May the invading forces had suffered heavy casualties and had only advanced a very short distance from the beaches; they were short of sleep, short of reinforcements, and short of supplies; and none of their base or rest areas were outside the range of the enemy's artillery. As the summer wore on other factors contributed to the discomfort of the expeditionary force. The Official History of the Gallipoli campaign has described the conditions:

> The heat of the noon-day sun was intense; there was little or no shade; and the scanty water supply in the trenches was rarely sufficient for men with a parching thirst. The sickening smell of unburied corpses in No Man's Land pervaded the front areas; dense clouds of dust were incessant; and despite the preventive care of the doctors there was such a loathsome plague of huge flies (known to the troops as 'corpse flies') that it was difficult to eat a mouthful of food without swallowing the pests. . . . The number of sick was increasing by leaps and bounds and there was not a man in the peninsula who was not a victim of the prevailing epidemic of dysenteric diarrhoea.

All through the stifling summer months of July, August and September the expeditionary force endeavoured without success to push back the enemy and to enlarge its foothold. A new landing was made at Suvla Bay to the north of the Gallipoli peninsula, but owing to the inefficient planning and lack of artillery support the exhausted troops were soon checked and thrown on the defensive.

The approach of wintry weather was accompanied by new torments for the invading forces. Storms swept the coast, disrupting their supply vessels and wrecking the makeshift piers on which they relied for their survival. At the end of November a gale of unusual violence devastated the peninsula for three days. At first it blew from the south-west, bringing with it a tropical downpour; then it veered to the north, the temperature fell and the rain was transformed into a blinding blizzard of snow. Thousands of men went sick with frostbite and over 200 were drowned or frozen to death in their trenches.

At the beginning of December the British War Cabinet had decided to abandon the Dardanelles project and to evacuate two out of the three bridgeheads in Gallipoli without delay. The withdrawal was successfully completed by 20 December. The remaining bridgehead was completely evacuated by 9 January 1916. A total of 410,000 British, Australian, New Zealand and Indian troops had served at Gallipoli. Out of these 205,000 were recorded as killed, wounded or missing, and 90,000 men were removed from the peninsula through sickness. The Official History adds a final comment on the failure of the operation:

> Many reasons combined to frustrate an enterprise the success of which in 1915 would have altered the course of the war. But every reason will be found to spring from one fundamental cause – an utter lack of preparation before the campaign began.

A new theatre of operations had opened for the Allies in the autumn of 1915 when an Austro-German Army had struck southwards into Serbia, and at the same time a large Bulgarian force had advanced into southern Serbia in the rear of the main Serbian Army. In response to Serbia's urgent call for assistance France and Britain had sent a combined expedition to Salonika in October, the British contribution to which consisted in the first place of the 10th (Irish) Division from Gallipoli.

The first execution of the Gallipoli campaign occurred in the 29th Division, which had been stationed in India on the outbreak of war and was the only Regular formation to take part in the initial landings on 25 April. The 29th Division had encountered desperate resistance from the start. Within three days their effective strength was reduced from over 17,500 men to just under 7,000, and by the end of May they had only managed to advance a little more than three miles from their main landing beach. The condemned soldier, Private K, belonged to an Irish regiment. On 20 June he had been a member of the guard at his battalion headquarters. At one o'clock in the morning the guard-sergeant had posted him on a two-hour duty as a 'flying sentry' to patrol around the perimeter of the headquarters. An hour and a half later the sergeant had carried out a routine check on his sentries and had found that K was missing. No one saw K again until he reported back to the guardroom about three hours later.

Private K was charged with 'leaving his post without orders from his superior officer'. He was tried by court martial at the end of June, a few days after he had committed the offence. Owing to the exigencies of the situation there was no field officer available to act as president of the court, the members of which consisted of two captains and a lieutenant. K maintained in his defence that he had continued on duty until just after two o'clock in the morning, when he had suffered from a severe pain in his stomach and had been obliged to find a latrine; he had remained there for the next two hours. His story was disbelieved and he was sentenced to death. Probably the court formed the opinion that K had lain down somewhere away from the area of his patrol and had fallen asleep. He was a man with a bad military record. Since he had landed in Gallipoli he had been court-martialled twice and he was subject to a suspended sentence of ten years' penal servitude.

The second soldier to be executed during the campaign was Private S, whose home was in the North of England. He was serving in the 13th (Western) Division which had arrived in Gallipoli during a crucial phase of the fighting at the end of June, and was mostly composed of Kitchener volunteers like S, who had received nine or ten months' preliminary training in England. Private S deserted from the front line on 1 November after he had been continuously in action for over four months. He was apprehended after ten days. At his court martial he put forward no defence, declining to give evidence or to make a statement. He had been absent without leave on two previous occasions in Gallipoli. In recommending that S should be shot, his brigade commander said there were no redeeming features in his character and his persistent efforts to get away from his unit showed that he had no intention of performing his duty in the future.

The third and last soldier to be executed in Gallipoli was another member of the 13th (Western) Division. Sergeant T, a regular of some years' service, had been court-martialled for disobedience early in December, just before the War Cabinet made their final decision to evacuate the peninsula. On 3 December, just after the abatement of the arctic storms, T had been detailed to accompany an officer on a patrol into no-man's-land and had refused to go on the ground that he was not feeling well enough. He was examined by his battalion medical officer who reported that his temperature and his pulse rate were perfectly normal. Again T was ordered to go out on patrol and again he refused, still maintaining that he was too ill. At his trial he said that he suffered from persistent bouts of fever as a result of his eight years' service in India. Perhaps the truth of the matter was that his courage and his will had been sapped by five months of arduous fighting in the climatic extremes of both summer and winter. Sergeant T was shot at dawn at the beginning of 1916, when the evacuation of Gallipoli was almost complete and the 13th Division was giving rearguard protection to the Helles beaches.

A 19-year-old soldier from the 10th (Irish) Division in Salonika was also sentenced to death for disobedience in December. Private B, who came from the west of Ireland, had enlisted as a volunteer in September 1914 at the age of 18. For some reason which was not explained he had stood fast when his company sergeant-major had ordered him to fall in on parade, and then had refused to put on his cap when an officer had told him to do so. B's commanding officer recommended that the sentence should be carried out owing to the poor state of discipline in his battalion. B was executed two days after Christmas.

The British failure at the Battle of Loos confirmed the growing doubts as to the ability of Sir John French to conduct a victorious campaign on the Western Front. In December 1915 he was replaced as Commander-in-Chief of the BEF by his old staff officer, Sir Douglas Haig. On his return to England French was made a viscount and was appointed Commander-in-Chief of Home Forces.

Notes

1. A. J. P. Taylor, *English History 1914–1918*.
2. Vera Brittain, *Chronicle of Youth*.
3. Vera Brittain, op. cit.
4. Report of the Committee appointed to consider the Education and Training of the Officers of the Army, 1902.
5. Robert Graves, *Goodbye to All That*.
6. Raymond Asquith, *Life and Letters*, edited by John Joliffe.

5
EXECUTION AT DAWN

S OON AFTER THE commencement of the First World War rumours
were beginning to circulate in Britain that soldiers were being
executed on the Western Front. When Roland Leighton was home on
leave in August 1915 he told Vera Brittain about his experiences in
France and as she noted in her diary:[1]

> He dealt too with many of the usually unmentioned and more unpleasant
> aspects of the War, such as the condition of the charnel-house trenches,
> or the shooting of sentries who go to sleep on duty and are described in
> the casualty list as 'Died'. Military discipline I suppose – but all the same
> it makes me feel sick to hear about it.

Since no sentries had been shot at that time for sleeping on their
posts and there had been no executions at all in Leighton's own
battalion his information on this subject must have been derived
entirely from hearsay. Discussing the state of discipline in the BEF
John Baynes has written that 'although most people knew at second-
hand about an execution by the firing squad it was extremely rare for
anyone to have personal knowledge of one'.[2]

With the passage of time the legend and reality of half-secreted
happenings become deceptively intermingled. In attempting to investigate what actually occurred at these dawn executions reliance
must be placed on the sparse contemporary directives and reports, and
on the recorded accounts of eyewitnesses, and purported eyewitnesses, which are inclined to be coloured by emotive embellishment and
even, on occasion, by downright fabrication.

After a sentence of death had been confirmed by the Commander-
in-Chief the soldier was usually executed within a matter of three or
four days. During this time, unknown to the condemned man, the
necessary preparations were made for the final ritual.

There had been a custom in the British Army in past ages that a
firing party should be composed of regimental criminals. Writing in
1786 Francis Grose said that it would generally be made up from
'hardened deserters or persons guilty of the same offence for which the
party is to suffer'.[3] That practice had fallen into abeyance, and during
the war the selection of the firing party was left to the condemned

soldier's own unit. They were also responsible, in conjunction with the APM, for choosing the place where the execution would be carried out, though occasionally they received a directive on this point from their divisional or their brigade headquarters. The 40th Brigade in Gallipoli issued an order that one shooting would take place 'on the beach 400 yards North of Gully Ravine'. In 1916 the 15th Brigade on the Western Front suggested to a battalion that a railway embankment in the vicinity of their positions would be a suitable location for an execution. Sometimes the instructions were less precise. A brigade headquarters in the Ypres Salient, when informing a commanding officer that a death sentence on one of his men had been confirmed, told him to arrange the execution 'in a secluded spot'.

On 22 March 1916, a staff officer of the 21st Division issued this terse movement order for a firing party:

The following detail from 10th Battalion of the ——— Regiment will be sent to Armentières tonight, returning to Strangeile on completion of the duty. Buses are to be arranged for –

Regimental Sergeant-Major
Provost Sergeant
Escort 1 NCO and 2 men
Firing Party 1 Officer
            1 Sergeant
          16 Men

The NCO in charge of the Escort should be able to identify [the condemned soldier].

On arrival at Armentières this party should be confined to the billets which will be allotted to them. The men need not be informed of the duty for which they have been detailed until the morning of the 23rd inst.

There were no prescribed numbers for a firing party, but a squad of 18 for a single execution was unusually large. The standard size in the BEF seems to have been one officer and ten men. An execution was carried out at Gallipoli in December 1915 by a squad consisting of an officer, two NCOs and 12 men. It was the practice in France for the officer in charge to load the rifles himself, putting live ammunition into nine of them and a blank cartridge in the tenth, or merely leaving it unloaded. It is difficult to believe that a trained soldier would not know as soon as he had pressed the trigger whether or not he had fired a live round; the fact remains that right up to the moment of taking aim each member of the firing party could continue to hope that he alone might be absolved from playing a part in the killing of a comrade. The officer did not have a rifle but was armed with a loaded revolver. It was his duty to give the executive orders, and if the prisoner showed any signs of life after the firing of the volley, to approach him and to administer the *coup de grâce*.

It was customary for a firing party to be supplied from the condemned soldier's own unit, but there was no inflexible rule to this effect. Sometimes the men were found from another battalion in the same brigade, and on one occasion in France in 1916 the firing party was made up of detachments from two different battalions.

The night before his execution the prisoner was kept at a camp or in a billet as near as possible to the place where he was going to be shot. If the death sentence had already been promulgated to him he could receive, if he wished, a visit from a chaplain of his own religious denomination. Meanwhile the last preparations were put in hand. A grave was dug and the necessary stores were collected. A message from a brigade to a condemned soldier's battalion in April 1916 told them they must provide 'a chair, a blanket and two ropes', and that their medical officer must have available in the morning 'a bandage and a piece of white cloth to mark the heart'. The message also said that two men were to be standing by with spades to fill in the grave after the prisoner's body had been put into it.

Executions were ordered to be carried out, according to various divisional orders, 'at daybreak', 'at as early an hour as may be found convenient', or 'as early as possible after first light of dawn'. A chaplain was always at hand to support and to comfort the prisoner, if he could do so, on the final morning. An order for an execution in January 1915 instructed the chaplain to visit the condemned soldier 'at least an hour' before he was to be shot, and in the autumn of the same year a divisional directive for a double execution decreed, 'A chaplain of the prisoners' denomination should be present and have access to the prisoners until the time of their execution. The chaplain must be near at hand so that the prisoners can see him just before their execution, if desired.'

It appears that an execution was sometimes carried out in private: sometimes it was carried out before an audience of compelled spectators. An order from a divisional headquarters in the early part of 1915 left it to the brigade commander concerned to detail 'such troops as you consider desirable' to witness the shooting. On the other hand, a divisional commander in September 1915 directed that the whole of the accused soldier's own battalion should be paraded to watch, and in March 1916 a message to the commanding officer of an infantry battalion from his brigadier told him, 'The Divisional Commander wishes one platoon from each company of your battalion to be present at the execution.' Since the death penalty was supposed to be exemplary the desire for a large attendance at the scene might emanate from the commanding officer himself. In a note to brigade headquarters in

May 1918 the colonel of an infantry battalion, one of whose privates had been sentenced to death for desertion, complained about a prevalent mood of insubordination amongst his men. 'In order to restore discipline,' he wrote, 'and to show the men of my battalion that the death sentence is sometimes carried out, I earnestly request that Pte. ―― may be shot in front of my whole battalion on parade.'

When two men were being executed in the same place on the same occasion they were shot simultaneously by a double firing party, each member of which had been detailed to aim at one specific prisoner. In the days of the British Army's notorious flogging parades the procedure had been different; when several men were being flogged on the same occasion they were dealt with one at a time and those who were awaiting their punishment were compelled to witness the sufferings of the earlier victims. Just before his execution the soldier was tied to a chair, a tree or a stake in the ground and a handkerchief, a cloth or a towel was wound around his eyes. In order to spare his ultimate anguish the officer in charge of the firing party avoided the shouting of orders and ordinarily instructed his men to take aim and to fire by a prearranged code of signals.

After the execution volley had been fired it was the duty of the medical officer present to confirm that the victim was dead and to certify whether or not death had been immediate. In the vast majority of cases the doctor was able to employ the set formula 'death was instantaneous'. Indeed, it is difficult to imagine how, if a party of nine trained soldiers had been aiming at the prisoner's heart from a minimal distance, their shots could have failed to kill him outright. However, this did not always happen. On one occasion a medical officer reported 'death was practically instantaneous' and on another that 'death not instantaneous'. At an execution in France in March 1917 the doctor's certificate stated, 'Death was not instantaneous. The coup de grâce had to be given by the officer in charge of the firing party.'[4]

As soon as the doctor was satisfied that life was extinct the corpse was rolled up in an army blanket and lowered into a shallow, temporary grave, the map reference of which had been recorded by the APM. The chaplain then recited the brief and poignant invocations of the burial service in the field – and the execution ceremony was at an end. Thus the disposal of the condemned soldier's body and the ultimate rights accorded to it were identical with those granted to the bodies of his erstwhile comrades who had met an honourable death at the hands of the enemy.

In due course the corpses of the executed were collected, like those of soldiers who had been slain in battle, and removed for reinterment at military cemeteries. An order from the Adjutant-General in September 1916 stated:[5]

There is no rule that any man who has suffered the extreme penalty of the law should be buried near the place of execution. Any man who suffers the extreme penalty of the law may be buried in a cemetery, the inscription being marked 'DIED' instead of 'KILLED IN ACTION' or 'DIED OF WOUNDS'.

It is sometimes said that towards the end of the war it became increasingly difficult to organize effective executions because members of firing parties were declining to shoot at the condemned men. There is no reason to believe that this rumour has any substance. No doubt, before the firing party was marched to the scene of the execution an officer, a sergeant-major or a senior NCO used to impress on them the importance of shooting to kill from motives of sheer humanity. There might have been some soldiers, and there probably were, who deliberately ignored this injunction, but it seems quite clear that the majority of the men concerned carried it through to the letter and that executions towards the end of the war differed in no way from those at the beginning.

Stephen Graham gave his account of an execution on the Western Front in his memoirs published in 1919.[6] When Graham was posted to France during the last year of the war he was allocated the task, as a professional writer, of editing his battalion's diaries for the campaign and supplementing them by speaking to men with a first-hand knowledge of the events in question. Although the execution he described had taken place as early as March 1915, it is probable that he was still able to find some survivors who had been serving with the battalion at the time.

Reveille had been early on the morning of the execution, said Graham, and the battalion had dressed in the dark. They had had to wear full fighting order with packs and they had formed up at dawn on three sides of a square. The condemned soldier had been comparatively free at first and had chatted to several of his old companions, saying 'good-bye' to them happily and calmly. He had been allowed to smoke a last cigarette and then had strolled over to a tree to which he was tied by his hands and feet. According to Graham, an attempt had been made to find volunteers for the firing party, but as none were forthcoming ten of the battalion snipers had been detailed for the task. Before his eyes were bandaged the condemned man besought them to aim at his heart and to make sure they did not miss. The battalion had then come to attention, fixed bayonets and sloped arms. An officer had read out the charge, the firing party had aimed and fired, and the victim had dropped dead. It had only remained for the parade to order arms, unfix bayonets and to march off to their ordinary duties.

A few years after the Armistice a persistent campaign for the abolition of the death penalty for military offences was being led by Ernest Thurtle, a Labour Member of Parliament.[7] In 1924 Mr Thurtle published a small pamphlet designed, so he said, to establish that the executions during the war for cowardice and desertion had been miscarriages of justice.[8] In his introductory remarks he stated that the relevant records were all in the hands of the War Office and access to them was not permitted; he had therefore found it necessary to collect his information from the comrades of the victims and it had been impossible to construct anything like a complete picture of the operation of the military death penalty in wartime. He continued:

I have, however, succeeded in obtaining the facts in regard to a number of executions, and I think these will be sufficient to convince the public of the barbarity and gross injustice of this particular part of Military Law. All the cases quoted are supported by complete details, which are in my possession, as to names, units concerned, dates, places, and offences. My informants, who certainly have no motive for departing from the truth in regard to these cases, are prepared to maintain the accuracy of their statements before any competent tribunal.

It was, perhaps, somewhat naive of Ernest Thurtle to have placed so high a trust in the probity of his witnesses. For one thing, the subject-matter of his investigation was heavily charged with emotive impulsion; for another, after the comparatively brief interval since their demobilization there must have been many ex-soldiers who were still retaining a smouldering resentment against some of the harshness of army discipline. It is prudent, therefore, to examine the examples which he cites with extreme care.

The first of Thurtle's cases is easily identifiable as the second military execution to be carried out in the war.[9] His informant was well conversant with the facts, but mis-stated the prosecution evidence in one material particular which gave the false impression of a totally unfair conviction. Consequently, one must view with a little suspicion the description of the actual shooting:

To get the firing party, as we were going into the line that night, they called for twelve men to carry tools. Now the men who carried tools at the time had the first chance of using them, so you see there were plenty of volunteers, but once on parade they realized their job was to shoot [the accused]. On being brought out he broke away from the sergeant of the guard, and the firing party fired at him on the run, wounding him in the shoulder. They brought him back on a stretcher, and the sergeant of the guard was ordered by the Provost-Marshal to finish him off as he lay wounded.

Thurtle's second case, which can also be identified, was only included in his pamphlet to exemplify the extreme youthfulness of some of the soldiers who were executed. Private 'B', he says, was shot for desertion in April 1916 when he was eighteen and a half, having joined the Army in August 1914 at the age of seventeen. There is no reason to doubt that these details are correct as the other circumstances of the matter which Thurtle mentions seem to be fairly accurate. Private 'B''s battalion had been heavily engaged at Vermelles; a number of men had deserted during the action and had hidden themselves in cellars in the town. Five of the most blatant offenders were put up for court martial but owing to difficulties with prosecution evidence only Private 'B' had actually been tried. This man had a bad military record with several entries on his conduct-sheet for absence without leave, one for disobedience and one for sleeping on his post.

The third of Ernest Thurtle's informants had been a transport driver with the BEF and claimed that he was present at an execution in May 1916. The full particulars he supplied match up with those of an execution which did occur around that time. The brigade transport group, he said, were paraded at 3.30 a.m. in full equipment on the outskirts of a village. The prisoner and his escort were marched out in front of them and the APM read out the details of the charge and the findings of the court martial. The account continues:

> We were then ordered to turn about, and the Brigade Transport Officer threatened us that any man who turned round would be put on a crime. So we stood in silence for what seemed hours, although only minutes. Then the shots rang out and one of the Yorkshires fainted, the strain was that great. Still we stood in silence until we heard another shot, which I afterwards ascertained was the doctor's shot to make sure he was dead.

The fourth of Thurtle's informants, who had been a sergeant in a North Country regiment, referred to the executions of a lance-corporal and a private which had taken place within a week of each other during the month of February 1916. No soldiers from this man's battalion were executed in the month which he mentioned, but two executions, very similar in detail, took place during the month of February 1915. The sergeant's connection with the first shooting, that of the lance-corporal, was that he was told to pick out two of the toughest characters in his platoon to form part of the firing party. After the execution, he said:

> tough characters though they were supposed to be, they were sick, they screamed in their sleep, they vomited immediately after eating. All they

could say was: 'The sight was horrible, made more so by the fact that we had shot one of our own men.'

A week later, the ex-sergeant continued, he had been in charge of the regimental guard and had received orders to select 12 prisoners from the guardroom to form the firing party for the execution of the private soldier who had been sentenced to death for desertion. He described his difficulties:

> It was then I witnessed a scene I shall never forget. Men I had known for years as clean, decent, self-respecting soldiers, whose only offence was an occasional military 'drunk', screamed out, begging not to be made into murderers. They offered me all they had if I would not take them for the job, and finally, when twelve of them had found themselves outside, selected for the dreaded firing party, they called me all the names they could lay their tongues to.

Thurtle went on to quote a lengthy extract from an article which he said had already been published, purporting to be a description by an ex-soldier of a triple execution in France which he had been forced to witness. In endorsing the veracity of the account Thurtle said that he had the complete details of the case in his possession. He added that the victims had been a sergeant and two corporals belonging to a light infantry regiment, which he named, and he explained that their alleged offence had consisted of carrying out the orders given to them by a captain who was dying from wounds. The matter can be disposed of very shortly. During the whole war this particular regiment never had a triple shooting, and none of its sergeants was ever executed. Furthermore, there was no capital court martial in any unit the facts of which were in any way similar to those attributed to this case.

In the days when Thurtle was collecting his information there must have been a number of demobilized soldiers in Britain with experience of wartime executions. His difficulty, no doubt, was to distinguish between veracity and falsehood. He had received one letter from a man who said that during his service in the infantry he had been a member of a firing party at the execution of two men, to whom he refers as 'E' and 'G'. The writer gave details of his regiment and battalion, and his claim appears to be authentic since two private soldiers from that unit, the initial letters of whose surnames happened to be E and G, were executed together in February 1916. The account of the shooting is brief and unadorned:

> We were told that the only humane thing that we could do was to shoot straight. The two men were led out blindfolded, tied to posts driven into the ground, and then we received our orders by sign from our officer, so

that the condemned men should not hear us getting ready. Our officer felt it very much, as he, like me, knew the fellow 'E' years before. 'G' I never knew, but his case was every bit as sad, as he was only a boy.

Another ex-serviceman who wrote to Thurtle told him that he had been the sergeant in charge of an execution party, two members of which had refused to fire. 'Of course, they were tried', his letter continued, 'but they were found to be medically unfit – their nerves had gone.' As no particulars were provided with regard to the date, the place or the circumstances of the episode it is impossible to verify its authenticity.

A depiction of a military execution in France was given by William Moore in a book published in 1974.[10] The condemned man, whose unit was specified, is said to have been shot for desertion in the summer of 1916. The details were supplied to the author by a man who claimed to have been serving in the same battalion as the victim, but it is not clear whether he purports to speak as an actual eyewitness or as one who has derived his knowledge from others. In fact, no soldier in the battalion mentioned was executed that summer; only two of its members were shot by sentence of court martial throughout the entire war and their executions took place in November and December 1916. The ascertainable facts of both these cases are very different from those which are stated in Moore's book.

One of the most reliable descriptions of an execution on the Western Front was given by Doctor M. S. Esler, who served as a medical officer in the RAMC.[11] His battalion, he said, had been having two weeks' rest in a village a few miles behind the line when the commanding officer had sent for him and told him, 'I have a very unpleasant duty for you to perform which I won't like any more than you do.' The colonel went on to explain that a soldier in the battalion had been sentenced to death by court martial for deserting from the front line. He instructed Esler to attend the execution on the following morning, and before it took place to pin a piece of coloured flannel over the condemned man's heart so that the firing party would know where to aim.

Doctor Esler lay awake all night thinking about the execution. Early next morning he took a cup of brandy to the condemned soldier and urged him to drink it. The man refused saying that he had never drunk spirits in his life and there was no point in starting then. 'That to me,' Esler commented, 'was a sort of spurious courage in a way.' Esler's account continues:

Two men came and led him out of the hut where he'd been guarded all night. As he left the hut his legs gave way; then one could see the fear entering his heart. Rather than marched to the firing spot he was dragged along. When we got there he had his hands tied behind his back, he was put up against a wall, his eyes were bandaged and the firing squad were given the order to fire.

The firing squad consisted of eight men only two of whom had their rifles loaded. The other six carried blank ammunition – that was so that they wouldn't actually know who had fired the fatal shot.[12] I wondered at the time, 'What on earth will happen if they miss him and they don't kill him completely?', and I was very anxious about that, but when they fired he fell to the ground writhing as all people do – even if they've been killed they have this reflex action of writhing about which goes on for some minutes.

I didn't know whether he was dead or not, but at that moment the sergeant in charge stepped forward, put a revolver to his head and blew his brains out, and that was the coup de grâce which I understood afterwards – I learnt afterwards – was always carried out in these cases of shooting.

Notes

1. Vera Brittain, *Chronicle of Youth*.
2. John Baynes, *Morale. A Study of Men and Courage*.
3. Francis Grose, *Military Antiquities*.
4. A similar phrase was used by a doctor when a member of the Macedonian Mule Corps was executed for murder in Turkey in 1919.
5. Reproduced in instructions issued by the Brigadier-General Director of Graves Registration and Enquiries, 30 June 1917. Also see note 11 on p. 94.
6. Stephen Graham, *A Private in the Guards*.
7. Ernest Thurtle (1884–1954), accountant and salesman. Served with BEF in the ranks and then as an officer. He was severely wounded at Cambrai. Later he became a junior Minister from 1930 to 1931 and was Parliamentary Secretary at the Ministry of Information from 1941 to 1945.
8. Ernest Thurtle, MP, *Shootings at Dawn. The Army Death Penalty at Work*.
9. Ante, p. 14.
10. William Moore, *The Thin Yellow Line*.
11. Imperial War Museum Oral History Recordings, Western Front, 1914–18, Doctor M. S. Esler.
12. Dr Esler's information or his recollection was surely at fault on this point. It is far more likely that six rifles were loaded with live and two with blank ammunition.

6

THE YEAR OF THE SOMME

D URING THE COSTLY and relentless fighting at Loos and Gallipoli a profound change had taken place in the attitude of the British civil population towards the war. As the nation roused itself to the sembl- ance of a national effort the mood of levity and illusion had given way to a sombre sense of realism. Gone were the hopes of a quick and easy victory and gone, too, were most of the facile fantasies of martial glory. The mass of the people had now become aware – albeit only dimly aware – of the ugliness and horror of the modern battlefield. There was a growing belief that every able-bodied man of military age should be in uniform, and women went about distributing white feathers, the traditional emblems of masculine cowardice, to all those they thought were shrinking from the duty.

As more and more voices were raised to demand the commence- ment of conscription several government ministers, led by David Lloyd George, the Minister for Munitions, threatened to resign unless it was brought in forthwith. On the other hand there were many members of the Labour and Liberal parties in Parliament who were equally vehement about retaining the voluntary principle. Eventually a compromise was adopted and in October 1915, Lord Derby, the newly-appointed Director-General of Recruiting, introduced a national register for service. Under the 'Derby Scheme' men between the ages of 18 and 41 could either enlist as volunteers or could attest, whereby they entered into an obligation to join the forces if and when they were called upon to do so. When registration was completed in December 1915, 215,431 men had enlisted and 2,184,979 had chosen to attest.

In fact the Army had so many voluntary recruits already that it would have had difficulty in training and equipping them all by the end of 1916. Norman Gladden has told how, as an 18-year-old post office clerk, he enlisted under the Derby Scheme during the winter of 1915, and having received a day's army pay and a special khaki armlet to wear he was sent away to await his call-up, which did not happen until the following May.[1]

The Military Service Act was passed by Parliament in January 1916. It provided that all voluntary enlistment should cease and that any man between the ages of 18 and 41 who was either unmarried, or a widower without dependants, would be liable to be called up for general service. Conscripts would have no right to select the arm or the unit into which they were drafted. Apart from the resignation of Sir John Simon, the Home Secretary, and a certain amount of protest from the Labour and Liberal benches, the introduction of conscription had no significant political consequences for the Asquith government and in May 1916 it was extended to include all married men in the same age-group.

The Official History of the Great War records this comment:

> Whatever result the introduction of compulsory service may have had in Great Britain, and it was much less than had been anticipated since volunteering had already taken the cream of the nation, it had an immense effect on public opinion in Germany, where it indicated that at last Great Britain was taking the war in grim earnest.

Up to the end of 1915 the British Army had suffered the loss of 21,747 officers and 490,673 other ranks, the killed and missing making up about two-fifths of these totals. Although Britain by now had more men under arms than at any time before in her history the demand for reinforcements was still insatiable from the Western Front and from the other theatres of operations in which she was involved.

On 1 January 1916 the BEF consisted of 38 infantry and five cavalry divisions, with a total strength of 987,200 officers and men. It was divided into three armies, a fourth being added two months later. By the early summer 20 more infantry divisions had joined the BEF from England. Britain also had considerable forces on active service in Salonika and Mesopotamia which made additional inroads on her available manpower.

After the fighting on the Western Front during the closing months of 1915 the German positions were superior to those of the British in almost every sector, as they were dug on ground which was both higher and better drained. The German Army also enjoyed superiority in equipment for this sort of warfare, being amply provided with hand-grenades, rifle-grenades and light mortars, capable of lobbing bombs in quick succession from one set of trenches into another. At this stage the opposing lines were continuous and were divided from each other by a strip of no-man's-land which was never more than a few hundred yards wide. The BEF had adopted a defensive system comprising three rows of trenches, known respectively as the firing, the support and the reserve lines. Each of these had its own dugouts which provided adequate protection from shrapnel splinters but were rarely strong enough to withstand a direct hit from a shell.

During the hard winter months of cold, wet immobility the British higher command were seeking continuously to instil an offensive spirit into the troops in the line. They insisted upon a constant programme of limited attacks, sniping, patrols and night raids, in an effort to procure the complete domination of no-man's-land. This policy frequently evoked a retaliatory effort by the enemy and it accounted for an average of about 35,000 British casualties a month. Nevertheless, it is an undoubted fact that when two armies are face-to-face in a static role it is quite possible for one of them to achieve a psychological supremacy over the other by the energy and the aggressiveness of its behaviour.

When units were relieved from the line they were sent to reserve or to rest areas, where to the irritation of both the junior officers and the men the bulk of their time was occupied in drill parades, training and inspections. Norman Gladden bitterly complained[2] that the old regular officers 'were still living in a little world of their own, a world of parades and drill-books. . . . They treated us as they had learned to treat their peacetime soldiers, as automata made of a different clay to themselves.' Raymond Asquith was equally impressed by the fatuity of the situation. In a letter[3] to his wife in January 1916, he told her about his new commanding officer who, he said, was wonderfully efficient but patently limited and did not allow his battalion a moment to themselves. He went on:

> All subalterns parade at 8 A.M. and do the most elementary form of drill under a sergeant-major. I cannot believe that this helps us to win the war, and I would rather be shelled for an hour than drilled for an hour.

Throughout the months of January, February and March in 1916 there were sporadic attacks by both sides on the Western Front, designed as minor demonstrations of strength rather than the fulfilment of any tactical plan. From the British point of view these brief and localized actions provided an opportunity for some of the new formations to have their initial insight of active combat. During one such encounter Siegfried Sassoon's veteran battalion was relieved in the front line by troops who were freshly arrived from England. 'They were mostly undersized men,' he wrote,[4] 'and as I watched them arriving at the first stage of their battle experience I had a sense of their victimization.'

A 19-year-old deserter was the first British soldier to be court-martialled and shot in 1916. He had given every satisfaction in his battalion until he had gone absent, and could only plead that his mind had been affected by the constant heavy shelling. Debility of nerves induced by the conditions of battle was still not regarded as a defence, or even as a mitigation, on charges of cowardice or desertion. A private in a Scottish regiment was arrested by the military police in Béthune during January 1916, having absented himself from the trenches on the previous day. A week after his court martial he was examined by two medical officers who reported that he was suffering from a marked degree of neurasthenia, but were unable to say whether or not this was due to shell-shock. Unfortunately for this man there had recently been several other cases of desertion in his battalion and it was considered that an example was called for. He was executed in the abattoir at Mazingarbe on 15 February.

It is always a temptation to pass judgement on the events of recent history according to the outlook of the moment. It must be remembered, however, that more than 60 years have elapsed since the end of the First World War, and that the intervening period has witnessed, amongst the nations of the West, a major reappraisal of the tenets of moral ideology and a by no means inconsiderable advancement both in sociological and in humanistic principles. It is also as well to remember the setting in which those courts martial took place. When a soldier deserted on active service he left a gap in the ranks, to the prejudice of all his more-dutiful comrades. When he committed an act of cowardice in the face of the enemy he might have been jeopardizing the safety of the men around him; and panic on the battlefield can spread with the speed of light, affecting even those who until then have been entirely resolute. In addition, the generals who had to make the fateful decision as to whether the prisoners were going to live or die were inured to the paltry value of the lives of the men they commanded. They were, of necessity, dealing out death warrants in the abstract almost daily. It happened each time they ordered an offensive operation: it happened each time they sent a battalion up the line. To terminate the existence of some remote and numbered soldier at such a time was scarcely a matter of very great significance.

But when all this has been said the fact remains that there were certain decisions to implement the death sentence for military offences in the field which, at the present day, can only be regarded with amazement and horror. One case at the beginning of 1916 stands out. A private from a North Country regiment was tried in February on two charges of desertion and the following facts emerged at his court martial. The accused had left school at the age of 14 and had gone to sea for two years. He had then joined the Army when he was 16, pretending that he was two years older. He was posted to France in January 1915 and had served with his battalion for just under nine months; during this time he had been in constant trouble and, in his own words, he had 'lost heart' with soldiering. He had deserted at the end of September 1915 and had been recaptured two months later. He had then escaped from custody because he had heard that deserters from the BEF were being shot, but he had been apprehended wandering in some woods in January 1916. His eighteenth birthday had occurred during his second period of absence. In other words, both his offences of desertion had taken place when he was aged 17 and when he really should not have been on active service at all. The accused's corps commander was of the opinion that the death sentence should be commuted owing to his extreme youth. The army commander and the Commander-in-Chief had had no hesitation in saying that he should be shot. This soldier was executed during the last week of February at an age of 18 years and just under two months.

It would seem that at this period of the war the only factors which might mitigate a death sentence were either the prisoner's good record of service at the front or the prospect that he would develop into 'a good fighting man' in the future. On the whole, the generals were not swayed by instincts of compassion. A 21-year-old deserter was shot in the abattoir at Mazingarbe in February 1916, although he had a dependent child at his home in the Midlands. He had offered as a reason for his offence that he had been continually victimized by his platoon sergeant. Another man, who was shot for desertion about three weeks later and who had been in France for five months, was said at his trial to have been a satisfactory soldier until he had been told of his mother's death a short while before he went absent. This man was a volunteer, having enlisted in the Army at the beginning of September 1914.

It was only too easy for men who had had enough of the dangers and discomforts of the front to feign a mental or physical illness, and medical officers in the forward areas had to be constantly on guard against malingerers. For the most part it must have been easy enough for a doctor to recognize these fictitious symptoms without much difficulty. There may have been occasions, however, when a cursory examination at a regimental aid post had failed to reveal some perfectly genuine neuropathic disorder. The terror which can dominate the mind and the extent to which it might affect the thoughts and actions cannot be measured by any outward gauge. It is natural for normal persons to be afraid when under hostile fire. A soldier is expected to subdue his fear, but if he gives way to it under the stresses of the moment it may be a policy of prudence and humanity to remove him temporarily from the atmosphere of danger until he has reasserted his self-control. This was not the practice in the wartime British army.

On 13 February 1916, a private in the infantry, a soldier with a good military record, went absent from the firing line and reported back to his rear company headquarters saying that a grenade had burst just beside him and he was suffering from shock. The man was seen by his company quartermaster-sergeant who formed the impression that he was in a nervous condition and told him to report to the nearest MO. He did so, but the doctor could find nothing wrong with him and ordered him to return to the trenches. Instead of going back to his unit the private went to a farmhouse behind the lines where he told the farmer's wife that he was on his way back to England. He said he was cold and asked her if he might come inside to warm himself by the fire for a while. She had invited him in and a short while later he had been found there by a captain from another regiment who had placed him under arrest as a suspected deserter. At his court martial the soldier had pleaded that the explosion of the grenade had undermined his nerves and that thereafter he had not been properly responsible for what he was doing. His story was not accepted. He was convicted of desertion and was shot on 20 March. This man had originally been posted for duties at his regimental depot and when his battalion had been sent to France he had applied successfully to accompany them.

An unfortunate consequence of the vigilance shown by medical officers in the detection of pretended illness was that they came to be regarded with a certain amount of animosity and distrust by a large proportion of the front-line soldiers. Norman Gladden was probably expressing a widely-held reaction when he described a medical inspection at a rest-camp near Boulogne just after his draft had arrived in France. The medical officer walked quickly down the ranks, said Gladden,[5] 'with his face fixed in a supercilious stare. . . . If he wanted to create an impression of inhumanity he could hardly have done it more effectively.' Later on, when Gladden was in the line, he reported sick with diarrhoea and bleeding from the bowels. He was examined by his battalion medical officer who could not discover the cause of his trouble and graded him as 'medicine and duty', a category reserved for the most trivial complaints. 'MOs treated all sick as swingers', Gladden explained.

Doctor Harold Dearden, who had served in the RAMC with an infantry battalion on the Western Front, later wrote[6] that when a soldier reported sick, especially in or near the trenches, the average MO had endeavoured to prove, 'exclusively to his own satisfaction', that there was nothing whatever wrong with the man. On one occasion Dearden was asked to examine a soldier on the morning of his court martial for desertion. He was, said Dearden, 'a pitiful degenerate [who] had drunk a lot in his time and is obviously no use to anyone'. Dearden recorded in his diary:

I went to the trial determined to give him no help of any sort, for I detest his type; and seeing so many good fellows go out during the night's shelling made me all the more bitter against him for trying to back down. I really hoped he would be shot as indeed was anticipated by all of us.

Even when a soldier deliberately evaded the medical officers in the forward localities and placed himself in the hands of the doctors further to the rear, he did not find them to be any more sympathetic towards those whom they believed to be malingerers from the front. At the beginning of February 1916 a man who had enlisted voluntarily in an Irish regiment in September 1914 disappeared from the firing line, walked back about 25 miles, and obtained admittance to a field ambulance hospital. He was complaining of pains all over his body and said that he had been wandering about in a dazed condition since he had left his unit. The doctor who examined him reported that he was perfectly fit, physically and mentally. He was promptly returned to his battalion and three weeks later he was executed for desertion.

Sometimes after a court martial the accused was ordered to undergo a medical board before it was decided whether or not his sentence should be confirmed. The members of the board were usually an Assistant Director of Medical Services (ADMS), and two other officers from the RAMC. At his court martial for desertion in February 1916 a corporal from a Highland regiment claimed that he had been blown up at a factory explosion in Canada a few years before the war and that ever since then he had suffered periodically from fits and from loss of memory. He was examined by a medical board soon after the court had found him 'guilty' and sentenced him to death. The three doctors, the ADMS, who held the rank of colonel, a captain and a lieutenant, could find no present signs of mental derangement but pointed out that if the corporal had told the truth about his accident they had no means of testing the accuracy of his statement about the after-effects he had suffered from it. Apparently this non-committal report was taken to be a refutation of the corporal's defence as he was shot in the abattoir at Mazingarbe ten days later.

At times even junior officers encountered the suspicion of army doctors that they were using their physical ailments to avoid returning to the line. When Siegfried Sassoon was recovering from a wound he had received in France he was sent to a hotel in London which had been commandeered for the accommodation of convalescent officers. He had been warned that the doctor in charge there took a pleasure out of tormenting his patients by assuring them that they would remain at the hotel until they were passed fit for duty. This doctor, said Sassoon,[7] was a youngish man holding the rank of captain in the RAMC. At their first meeting Sassoon expressed the wish to continue his convalescence for a few weeks in the country. He had described the doctor's reactions to this suggestion:

He replied that I was totally mistaken if I thought any such thing. An expression, which I can only call cruel, overspread his face. 'You'll stay here; and when you leave here, you'll find yourself back at the front in double-quick time. How d'you like that idea?'

Siegfried Sassoon, who was an extremely gallant officer and had just been awarded the Military Cross, succeeded in obtaining a transfer to a convalescent home in Sussex in spite of the medical officer's vindictive warning.

A medical board which was reporting on a soldier under a sentence of death usually spent a matter of an hour or two in investigating his mental condition. Although at that time psychiatry was a branch of medical science which had scarcely come into existence, in the majority of cases this should have been sufficient time to satisfy the purpose of the enquiry. When the condemned man was claiming, as so many did, that he had been suffering from temporary loss of memory when he had gone absent from his unit, a series of exploratory questions would have established whether or not he might really have undergone a period of emotional amnesia. In cases where the prisoner had attributed his behaviour to a previous head injury the members of the board would probably have carried out both a clinical and interrogatory examination to see whether there was any evidence of neurological impairment. If the doctors had observed the merest suspicion of brain damage they should have endeavoured to obtain the man's past medical records before they came to a final conclusion about him. This seldom, if ever, happened if he was maintaining that some accident had befallen him before the war.

There can be no doubt that medical boards sometimes went to extreme lengths in attempting to discover the state of a condemned soldier's mental and emotional stability. A board consisting of a colonel and a major in the RAMC reported on a man in March 1916, to the effect that they had kept him under observation for four days and continued:

There is nothing in this man's condition to remark on except that he shows a want of intelligence in answering slowly and with hesitation questions put to him. Physical condition normal.

Medical boards often commented upon the extremely low intellectual capacity of the prisoner they had examined. Perhaps the duller type of man was more prone to run foul of military authority or perhaps the British Army was reflecting the standard of intelligence of the nation as a whole. Most infantry soldiers had received only a minimal education as compulsory schooling in the pre-1914 period had terminated at the age of 13. Furthermore, the average recruit from an urban background had been born into the aftermath of the Industrial Revolution with its depressed living standards and its stultifying restraints on initiative, opportunity and development.

Another type of problem soldier was the man who had no interest in the purpose of war, no patriotic impulsion and no will to submit himself to personal danger. A private from the south-east of England who was executed for desertion in March 1916 was such a person. He had been a rag-merchant in civilian life, which probably meant that he was a rag-and-bone collector, and he was believed to be between the ages of 30 and 35. He admitted that he had had many convictions for housebreaking and had served numerous sentences of imprisonment. He had proved to be a bad soldier from the start, being described as indifferent, ignorant and dirty. Having been posted to France with a draft of reinforcements in February 1916 he was sent up to join a battalion in the line, but he only remained with them for five days before he went absent. Inside of a week he was arrested by the Military Police in the town of Béthune and he informed his captors that he hoped he would be sentenced to five years' penal servitude so that he would never have to return to the trenches.

There is good reason to doubt whether a murder charge in the field, which was triable by the ordinary English law, should ever have come before an FGCM sitting without the assistance of a judge-advocate. Two murder trials took place in the BEF during February 1916, which would have required a very careful legal direction before the members of the court could have been sure they were reaching a proper verdict. In the first case a noncombatant soldier, who was stationed at a town behind the lines, shot and killed one of the men sharing his hut. There was no apparent motive for the crime which remained completely inexplicable. It came out in evidence that the accused soldier's mother was confined in a lunatic asylum and he stated in his defence that he believed that he, too, was out of his mind. He was convicted and sentenced to death without a report being obtained on his mental condition. It is impossible to know at this stage whether the members of the court had been informed of the significance of the M'Naughten Rules[8] with regard to insanity, or of the vital importance of malice aforethought in distinguishing murder from manslaughter, which was not, of course, a capital offence.

The circumstances of the second case were entirely different. A private in an infantry battalion, which was resting at the time, spent the morning in an estaminet and became very drunk. He was seen by a lance-corporal from his platoon, with whom he was on very friendly terms, and ordered to leave. The private then returned to his billet, collected a rifle and was seen to climb a ladder leading to a loft. From there he shot and killed the lance-corporal as he was passing through the yard below. A member of the Military Police who went up to the loft a few minutes later to arrest the private described him as being very drunk, crying and mumbling stupidly. Another witness said he seemed to be delirious. This man was also convicted and sentenced to death. It would have been very difficult for the court, without proper legal guidance, to have fully appreciated the degree of intoxication which is necessary in order to establish a defence to a charge of murder.

Both these soldiers were executed, and it may well be that after the most meticulous legal directions they still would have been convicted. Nevertheless, it seems wrong when the lives of the prisoners were at stake that the members of the courts which were trying them should not have received the clearest elucidation of the law from a legally-qualified adviser.

Notes

1. Norman Gladden, *The Somme 1916*.
2. Norman Gladden, op. cit.
3. Raymond Asquith, *Life and Letters*, edited by John Joliffe.
4. Siegfried Sassoon, *Memoirs of An Infantry Officer*.
5. Norman Gladden, op. cit.
6. Harold Dearden, *Medicine & Duty, A War Diary*.
7. Siegfried Sassoon, op. cit.
8. The M'Naughten Rules lay down that to establish a defence on the ground of insanity it must be proved that at the time of committing the act the party accused was labouring under such a defect of reason from disease of the mind, as not to know the nature and quality of the act or, if he did know it, that he did not know he was doing what was wrong.

QUESTIONS IN THE HOUSE

W HEN MILITARY EXECUTIONS were receiving so much publicity amongst the troops both in France and in Gallipoli it was hardly surprising that rumours about them, and probably highly exaggerated rumours, began to circulate amongst the civilian population in Britain. This created an awkward situation for the government, for shootings at dawn were scarcely the best form of advertisement for the Army during a massive recruiting campaign.

On 9 June 1915 the Under-Secretary for War was asked in the House of Commons[1] whether any soldiers had been put to death by the sentence of a court martial since the outbreak of hostilities and, if so, of what offences had they been convicted. The Minister's reply was brief and unenlightening. He affirmed that executions had taken place and stated that the Army Act enumerated the offences which carried the penalty of death.

It looked as though the government were intending to adopt one of the recognized ministerial methods of dealing with sensitive subjects, namely by avoiding direct answers and by citing the authorized regulations. This was borne out eight days later when the Under-Secretary was asked whether a soldier convicted by court martial had an opportunity of making 'any representation to the confirming authority with regard to his sentence or to any question of law or fact arising at his trial'. The same questioner also enquired whether the Army Council had issued any instructions for the guidance of confirming authorities. The Under-Secretary replied:[2]

A soldier who is tried by court-martial has every opportunity of raising in his defence any question of law or fact at his trial, and if the trial results in a conviction the soldier has the right of complaint under Section 43 of the Army Act. The regulations as to the duties of a confirming officer are contained in the Rules of Procedure, 1907.

Section 43 of the Army Act then in force would seem slightly inappropriate in the context of this particular question, as it came under the heading 'Redress of Wrongs' and laid down the method by which a soldier could make a complaint against an officer or against another man. He had first of all to complain to his captain. If he did not receive satisfaction he could take the matter to his commanding officer. Then, if he was still aggrieved, he was permitted to bring his complaint before his general. It is difficult to envisage a soldier who had just been informed of his impending execution carrying out this procedure, even if he knew of its existence. As for the rest of the answer, it is true that the Rules of Procedure prescribed the duties of a Confirming Authority, but they gave no indication of the principles on which they were to be applied.

When a Member enquired on 1 July 1915 how many courts martial had been held during the war and how many death sentences had been imposed,[3] he was met with the answer that it would not be in the public interest to supply this information. But on 5 July when another Member asked about the method of notifying relatives when soldiers were executed the Under-Secretary was more forthcoming.[4] The next-of-kin, he replied, were informed of the facts by the Record Office as soon as the official report was received from the base. According to William Moore, in April 1916 a letter in the following terms was sent from the Infantry Records Office to the parents of a young soldier from the East End of London:[5]

> I am directed to inform you that a report has been received from the War Office to the effect that [the number, rank, name, battalion and regiment of the soldier] was sentenced after being tried by court martial to suffer death by being shot, and his sentence was duly executed on 20 March, 1916.

At the end of January 1917 Basil Liddell Hart,[6] who was still recovering from being severely gassed in the Somme, was posted to York as assistant to the Colonel-in-Charge of Infantry Records. A 'nauseating' feature of his work there, he said in his memoirs, was the despatch of formal letters to the widows and parents of men who had just been executed.[7] He described his reactions:

> Until then I had imagined, like most soldiers, that such executions were camouflaged in some way as accidental death. When I protested at the callousness of these bald announcements, I was told that it was a means of saving the Government's money on pensions.

Some parents were so horrorstruck on being notified of their sons' executions that they wrote in desperation to their Members of Parliament. In January 1916 an attempt was made by an MP at Question Time to obtain information about an Irish private who had been shot almost a year previously. He asked the Under-Secretary for War the circumstances under which the soldier, whose name he mentioned, had been court-martialled and shot in France for desertion; whether he had had an advocate to defend him at his trial; and if it was true that he had only been told of his sentence within an hour of his execution.[8] The Minister replied that counsel could not be employed at courts martial in the field. He continued:

> It is well-known to all soldiers that desertion in the face of the enemy is liable to be punished by death. Private ———— was informed of his sentence more than twelve hours before it was carried out. The sentence was passed on the 14th February, and was most carefully reviewed before it was confirmed by the Commander-in-Chief on the 27th February. Such confirmation was strictly in accordance with the law.

The soldier in question had deserted two days before Christmas in 1914. His battalion was in the line at the time and he had been detailed with three other men to form a company ration-party. He had been seen at the ration-dump, about half-a-mile to the rear, but had not been with the party on their return to the trenches. When he was arrested in Armentières the following February he had been wearing the chevrons and the badges of a lance-corporal in the Military Police and at first he had refused to disclose his real name. At his trial he said that on his way back with the ration-party he had lost his way and been captured by the Germans. After a while he had escaped and had managed to cross back into the Allied lines. He explained his presence in Armentières by saying that he was looking for his battalion. Not surprisingly, his story was disbelieved by the court.

The MP who raised the matter also enquired 'whether it was brought to the notice of the court that on several occasions the man had exposed himself gallantly in trench warfare before the German lines, thereby proving that he was not a coward or a shirker of his duty?' Presumably this information had come from the executed soldier's relatives or friends. The Minister replied that no such evidence had been given at the trial. He might have added that when a capital sentence had been imposed the condemned man's past behaviour in action was automatically reported to the confirming authority by his commanding officer.

On 26 January 1916, Philip Snowden, the Labour MP for Blackburn, made a further attempt to discover how extensively the death penalty was being employed in the Army, when he asked the Under-Secretary for War to disclose the number of British soldiers who had up to then been shot for desertion or for other military offences. Snowden, a future Chancellor of the Exchequer, was the accepted leader of a small group of Labour politicians who were opposed to the continuance of the war. The Minister told him that no British soldiers had been shot in the United Kingdom since the commencement of hostilities. He went on to say:

It is not in the public interest to give statistics of the numbers who have suffered the death penalty in the forces overseas, but I will ask my honourable friend to be good enough not to believe that the number has been considerable.[9]

When the Army (Annual) Bill was being considered in Committee at the end of March 1916, a back-bencher proposed an amendment to the effect that no sentence of death should be passed by a General Court Martial without the concurrence of all the officers sitting on the court.[10] By the terms of the Army Act a GCM had to consist of at least five members, and in practice it usually used to consist of nine. No death sentence could be passed on a prisoner unless at least two-thirds of the members concurred. It might not have been appreicated by the House that at that time GCMs were only being convened for the trial of officers, and that every capital charge against a soldier was then being tried by an FGCM, which could not sentence to death unless all the members were in agreement.

The Under-Secretary for War successfully resisted this proposal. His reason for doing so was rather curious. A soldier might have been convicted of a grave offence for which he ought to be executed, he said, but out of nine members of the court which had tried the case there might be one officer who was conscientiously opposed to the death penalty. 'It would defeat the ends of justice', he continued, 'if you were to have such a proceeding by which one solitary dissentient could prevent the death penalty being carried out.'

On 5 April 1916 the Under-Secretary refused once again to make public the number of executions which had taken place in the field, and he repeated that it would be impossible for men court-martialled on capital charges to be granted the right of being defended by a trained advocate.[11]

It was probably justifiable in the grave and perilous circumstances of the war for the government to be unwilling to disclose any precise details with regard to military executions overseas. It was proper, however, for such matters as the fairness of capital courts martial and the frequency with which the death penalty was being applied to be ventilated in Parliament. Although a great deal of the relevant information was not available to back-benchers at the time, the conclusion is unavoidable that if the Members who were raising these matters had prepared their ground with a little more care it would have been much more difficult for the Minister concerned to have side-stepped so many of their questions with such manifest ease.

The Under-Secretary for War was subjected to further questioning on this subject on 4 May 1916, when an MP referred to a recent court martial in which, he said, a boy from East London had been sentenced to death.[12] He asked for the record of the trial, together with the names of the officers constituting the court and the name of the officers who had confirmed the sentence to be laid on the Table of the House. The Minister replied that it was not possible for him to comment upon sentences which had been approved by the Commander-in-Chief. Philip Snowden then enquired if it was a fact 'that this boy, only nineteen years of age' had been shot. The Minister confirmed that the sentence had been carried out, but added that he did not know the soldier's age. Another Member stated that sentence of death had been passed 'within a month of this boy leaving hospital, where he had been for a nervous breakdown caused by wounds due to a mine explosion'. The allegation was neither accepted nor denied by the Minister who replied noncommittally, 'I was not aware of that fact.'

This was the last occasion on which the subject of capital courts martial was raised in Parliament until the autumn of the following year.

All through the spring and the early summer of 1916 preparations were going ahead on the Western Front for a massive British attack across the Somme valley. Originally it had been intended as a combined Anglo-French operation, but with the French Army needing more and more of its resources to contain the crushing German onslaught at Verdun it soon became clear that the BEF would have to carry out the Somme offensive completely on its own.

In spite of the Derby Scheme and conscription the BEF was continually below its authorized establishment of manpower. It had been estimated by the High Command that a recruit would require four months' training at home before he was properly fitted to take his place in the line; it was found, however, that the men enlisting in 1916 required a slightly longer period of training. Haig had considered at the beginning of the year that he would be able to commence his great attack in April, but in view of the manifold difficulties which had arisen it was decided that the earliest practicable date would be some time in June or July.

One of the problems facing the British Army on the Western Front – indeed, a problem which faced the armies of all the participants – was the limit of endurance for the average soldier to the stresses and privations of this form of warfare. Early in 1916 Robert Graves was posted for a while to the staff of an infantry training school at Harfleur. He found that the other instructors there, all officers fresh from the trenches, were generally agreed that about a third of the troops in the BEF would be 'dependable on all occasions'; a third were 'variable'; and the remaining third were 'more or less untrustworthy'.[13] The suspicion of latent instability was not confined to the newcomers to the line but even applied to the battle-tested veterans, as nobody knew for how many months the nervous system of the normal person could be expected to withstand the protracted stresses of perpetual bombardment. Edmund Blunden has described how a young soldier in his platoon was so badly shaken by a violent burst of shelling that he could only lie moaning and sobbing on the bottom of the fire-trench.[14] And in discussing a sergeant who had been in France for nearly a year, Siegfried Sassoon remarked that it was 'far longer than most men could stick such a life'. He added ruminatively, 'Sooner or later I should get windy myself. It was only a question of time.'[15]

Most memoirs of the Western Front speak of the hordes of bloated rats which fed on the unburied corpses and bored voraciously into the shallow graves; also, the lice which impregnated the blankets, the clothing and the dugouts causing perpetual irritation and discomfort. Hygiene and cleanliness were impossible in the line, where clean water was so precious it was only used for drinking. 'For washing ourselves', said Frank Dunham, 'we had to use ditch-water, and usually we would manage to heat some in an old tin hat on top of a brazier.'[16] As an occasional luxury when troops were resting or in reserve they would be marched to a bathing centre where they could enjoy a hurried shower.

Then there were the stagnant malignity and the brooding oppression which are endemic to a field of battle. The mutilated trees with their clumsily-amputated branches, and the motley clusters of rags, weapons, equipment and bodies, sprawled around in abandoned squalor. In a letter from the front in June 1916, Raymond Asquith wrote:[17]

> I never saw anything like the foulness and desolation of this bit of the Salient. There were two woods near to us on which we roamed about picking up gruesome relics in the dusk – Magpie Copse and Sanctuary Wood – not a leaf or a blade of grass in either of them, nothing but twisted and blackened stumps and a mesh of shell holes, dimpling into one another, full of mud and blood, and dead men and over-fed rats which blundered into one in the twilight like fat moths.

Twenty-three of the death sentences passed on the Western Front during the months of April, May and June 1916 were confirmed by the Commander-in-Chief. Nineteen of these were for desertion, two were for disobedience, one was for cowardice, and one was for striking a superior officer.

In three of the cases of desertion doubts had been raised with regard to the mental condition of the condemned men. A 21-year-old private who was court-martialled in May was described by his commanding officer as 'useless and good for nothing'. Since he had joined the Army as a volunteer within the first few weeks of the war he had been in constant trouble and the commanding officer added, 'My opinion is that he is not entirely responsible for his actions and should be shut up in a lunatic asylum.' Two weeks before his execution this soldier was examined by three doctors who pronounced him 'physically and mentally fit for service'. Another private, a coal-miner in civilian life, told the court at his trial that he had reason to suspect his own sanity. His brother had died in a lunatic asylum, he said, his sister suffered from fits, and his mother 'had been troubled with her head all her life'. It was suggested in this man's defence that a particularly severe bombardment just prior to his desertion might have activated some dormant hereditary disorder of his mind. The medical officer of his battalion, a captain in the RAMC, had been unable to discover anything wrong with him but had tentatively proposed that a fuller investigation by a specialist in lunacy would be necessary before a definite conclusion could be reached. In fact, the Commander-in-Chief had felt able to confirm the death sentence without requiring any further reports at all.

The soldier in the third case had been another early wartime volunteer. When he deserted from the front line in May 1916 he had already been convicted of 'carelessly wounding himself', and had been punished no less than ten times for being absent without leave. He said in his defence that he had been afflicted with 'a wandering mind' for the past 18 months. He was not the only person who felt dubious about his sanity for his commanding officer had written, 'I consider he is not of normal medical development . . . he should be carefully examined by a specialist in mental diseases.' In spite of this forthright statement no medical opinion upon this man was ever sought and he was executed the day after the opening of the Somme offensive.

Some of the deserters who were shot in this period were so utterly unsuited for military service they should never have been in the Army at all. A private from London, who was court-martialled in June, said in his defence that since he was ten years old he had suffered from 'a wandering mania' and that on many occasions in the past he had been picked up by the police when he was roaming about in the streets. He had deserted from the front line and apparently the court had considered that there might be a grain of truth in his story because, although they sentenced him to death, they expressed the view that enquiries should be made to see if he was known to the Metropolitan Police. In due course a report was received from Bow Street police station which clearly revealed that before his enlistment this man had been a typical maladjusted urban vagrant who had found it a psychological impossibility to settle down for long in any place or in any occupation. He had been arrested in the West End for begging in 1911 and had been handed over to a probation officer who had tried unsuccessfully to install him in a mission home. Before the Commander-in-Chief confirmed the death sentence a medical board had examined the soldier and found him to be 'of a very low standard of intelligence but neither insane nor of unsound mind'.

As the war progressed it became increasingly apparent that desertion was not an offence which was peculiar to the young in age or to those who were unused to military constraint. During May and June four reservists were executed, each of whom had been instilled with many years of army discipline. Two of them were privates in the same battalion and had both enlisted for regular service at the conclusion of the Boer War. They had been together on a draft for France in October 1915 and had deserted from Waterloo Station while they were waiting for a train at the outset of their journey. They were arrested in the south of England in May 1916. Another was a gunner who had been sent on leave just before Christmas 1915 and had remained at his home until his apprehension the following April. The fourth, a Welsh soldier, was a married man with three children. He said in his defence that he had deserted from the front because, at the age of 44, he had found it very difficult to keep up with the younger men and had expected to be given a job behind the lines.

Although 'shell-shock' was by then a term in current use it was still viewed with considerable suspicion by the military hierarchy. A private charged with desertion told the court which tried him that his nerves had been completely shattered by the constant bombardments. He said he had been taking a drug called 'cocoa extract' to allay his fear in the trenches, but when he had been unable to get any more supplies he had gone to pieces. He was shot without being medically examined either by a board or by his battalion doctor.

At times it is difficult from the material now available to discover what principles were being applied by the Commander-in-Chief in deciding whether to confirm or to commute a sentence of death. A few men with excellent military records were executed during the spring of 1916. One had served in France for eleven months before his desertion and had been wounded in the head. He had volunteered for dangerous jobs on several occasions, said his commanding officer; he had always done his work in the trenches well; and up to the time of his offence 'he was regarded as a good and plucky soldier'. In another case it had not saved a man from the firing squad that he had spent five months in England during the previous year recovering from a wound.

A private in a Highland regiment, who had been court-martialled in France on 14 April 1916, was the first soldier in the war to be executed on a charge of 'striking his superior officer'. The incident had occurred in a training area during a morning rifle and turn-out inspection. Just after his platoon commander had reprimanded him for having a dirty rifle and dirty boots he had stepped forward from the ranks and kicked the officer twice on the knee. In his defence the man said that he had served in the BEF since November 1914 without being granted any leave. His mother had died two months before and he was worried about his crippled sister who had been left with nobody to look after her. He had also tried to establish that he was drunk when he had committed the assault, but all the prosecution witnesses were agreed that he had been perfectly sober.

The two cases of disobedience had taken place under entirely different circumstances from each other. The first of the executed men was a 23-year-old driver in the Royal Field Artillery who had enlisted in the Army in the summer of 1915 after being at sea for most of his working life. He had committed the offence at the outset of a sentence of 28 days' Field Punishment No. 1, passed upon him for a previous act of disobedience. Early one morning a sergeant had taken him from the regimental guardroom and ordered him to carry some horse-rugs to his company office. The driver had flatly refused saying that the British Navy had failed to make a slave out of him and the British Army was going to be no more successful. Apparently he was in a rebellious frame of mind because during the following week he was charged twice with using insubordinate language to an officer.

In the second case three infantry privates, all of whom had recently arrived in France with a draft of reinforcements, were tried together for disobedience to an order in the front line. On a night in April 1916, they had been members of a party consisting of a subaltern, a sergeant, a corporal and eight men which had been detailed to repair some wire in no-man's-land. When the sergeant had assembled the party, and before they had been joined by the officer, there was a great deal of grumbling about the increased danger of their task owing to the brightness of the moon. The sergeant had told them that he did not believe they would be sent out in such clear conditions. On the way up to the starting-point a message was circulated, some of the men believed it had come from the sergeant and others thought it had been started by the corporal, that if they were ordered to cross into no-man's-land they should all refuse to move. In spite of the visibility there was no cancellation, but when the subaltern in charge of the party had climbed over the parapet only the sergeant and the corporal had followed him. The company commander had then come on the scene, and having delivered a warning about the penalties for disobedience in the field, he had said that he would lead out the party to the wire himself. This time the two NCOs and five of the eight privates had accompanied him, and the necessary work had been successfully accomplished. The three who had stayed behind on the latter occasion were condemned to death. One of these sentences was confirmed and the other two were both commuted to 15 years' penal servitude.

The soldier who was executed for cowardice, a lance-corporal, had been in charge of four men in an outpost trench not far from the enemy lines. Their tour of duty was intended to last for 24 hours, from the early hours of one morning until the early hours of the next, and during this period they were forbidden to leave their position unless they were officially ordered to do so or they had been properly relieved. About six o'clock in the evening the sentry on duty had observed two men, in uniforms which he believed to be French, approaching the post. He challenged them but they took no notice and both jumped into the trench. At the same time that he realized the intruders were Germans he had noticed the lance-corporal and the rest of his own party running back toward the main British lines. The sentry had resolutely remained where he was and had seen the Germans leaving the trench and withdrawing hurriedly across no-man's-land. Meanwhile the lance-corporal had rushed into his company headquarters to report that the enemy had attacked and broken through the outpost. As soon as the true facts of the situation were known the lance-corporal was arrested and charged with cowardice. In his defence he said that he had been feeling unwell throughout the day of the incident and had tried to report sick before he had gone on duty. He was described by his commanding officer as an efficient NCO who had served on the Western Front for six months and had always performed his duties in a proper manner. He had joined the Army as a volunteer in 1914 within a few weeks of the outbreak of war.

Notes

1. House of Commons, written answers, 9 June 1915.
2. House of Commons, oral answers, 17 June 1915.
3. House of Commons, oral answers, 1 July 1915.
4. House of Commons, oral answers, 7 July 1915.
5. William Moore, *The Thin Yellow Line.*
6. Sir Basil Liddell Hart (1895–1970), military historian and strategist.
7. *The Memoirs of Captain Liddell Hart*, Vol. 1.
8. House of Commons, oral answers, 20 January 1916.
9. House of Commons, oral answers, 26 January 1916.
10. House of Commons, Army (Annual) Bill, Committee stage, 29 March 1916.
11. House of Commons, written answers, 5 April 1916.
12. House of Commons, oral answers, 4 May 1916.
13. Robert Graves, *Goodbye to All That.*

14. Edmund Blunden, *Undertones of War*.
15. Siegfried Sassoon, *Memoirs of an Infantry Officer*.
16. Frank Dunham, *The Long Carry*.
17. Raymond Asquith, *Life and Letters*.

8

THE SOMME OFFENSIVE

O N 5 JUNE 1916 Kitchener was drowned at sea when a ship carrying him on a mission to Russia struck a mine in the approaches to Scapa Flow. Before his death he had created an army of over two million men, imbued with the dogged courage and sustained by the perky, crude, satiric sense of humour which had always characterized the British soldier in times of danger and adversity. It was by far the largest volunteer force ever to go into battle, says A. J. P. Taylor, but it was in reality a clumsy instrument. 'The senior officers were elderly unimaginative professionals from the old peacetime army, who refused to contemplate the problems of trench warfare.'[1] They had failed to appreciate, even by then, the destructive power of the machine gun or the formidability of a scientifically-planned defensive line. As for the junior officers and the men of the New Armies, they had only received a rushed and rudimentary training in England before their committal to France on active service.

Haig had decided to launch his great attack in the summer of 1916 on a 14-mile front between Maricourt and Serre, using the 18 divisions of General Rawlinson's Fourth Army. The starting date was originally fixed for 28 June, but owing to bad weather it was eventually postponed until the 1st July. The initial assault would be preceded by a massive five-day bombardment designed to obliterate the German wire entanglements and to pulverize their forward trenches and their dugouts. Nothing could remain in existence after the barrage was finished, Rawlinson had informed his corps commanders; the British infantry would merely have to walk across no-man's-land and take possession of the German line. This mood of buoyant optimism was shared by Haig who wrote, as the preparations were proceeding, 'I feel that every step in my plan has been taken with Divine help.'

Gradually, 400,000 troops and 100,000 horses were concentrated in villages and in bivouacs in the locality chosen for the offensive. When all was ready the bombardment had begun. After it had continued for a few days battalions in the front line were reporting back that considerable portions of the enemy wire were still intact and that many of their machine-gun posts were still operating. Such information was dismissed by staff officers in the areas behind the line as the outcome of cowardly imagination.

It is now known that much of the British artillery was obsolete both in pattern and in range and many of its shells were defective. Further, the German dugouts were deeper and better constructed than had been foreseen and most of them were impervious to the fire of the British guns. In consequence, the barrage was failing completely to fulfil its intended purpose.

As the day of the attack approached the British infantry huddled in their rainswept trenches or waited patiently in the waterlogged bivouac areas for the summons to move forward to the line. On 30 June all the assault troops who could be spared took part in ceremonial parades at which messages of encouragement from their senior commanders were read out to them. At the front the final 24 hours was spent in relative inactivity. Haig had said that the assault would not take place unless the German defences had been sufficiently destroyed, but it was not considered necessary to probe the enemy positions on the eve of attack in order to test the strength of their resistance.

The 1st July 1916 was destined to be one of the saddest days in British military history. The assaulting troops had spent the night in their assembly trenches, the reserves were in places of readiness, and a couple of miles behind the line the Military Police had set up 'battle-stops' to deal with stragglers and deserters. Zero-hour was timed for 7.30 a.m. In a memorandum from GHQ it had been ordered that the attack should be carried out 'in successive waves or lines, each line adding fresh impetus to the preceding one when this is checked, and carrying the whole forward to the objective'. The advancing men, so heavily laden that they could only move at a slow walk, were supposed to keep a distance of two or three paces from each other. Even at this stage of the war many battalions still took pride in keeping their lines as straight as they would have been on a parade ground.

At last the moment arrived. On a beautiful summer morning under a clear blue sky, untinged with the faintest streak of drifting cloud, wave after wave of British soldiers went over the top to be mown down by machine-gun and rifle fire from the German lines. The Official History of the Campaign gives an account of the scene from the enemy side. When the barrage had lifted, says the narrator, the German troops left their dugouts and manned their posts. He goes on:

As soon as the men were in position a series of extended lines of infantry were seen moving forward from the British trenches. The first line appeared to continue without end to right and left. It was quickly followed by a second line, then a third and fourth. They came on a steady pace as if expecting to find nothing alive in our front trenches. . . .

The Germans held their fire until the leading waves were halfway into no-man's-land and then they opened up with every available weapon, devastating the British ranks.

Whole sections seemed to fall, and the rear formations, moving in close order quickly scattered. The advance crumbled under this hail of shell and bullets. All along the line men could be seen throwing up their arms and collapsing, never to move again. Badly wounded rolled about in their agony, and others, less severely injured, crawled to the nearest shell-hole for shelter.

The fields, glistening in the early morning sunshine, were suddenly littered with still and writhing bodies. In some divisions 80 per cent of the men in the foremost battalions became casualties, but everywhere the gaps were filled by those coming up behind and the onward movement was resumed.

Within a few minutes the leading troops had advanced to within a stone's throw of our front trench and whilst some of us continued to fire at point-blank range, others threw grenades among them. The British bombers answered back; while the infantry rushed forward with fixed bayonets. The noise of battle became indescribable. . . . Again and again the extended lines of British infantry broke against the German defences like waves against a cliff, only to be beaten back. It was an amazing spectacle of unexampled gallantry, courage, and bull-dog determination on both sides.

By the end of the day most of the assaulting forces had failed to penetrate the German line. The total British casualties had amounted to 57,470 officers and men, of whom over 19,000 were listed as killed or died of wounds. 'For this disastrous loss of the finest manhood of the United Kingdom and Ireland,' says the official historian, 'there was only a small gain, although certainly the greatest yet made by the British Expeditionary Force: an advance into the enemy's position some three and a half miles wide and averaging a mile in depth.'

Late in the evening on 1 July Haig issued orders that the offensive must be renewed next day. In fact the BEF attacked persistently for the whole of the month, sustaining heavy losses and making no appreciable gains of ground. At the beginning of August Haig informed the War Cabinet of his satisfaction with the results he had so far attained. Endorsing the callous conception of a war of attrition he promised to keep up the pressure until well into the autumn and gave his assurance that the German casualties would 'amply compensate' for those which the British would be bound to suffer. He ended with a misguided and self-deluding prediction:

It would not be justifiable to calculate on the enemy's resistance being completely broken by these means without another campaign next year. But, even if another campaign proves to be necessary, the enemy will certainly enter the coming winter with little hope of being able to continue his resistance successfully through next spring and summer, and I am confident it will prove beyond his power to do so.

And so throughout August and September the offensive continued with mounting losses and minimal achievements. A leading neurologist who had been attached to a field ambulance unit on the Somme spoke later of an infantry division which had been kept in the line until the majority of the men were in a state of nervous and physical exhaustion. This had resulted in massive sick parades. 'There was nothing wrong with them,' he said, 'except that they were absolutely fagged out. They had been over the top about eleven times in a fortnight and simply could not do it again.'[2] It seemed that nothing could shake the confidence of the Commander-in-Chief or his conviction that the German Army had almost used up its entire reserves. True to his undertaking to the government he was planning to maintain his attack even into the months of October and November.

During July, August and September, 24 soldiers were sentenced to death by courts martial and executed. Thirteen of them had been convicted of desertion, six of cowardice, two of leaving their posts without orders, two of striking a superior officer, and one of murder.

All the cowardice charges arose out of incidents during the most bitter fighting on the Somme. The first had occurred within a few days of the opening of the offensive. The condemned man, a private in a north of England regiment, had been detailed as a member of a working party led by a lieutenant which was to go out under cover of darkness in order to recover three portable bridges, abandoned the previous night by a British fighting patrol. No-man's-land in that sector was between 200–250 yards wide, and the bridges were estimated to be no more than 75 yards from the German trenches. The whole of the party, according to the officer in charge of it, had been in an extremely jittery state, and when the moment arrived to move forward from the British line the private had refused to go, saying that it would be certain death and that he had a wife and five children at home to consider. The court were obviously sympathetic to the man. Not only did they recommend him to mercy but they suggested that he should be examined by a medical board. He had pleaded in his defence that his nerves had been affected by an experience five months before when he had been buried for four hours after a shell exploded on top of his dugout. No doubt the members of the court also bore in mind that at the time of his refusal to accompany the party the man's battalion had been in the front line for 25 consecutive days without relief. Although the medical board found nothing wrong with him, his brigade, divisional and corps commanders had all favoured commutation of the death sentence. However, his army commander and the Commander-in-Chief thought otherwise.

The same situation occurred in the case of another private who was sentenced to death for cowardice a few days later, the court's recommendation to mercy being supported by all the relevant officers up to and including the condemned man's corps commander. This soldier had also been in action for more than three weeks at the time of the act which led to his execution. In the early hours of a moonlit morning he had disobeyed an order from his platoon commander to crawl to a listening post 40 yards out into no-man's-land and some 150 yards from the German front line. The post was in a clump of long grass and he would have had to lie motionless in it for an hour. His refusal had been respectful but adamant. He had told the officer that he was not feeling well and that his nerves were in a bad state; he said that if he went out he would only be a danger to other men as well as to himself. It was mentioned at his trial two weeks later that his father had been killed in action earlier in the war and that he was constantly worried about his mother who was looking after six young children at his home. In recommending the confirmation of the death sentence the army commander remarked, 'If toleration be shown to private soldiers who deliberately decline to face danger, all the qualities which we desire would be debased and degraded.'

One more soldier, a lance-corporal, was convicted of cowardice and shot during the month of July. He had been in charge of the rear section of a party carrying out a night raid on the German trenches. A short time before they were due to set out from the British line an officer came to the dugout where the rear section was resting and told the men to get into their form-up positions. The corporal immediately exclaimed, 'It's too light – it's bloody murder.' It took several minutes' persuasion before the men left the dugout as most of them were complaining about the clearness of the visibility. Eventually the whole raiding party assembled in an advance trench, but when they moved off into no-man's-land neither the lance-corporal nor any of his men followed. As a result of their conduct the raid had to be cancelled. There were no mitigating circumstances put forward on behalf of the lance-corporal at his trial, other than that he had served with the BEF for over 16 months in a battalion which had recently suffered enormous casualties. A disquieting feature of this case was that the brigade commander saw fit to submit to the higher commanders considering the confirmation of the death sentence a memorandum setting out his own recollections of the abortive raid, and including in it several facts which were highly prejudicial to the prisoner. There had never been any opportunity to test or to refute his statement during the court proceedings. A similar practice was followed by other senior officers after a number of capital courts martial and exemplified the contrast of approach between the judicial and the disciplinary processes.

The next two executions for cowardice took place early in September. Both the condemned soldiers were of a highly nervous disposition and had absented themselves from the front line because they had reached the limits of their endurance.

The first had joined the Regular Army only six weeks before the outbreak of war. He had left his position without orders during a German gas attack and had surrendered himself a few hours later a short distance behind the support trenches. His company sergeant-major described him as a man who practically went off his head from sheer terror the moment he came under shellfire. This was not a rational ground for mitigation in the opinion of the corps commander. 'Cowards of this sort are a serious danger to the army,' he wrote. 'The death penalty is instituted to make such men fear running away more than they fear the enemy.'

In the second case the soldier claimed in his defence that he had been treated in hospital for a nervous breakdown during the previous January after being buried in a dugout. He also said that two of his brothers had been killed in France and another had been wounded at Gallipoli. His offence had been committed when the Germans had shelled the locality through which he was passing with a ration party. He had walked away from the others after telling the officer in charge, 'I am getting out. I can stick it no longer. My nerves are gone.' Later he was found asleep in a dugout. The man's commanding officer expressed the opinion that he was so frightened of shellfire 'he deliberately preferred to take his chance of the consequences rather than remain under it'. Like so many others who were shot by firing squads during this period he had volunteered for service at the peak of Kitchener's recruiting campaign in the early autumn of 1914.

There was sometimes a very narrow dividing line between the various capital charges on which a soldier could have been tried. The first man in 1916 to be shot for quitting his post without orders might well have been court-martialled for either cowardice or desertion. The offence was committed during the preliminary bombardment before the disastrous offensive on 1 July. The condemned private was a member of a platoon manning two positions in the front line which had been under heavy shellfire for over two hours. Having told his platoon sergeant that he could stand no more he had wandered away from the post and hidden himself in a dugout a short distance to the rear. Evidence was given at his trial that he had appeared to be in an extremely distraught condition for some time prior to his departure. The court recommended him to mercy, both on account of his good character and because of the intense bombardment to which the positions had been subjected. The brigade, divisional and corps commanders were agreed that his life should be spared but the Army commander considered that unless the execution was confirmed 'the standard of courage in the British Army was likely to be lowered'. Sir Douglas Haig shared the latter view; indeed, he is believed to have written in red ink against the court's recommendation to mercy on the record of proceedings, 'How can we ever win if this plea is allowed?'

Another soldier, this time an infantry corporal, was shot for quitting his post a few weeks later. He had been in charge of ten men in what was termed a 'diehard' position in the front line, and because of its importance he had been told that it must be held at all costs. His tour of duty should have lasted for 48 hours without relief, but at the close of 42 hours, during which time the post had been under constant heavy fire, the corporal decided to evacuate it on his own authority. He did so, and on reporting his action to his company he was placed under arrest. Even allowing for the immensity of the casualties then being suffered by the BEF this NCO had obtained his promotion surprisingly quickly as he had only enlisted about six months previously.

During the month of September two soldiers serving in France were court-martialled and shot on charges of 'striking a superior officer in the execution of his office', one of the few capital offences which was neither concerned with lack of courage nor dereliction of duty in the face of the enemy. Both assaults took place on different days in the same artillery regiment, the victims being a 2nd lieutenant in one and a battery sergeant-major in the other.

The 2nd lieutenant had been taking the midday stable parade in his battery when he had noticed a gunner with a cigarette between his lips, apparently smoking. He had directed his sergeant-major to take the man's name and to place him under open arrest. Immediately the parade was finished the gunner had asked for permission to see the officer, but his request had been peremptorily refused. He had told the sergeant-major that there had been a misunderstanding and he was wrongly accused; the cigarette had been behind his ear, he said, and it had fallen down while he was tending a horse. He had only meant to hold it in his mouth for a moment because both his hands were occupied. The gunner had followed the 2nd lieutenant as he was walking away towards the officers' mess, and after an unsuccessful attempt to speak to him had struck him four blows – none of them very hard – on the head and body. Looked at in any way this was an act of grave misconduct which was bound to result in severe punishment. Unfortunately for the gunner he already had a bad military record and the brigadier had reported that the state of discipline in his regiment was far from satisfactory.

The second incident had occurred in a different battery six days after the assault on the officer. At half-past four in the afternoon the battery sergeant-major had ordered six teams of horses to be harnessed-up for the purpose of drawing replenishments of ammunition. One of the gunners in the detail had protested, using strong and insubordinate language, that if they went off at that time they would miss their tea. He was put under open arrest and replied, 'It's always the bastard same in this battery.' He then knocked the sergeant-major to the ground, fell on top of him and continued to punch him. Eventually he was pulled off by some NCOs but when the sergeant-major stood up he renewed his attack. At his trial the man could offer no real defence to the charge against him. He had told the court that he was fed up with serving in the regiment and that it had been 'absolute torture' being a member of his particular battery. The two gunners condemned to death for these assaults were executed together on a morning at the beginning of October.

During this period the usual length of time which elapsed between a soldier's arrest for a serious offence and his court martial was about 12 days, but on occasion it could be as little as six days or as much as five weeks. After a sentence of death had been passed the execution normally took place within a period of 10 and 15 days.

The capital cases of desertion were following the customary pattern. A proportion of the condemned men had been convicted of the same offence on a previous occasion and some were under suspended sentences of penal servitude or imprisonment. A number had been wounded in the earlier fighting in France and Gallipoli; one man who was executed had been wounded twice at Ypres and claimed that he had been troubled with his nerves ever since. Perhaps the confirming authorities had failed to appreciate that a soldier of reasonable fortitude might have his courage and his confidence impaired by even the mildest of wounds. One of the executed men had recently been treated for shell-shock, an amorphous term which was still regarded by most of the senior commanders as a psychopathic cloak for cowardice.

Recommendatons to mercy by the courts of trial did not seem to carry much weight as they were constantly disregarded. Similarly, suggestions that condemned soldiers had been suffering from nervous strain were unlikely to incite leniency. A commanding officer pleading in vain for the life of a man who had deserted in the early days of the Somme offensive said of him, 'He has a good reputation as a fighting soldier. I feel convinced that he would never have committed the offence unless he had been temporarily bereft of his wits after the action of the 1st July.'

There were plenty of tragic cases. A volunteer from September 1914, who had deserted in the middle of July 1916, stated in his defence that his mother had died whilst he was training in England and his father, a prisoner-of-war, was going blind. He had a sister of 13 and a brother of 10. 'I am the only one left,' he said; 'I have had to leave them in the charge of a neighbour.' In more merciful circumstances he might have qualified for a compassionate release from the Army: in the pitiless environment of universal slaughter he was sentenced to death and shot. Another man, a conscript, was executed less than six months from the date of his enlistment. He had made a forlorn attempt to return to England, but had been arrested by the Military Police within a few hours of leaving his battalion. He could offer no excuses except that he was ill, lousy and sick of the trenches. And there was a 35-year-old private whose father had committed suicide and who was recommended to mercy by the court 'on the ground of defective intellect'. The medical board which examined him before he was put before a firing squad reported, somewhat inconsequentially, that there was no evidence to suggest he had been 'insane' at the time of his desertion.

It must be remembered, of course, that the weaker brethren were only an infinitesimally small proportion of the men at the front. There were hundreds of thousands of others on the battlefields of the Somme who overcame their fear, their misery, and their personal tribulations and carried on with resolution in the performance of their duty.

Notes

1. A. J. P. Taylor, *English History 1914–1945.*
2. Per Dr W. Johnson, evidence given to the War Office Committee of Enquiry into Shell-Shock, 1922.

9

AUTUMN OF ATTRITION

A s THE WET weather set in on the Western Front halfway through September 1916, Haig's conviction that the German Army was rapidly exhausting its reserves became almost obsessional. Although some of the Ministers at Westminster were beginning to doubt whether the continuing human wastage in the BEF was being justified by the results, the government were still according the Commander-in-Chief their unqualified support.

On 7 October Sir Douglas Haig submitted to the War Cabinet his appreciation of the situation. He urged that 'the utmost efforts of the Empire' should be directed towards the prolongation of the offensive on the Somme without intermission. It was not possible to estimate how near to breaking-point the enemy might be, he said, but there was now a fair prospect of far-reaching success 'affording full compensation for all that has been done to attain it'. He hoped to keep up the pressure on the German defences throughout the winter and to open another offensive at the beginning of 1917.

In the autumn the conditions at the front deteriorated to such an extent that, according to the Official History, merely to exist at all became a severe trial of body and spirit. The ground was deep in mud and the infantry were often soaked to the skin for hours on end. On a day of continual rain John Glubb noted in his diary that the troops in the line seemed as though they had just been dipped in a swimming-bath. 'Their sodden khaki, looking almost black, clung to their bodies all over like wet bathing dresses,' he wrote; and he wondered how many of them would die from exposure.[1] Most units were under-strength as Britain was finding it increasingly difficult to replace the BEF's losses. The commanding officer of a battalion of the North-umberland Fusiliers said after the war that towards the end of 1916 recruits were being sent to France after only nine or ten weeks' training.[2]

The hardships on the Western Front might have been easier to endure if there had been a properly-organized system of leave in the BEF. As it was, the chances of an officer or a soldier enjoying a brief interlude at home were largely fortuitous. John Glubb considered that leave was allocated with a good deal of unfairness as there were some men serving on the Somme who had been in France without a break for as long as 18 months.[3] The period of leave for those lucky enough to obtain it was increased from seven to ten days in November 1915. Sometimes at courts martial for desertion accused soldiers revealed in their inarticulate ways the eternal suffering of their loneliness and their hopeless despair of ever seeing their homes and their families again.

Haig had decided to launch his next attack astride the River Ancre, using the Fifth Army commanded by General Gough, at the end of October. Owing to incessant bad weather the date of commencement was eventually postponed until 13 November. On that day a thick morning fog enabled the assaulting formations to take the Germans by surprise with the result that of the three corps involved one captured all its objectives and the other two achieved partial success with theirs. Pursuant to his tactical policy Haig ordered that the attack should be renewed immediately and for the next five days spasmodic fighting continued in increasingly wintry conditions.

On 18 November the weary British divisions went over the top in the first light of dawn and struggled forward over the half-frozen mud and slime through a blinding snow-storm. By nightfall no gains had been attained and the Fifth Army, which had sustained over 23,000 casualties in less than two weeks, had reached a stage of utter exhaustion.

Haig had recognized the impossibility of a further offensive that year. On 21 November he reported to the government:

> The ground, sodden with rain and broken-up everywhere by innumerable shell-holes, can only be described as a morass, almost bottomless in places; between the lines and for many thousands of yards behind them it is almost – in some localities, quite – impassable. The supply of food and ammunition is carried out with the greatest difficulty and immense labour. . . .

Although the British public were shocked and bewildered by the magnitude of the losses on the Somme they accepted them with a patient stoicism as though the whole nation was undergoing some terrible, predestined penance. This was varied by an outward display of emotional patriotism, exemplified in its simplest form by an anonymous letter from a bereaved mother published in the *Morning Post* and afterwards reprinted as a pamphlet, which contained the assurance that 'when the common soldier looks back before going over the top he may see the women of the British race at his heels, reliable, dependent, uncomplaining'.

In the mood of the moment little sympathy was wasted on those deemed to be 'shirkers' or 'funks'. Rumours were already beginning to circulate about troops retreating without orders being fired upon from the rear. Stephen Graham, who served with a battalion of the Scots Guards in 1918, assumed that this could occur for he wrote, 'In our army, undoubtedly, men who broke and ran might expect to be shot down by those in reserve and a party trying to arrange a surrender might be subjected to machine-gun fire.'[4] There were other reports of soldiers being driven forward at gunpoint by their officers. Norman Gladden has told from personal experience of two such incidents on the Somme. In the first, a private had become bogged down in the mud during the preliminary stages of an attack and had been warned by his platoon commander that he would be shot if he did not move on. In the second, there was some confusion at the start of a night assault and while some of the men hesitated on the fire-step, said Gladden, 'an officer pushed his way along the trench threatening with drawn revolver anyone who held back from going over'.[5] Sometimes the matter went further. Robert Graves was told in 1916 by a captain in a county regiment, 'In the last two shows I had to shoot a man in my company to get the rest out of the trench'.[6]

During the last months of 1916 there was no diminution of the number of death sentences being passed by courts martial on the Western Front. One of the three executions for cowardice in October was particularly disquieting. The accused was a regular soldier from Yorkshire who had joined the Army in 1910. He had arrived in France at the beginning of November 1914 and had been sent back to the base suffering from shell-shock in May 1915. The following October he had rejoined a battalion in the line. Obviously he had not fully recovered as his company commander wrote about him:

> I cannot say what has destroyed this man's nerve but he has proved himself on many occasions incapable of keeping his head in action and likely to cause a panic. Apart from his behaviour under fire his conduct and character are very good.

On a morning in the middle of September 1916 the Yorkshireman turned up at the transport lines of his battalion where he told a sergeant there that he had been taken sick and had fallen out from his company when they had been marching up to the trenches on the previous evening. The sergeant told him to report to the dressing station. In a short while the soldier came back and told the sergeant that the dressing station had refused to examine him because he was not wounded. At the time a ration party was just about to go up to the battalion and the accused had been ordered to accompany them. That evening the same sergeant had seen the man warming himself by a brazier in the transport lines. When questioned he had said that he could not bring himself to return to the trenches. A corporal was detailed to escort him back to the line, but the accused had screamed and struggled and had resisted all attempts to drag him along forcibly. Eventually he had been placed under arrest.

The Yorkshire soldier was condemned to death and shot without being examined by a doctor. Perhaps this was in accordance with what had become the general policy. According to Robert Graves, during the summer of 1916 an army order, secret and confidential, was circulated to all officers of the rank of captain and above informing them that cases of cowardice were always to be punished with death and that no medical excuses were to be accepted.[7]

Of the other two executions for cowardice in October one man had run off when his company was marching up to the front under heavy shellfire, and the other had absented himself when he was in a Lewis gun section in the line. The second man had pleaded that he could not control his nerves. When in the trenches, he said, he could neither eat nor sleep, and when a bombardment was in progress he seemed to take leave of his senses completely.

The first execution of the war for the offence of mutiny took place in the autumn of 1916 as the result of a disturbance in the British Army prison at Blargies near Rouen. Soldiers of the BEF who were sentenced to terms of penal servitude were normally returned to England, but those serving shorter sentences were kept in France.

The conditions in military prisons were far more rigorous than those in the ordinary English gaols. This was due to historical reasons. The Army had never considered that imprisonment as such was an effective punishment. Without exception the senior officers who gave evidence before the Royal Commission on military punishments in 1835–6 advocated the continuance of flogging on the ground that there could be no adequate alternative for it. One general said that if it were abolished 'the command of the British Army would be virtually given up'.[8] During the years that followed the retentionist lobby did not deviate in any way from its uncompromising stance; as late as 1880 a distinguished soldier, Lord Wolseley, was emphasizing in this context that 'the greatest ruffians and criminals in three kingdoms enlist in our army'.

When the government, yielding to the pressure of public opinion, finally abolished military flogging in 1881, they substituted for it 'summary punishment' in the field. Regulations were made under the authority of the Army Act which provided that a soldier undergoing detention might be kept in iron fetters and handcuffs for a term not exceeding three months; during this time he could be 'attached to a fixed object' for two hours a day in three out of any four consecutive days, up to a total of 21 days in all. These new forms of sentence, first used during the Egyptian campaign of 1882, were known as Field Punishment Number One and Field Punishment Number Two, the only difference between them being that with Field Punishment Number Two the prisoner was not liable to be attached to a fixed object.

In the early years of the twentieth century, in pursuance of the proposals of the Gladstone Committee, many of the more inhuman practices were eradicated from civil imprisonment in Britain. The military system, however, was unaffected by these reforms. Throughout the First World War the Rules of Field Punishment, approved in 1907, were applied to both the Army and the Royal Marines. There had been no modification in the original concept of the sentence except for a minor amendment permitting straps and ropes to be employed for the shackling of prisoners in place of irons. Field punishment could be awarded by a court martial or a commanding officer and was habitually used for a number of fairly trivial offences. Robert Graves' batman was given 28 days' Field Punishment Number One for drunkenness. Graves saw him in the corner of a farmyard as he stood 'spread-eagled to the wheel of a company limber, tied by the ankles and wrists in the form of an X'. He would be kept in this position, known to the troops as 'crucifixion', for several hours a day while the battalion was in billets, said Graves, and the sentence would then be continued after their next spell in the trenches.[9]

Following the mutiny in the army prison at Blargies seven soldiers were tried by a general court martial, the members of which consisted of a colonel, a lieutenant-colonel, a major and two captains, sitting with a judge-advocate. The disturbance had started as a protest by the prisoners at having to wear leg irons, and on account of the frequent imposition of dietary punishment. They had numerous other grievances as well. According to their evidence at the trial there were 14 latrines at the camp for approximately 300 inmates and these could only be used for a quarter of an hour each day between 1.15 p.m. and 1.30 p.m. Their blankets and their underclothing were lousy, they said, and they were not allowed to obtain any soap for the purposes of laundry. Several of the accused alleged that the prisoners at the camp were habitually tied to poles, sometimes being left there until they fainted. If they complained at this treatment they were punched in the ribs by the staff. Men undergoing field punishment were blindfolded for two hours every evening and were often kept in irons for a longer period than had been specified in their sentences. Two days before the mutiny a group of about 35 Australian prisoners at the same camp had demonstrated against the living conditions; as a result, a number of their complaints had been rectified. This had, no doubt, encouraged the belief that similar behaviour might succeed once again.

On the afternoon of the mutiny when the prisoners formed up for work after the midday meal-break 67 men in leg irons collected in the rear of the column. A sergeant-major ordered them to get on parade with the rest, but they refused, saying that they wanted to see the deputy-governor of the camp. They continued to ignore the sergeant-major's orders and the deputy-governor, a captain, was called to the scene. Upon his arrival the recalcitrant prisoners began to insist, noisily and abusively, that their chains should be removed and that all awards of dietary punishment should be immediately cancelled. The captain declined to listen to their demands and commanded them to fall-in in an orderly manner, but no one obeyed and the shouting continued. Deciding that drastic action was necessary, he directed that the whole party should be placed in handcuffs. With an armed escort on either side the handcuffing was started amidst a tumult of catcalls, booing and hissing. When several prisoners offered violent resistance the members of the staff drew their revolvers and the escort fixed bayonets. For a moment the atmosphere was explosive, the men shouting insults and threats at the deputy-governor and challenging the staff to open fire. The captain then ordered that the handcuffing should be discontinued and that all the mutineers should be driven into an isolated part of the prison compound.

During the remainder of the afternoon the mutiny subsided. Eventually all the men returned to work and the seven who were believed to have been the ringleaders were arrested. At their trial they offered no defence but repeated their allegations of the unjustified and brutal treatment they had been receiving at the camp. The prosecution was given leave to call in rebuttal a brigadier-general who held the appointment of Director of Military Prisons in the Field. He stated in his evidence that the trouble at this prison camp had only commenced after the arrival of the Australians. No instances of the ill-treatment of prisoners there had ever been reported to him, though he admitted that it was very common for men to faint when they were undergoing the punishment of being tied to a post. There was nothing in the regulations, he went on, which prohibited the blindfolding of prisoners serving terms of field punishment, provided it was done for some particular reason, for instance if they had been pulling faces or otherwise misbehaving themselves. Finally, he assured the court that it was permissible to keep military prisoners in leg irons without any limit of time.

Six of the seven accused were sentenced to death, but only one of them was actually executed, the remainder having their sentences commuted to terms of imprisonment or penal servitude varying between two years and 15 years.[10]

Towards the end of 1916 the strains of the interminable battle were having an appreciable effect on the troops, and men who had formerly been courageous soldiers were sometimes yielding to the impulse of uncontrolled panic. A sergeant, executed for 'shamefully casting away his arms in the presence of the enemy' was a typical instance of this. He had taken over as NCO of the watch at one o'clock on a bleak November morning when his battalion was manning a sector of the front line. About an hour later he was accompanying the duty lieutenant on a tour of an isolated and unoccupied trench when they suddenly encountered a German raiding party. The officer was shot and the sergeant dropped his rifle and bayonet and ran off. After a brief fight the Germans succeeded in occupying a small portion of the British fire-trench. While an immediate counter-attack was being prepared, the sergeant, acting without orders, asked a private to guide him to the rear headquarters of the company in order that he might give the alarm. The private thought that the sergeant looked ill at the time, and on their way back he had to sit down several times as he appeared to have lost control of his legs. They were stopped at a Military Police post and ordered to return to the line. The NCO in charge of the post noted that the sergeant was trembling, exhausted and seemed scarcely able to walk. A short while later the private reported to his forward company headquarters that the sergeant's legs had given out completely and he was lying in a dugout unable to move.

The sergeant had served with the BEF continuously for 11 months and had gone right through the summer and autumn campaigns on the Somme. His company commander spoke highly of his keenness and his bravery, but added that just recently he had been in very poor health. Before his court martial he was seen by his battalion medical officer who, without commenting upon his general condition, reported that a clinical examination of his legs had failed to reveal any symptoms of muscular rheumatism.

As a result of that German night-raid two lance-corporals and four privates from the same battalion as the sergeant, but from a different company, were jointly charged with 'shamefully abandoning their post'. They had all been members of a sentry group manning a traverse in the front line. Although their position had not been directly attacked by the raiding-party it had come under an intensive bombardment which had caused considerable damage to their trench. There had been the inevitable confusion as to what was happening and a rumour had reached the sentry group that the enemy had captured a neighbouring portion of the line. Suddenly a soldier, who was never identified, shouted out, 'Run for your lives, the Huns are on top of you!' Without waiting for further orders the two lance-corporals withdrew from the traverse and led the privates down a communication trench to the rear.

The men, none of whom were regular soldiers, were tried on Boxing Day and all six were sentenced to death. They had joined the battalion with the same draft in February 1916 and, according to their company commander, although none of them had served with any special distinction in the Somme battles each one had done everything that had been required of him. The divisional commander considered that the offence had shown the 'mental and physical degeneracy of the accused'. On his suggestion the sentences passed on the two NCOs were confirmed and those passed on the four privates were commuted to terms of 15 years' penal servitude.

One of the lance-corporals was 21 and had been a miner in civilian life. The other was 28 and had been a labourer. They had both volunteered for the Army at the beginning of March 1915. They were shot, together with the sergeant who had cast away his arms, in January 1917.

Twenty-four men from the BEF were convicted of desertion and executed during the last three months of 1916. Nearly all of them had been on active service for a considerable length of time, and at least a third of them were known to be suffering from some form of neurosis induced by their experiences in battle when they went absent.

There was a private in a Lancashire regiment who had enlisted very soon after the outbreak of war, and had served in France with his battalion for 16 months when he deserted in September 1916. He was said to have had a good fighting record until a short while before his offence, when he had started to exhibit 'signs of extreme nervousness' each time he went into action. A reservist of 30, he had joined the BEF in February 1915 and had stayed with his unit throughout the campaign except for a period of a few months in hospital while he was recovering from a slight wound. He had deserted in May 1916 and had been returned to the front with a suspended sentence. The following August he had deserted for the second time but had surrendered voluntarily to the Military Police. He told the court that he could not help himself because he seemed to always lose his nerve completely when he came under shellfire.

Sometimes there was independent evidence of the accused soldier's obvious state of emotional disorder. One of the executed men was a 23-year-old private who had been gassed on two occasions. Both his company commander and his company sergeant-major were agreed that out of the line he was keen and well behaved, but in the trenches he seemed to have no control over himself and his face and hands were continually twitching. They expressed their opinion that his nerves were completely shattered and that he was no longer fit for active operations. Another man, a lance-corporal who had volunteered in November 1914 and had joined the BEF eleven months later, was described by his company sergeant-major as being one of the best of soldiers and very well behaved. His conduct in action had been impeccable until an incident in December 1915 when a shell had burst close to him in the trenches spattering the head and brains of one of his comrades into his face. After that his demeanour had changed and he appeared to have never recovered from the shock. He was continually reporting sick until he eventually went absent in May 1916.

Two of the men who were shot around this time had been treated for shell-shock prior to their desertion. The first was a soldier from Somerset, an August 1914 volunteer, who had been wounded in June 1915. After his recovery he had rejoined his battalion but was admitted to a base hospital suffering from a nervous breakdown in November 1915. He was posted back to the front at the beginning of 1916 and had deserted soon after the opening of the Somme offensive. The second, a 22-year-old Yorkshireman, went absent while he was a member of a wiring-party in no-man's-land on a night in September 1916. During his initial period in the trenches, in July 1915, he was sent back to hospital in a state of nervous collapse. It might have been foreseen that he was totally unsuitable for active service, but following a spell with a labour company behind the line he had been reposted to his battalion a few weeks before his desertion. His commanding officer commented, 'I believe his terror under fire is such as to render him quite incapable of self-control.'

Excessively nervous soldiers in front-line units were a constant problem; for this was an age which still regarded cowardice in a male as one of the vilest types of degradation. To send back these men to a place of safety seemed utterly unthinkable; in any event, there was no recognized procedure for doing so unless they had been passed as unfit by a medical officer. Nevertheless, a colonel who pleaded unsuccessfully for the life of a deserter in October 1916, and recounted how he had seen the man during a heavy bombardment 'hiding in an old gunpit and trembling with fear', was mildly reproved by his corps commander. When the colonel had first become aware of the soldier's cowardly disposition, said the general, he should have had him withdrawn from the line or else have taken 'such disciplinary action as was necessary'.

The last batch of deserters to be executed in 1916 included the usual proportion of soldiers who were either dull-witted or mentally retarded. Having heard an accused private giving evidence on his own behalf in early October, the members of a court strongly recommended him to mercy 'owing to his low intellect'. A few weeks later a condemned deserter was described by his commanding officer as being 'a useless soldier with a weak intellect'. This man was a rather pathetic character who had obviously been treated as his company buffoon. He had been driven to desertion, he said, because he had spent 18 months in France without leave and he could not put up any longer with the incessant teasing of his comrades; each time he had gone into the trenches they used to throw stones at him pretending they were shrapnel. Some senior army officers seemed to consider that the mental dullness of a soldier was a form of self-induced depravity. A colonel, supported by his divisional commander, put forward the view in December that the 'moral degeneracy' of a convicted man caused by his own lack of intelligence should not be a ground for reprieving him from the firing squad.

Several of the deserters who were condemned to death and shot at this time had only been apprehended on the final stage of their bid to return to England. One was stopped by the Military Police in a street in Boulogne on the outskirts of the harbour. Another had presented himself at Le Havre claiming that he was on leave from the front and had lost his travel documents. A pioneer from the Royal Engineers had managed to insinuate himself into a home leave party and was arrested as he was preparing to join the boat. And a private from a Manchester regiment had been caught in civilian clothes on board a Swedish ship about to sail from the port at Dieppe.[11]

Towards the end of 1916 it was very obvious that the great offensive on the Western Front had failed to make any headway, although it became known in after-years that it had played an appreciable part in exhausting the military might of the German Army. The principal blame for the catastrophe was laid on the shoulders of Herbert Asquith, the Prime Minister. Attacked by the press and deserted by some of his most influential colleagues, he resigned on 5 December and was replaced by the dynamic Welshman David Lloyd George, who was already advocating a 'change of direction' in the war.

The other person primarily responsible for the misjudgments and disasters of the Somme received wholly different treatment. On 27 December 1916, Sir Douglas Haig was promoted to the rank of Field-Marshal.

Notes

1. John Glubb, *Into Battle*.
2. Report of the War Office Committee of Enquiry into Shell-shock, 1922.
3. John Glubb, ibid.
4. Stephen Graham, *A Private in the Guards*.

5. Norman Gladden, *The Somme 1916*.
6. Robert Graves, *Goodbye to All That*.
7. Robert Graves, op. cit.
8. Report of the Royal Commission for Inquiry into the System of Military Punishments, 1836.
9. Robert Graves, op. cit.
10. There was another mutiny at the prison camp at Blargies exactly two weeks after the first one as a result of which a New Zealand soldier was executed.
11. This soldier of the Manchester Regiment is buried in the Bailleulmont Communal Cemetry in France. His headstone bears the unusual inscription "Shot at Dawn". It is interesting to note that his death is recorded in official records as "Died of wounds" although it is clearly recorded on his Death Certificate as "Shot by sentence of FGMC for 'Desertion'."

10

THE EXECUTIONS OF TWO OFFICERS

O N 23 FEBRUARY 1918 a two-page article appeared in the popular weekly magazine *John Bull* under the title of 'Shot At Dawn'. It was written by the editor, Horatio Bottomley, and commenced:

> I have often pleaded the cause of Tommy. Today I want to plead that of the young officer – the mere boy, who at his country's call left his profession, his University, his home, to take command – as he well knew at the risk of his life – over those who, content with the rôle of private, had also rallied to the colours.

There followed an emotive account of the court martial and execution of a 21-year-old sub-lieutenant in the Royal Naval Division at the end of 1916. 'I tell this story', said Bottomley, 'because, after having made such inquiries as are possible into it, I believe that there was a grave miscarriage, if not of justice, shall I say of mercy?'

Although *John Bull* did not reveal the officer's name it was easily ascertainable from the records and it was disclosed in a book published in 1974.[1] Temporary Sub-Lieutenant D—— was tried for desertion on 26 December 1916. He was sentenced to death and was executed on 5 January 1917. It has often been suggested that A. P. Herbert, who was serving in the Royal Naval Division at the time, has based his sensitive novel *The Secret Battle* on the facts of this case.

Sub-Lieutenant D——, according to Bottomley, came from a family with a long tradition of service in the armed forces. He had joined the Royal Naval Volunteer Reserve after the outbreak of war and had been transferred against his wishes to the Royal Naval Division to serve upon land. He had taken part in the operation at Antwerp in 1914 and was 'a popular officer, but not a particularly efficient one' as he lacked the qualities of responsibility and leadership.

The Royal Naval Division had been formed during the summer of 1914 from naval personnel, mainly reservists, who were supernumerary to the requirements of the Fleet. It was sent to Antwerp the following autumn to fight alongside the Belgians, but it was ill-trained and ill-equipped for an infantry role and it was soon withdrawn to be reorganized. The division served with distinction in the Gallipoli campaign and was later sent to the Western Front. D——'s commanding officer, said Bottomley, was well aware of the young man's failings and when the battalion first went into action on the Somme, D—— was left at the base.

Horatio Bottomley quoted from a letter written by D—— to a friend on 13 December 1916, while he was still waiting to hear whether or not he was going to be court-martialled, in which he gave his own version of the incident which had led to his being placed under close arrest. After the division had taken part in a morning attack, said D——, he and another officer had been ordered to report back to their battalion as casualty replacements. They had crossed together into no-man's-land but were unable to locate anyone from their unit so they had separated and he had continued to search by himself. 'I rambled about,' he went on, 'and lost touch with everybody, and my nerves, not being strong, were completely strung up.'

D——'s letter was somewhat vague as to what had happened next. He had met an officer, he said, who was taking forward a party and who ordered him to join it, but he refused as he had wanted to find his own company. The other officer had then sent 'a startling message of sorts' to his brigade headquarters with the result that enquiries were commenced about D——'s conduct. He concluded:

> They have kept me a month hanging on. I am hoping for news any day now, and if there is nothing in it I do not see why I should worry my people by telling them. Now I have all the company mail to censor, so please excuse more.

The general tone of this letter implied that D—— did not expect the matter to be taken any further. His attitude had not changed when he wrote to another friend on 26 December telling him there was no need to be concerned about the outcome of the enquiry. He mentioned that at the beginning of November he had put in an application to his commanding officer to be sent back to sea as his nerves were not strong enough for the infantry battlefield, and he went on to describe the situation in no-man's-land on the day he had been searching for his battalion:

> There was considerable hostile artillery, gas and tear shells falling all round us, and snipers were all over the place; we had very narrow shaves more than once. We could not find our unit and rambled about.

He had then elaborated on the later episode. According to the quotation in *John Bull* he had written:

When it was dark we met a body of men with an officer in charge; they were wanted by Col. Freyburg V.C.; there was much confusion and disorder going on and my nerves became strung to the highest extreme. I found that my companion had gone off somewhere with some men. The officer who was leading the party we met was my 'one and only enemy', so we were not polite to each other, and as he is junior to me I practically ignored him except for telling him I was going back to B.H.Q., which I had left an hour or two before in daylight, but finding those places was not as easy a matter as I thought with the result that I got lost for the second time.

He had finished up, he said, by spending the night in a dugout. He felt certain that when he had given his explanation of what had really taken place the whole incident would appear in a different light.

Without stating the source of his information Bottomley alleged that D——'s defending officer had not seen him until about half-an-hour before the court martial had commenced. Even after the trial was over, said Bottomley, D—— had believed in the event of a conviction the worst punishment which could befall would be the loss of his commission. In fact, he had been sentenced to death with a strong recommendation to mercy. The article continued:

He waited, and the blow fell with sharp and cruel suddenness. One night, at the place to which he had been taken by two brother officers, they were playing cards, when another officer entered, opened a big blue envelope, and read out the Death Warrant – he was to be Shot at Dawn! Not much time to make peace with God – just a quiet hour with the Padré – Heaven bless them in their mission of comfort – just a last letter to the dear ones at home; just a fitful sleep, and then death in the chill dawn of a winter's day.

During the same week in which the article had appeared in *John Bull* an MP referred to it in the House of Commons, expressing the view that if the facts given were not accurate Horatio Bottomley should be prosecuted, but if they were true there was a case for investigation of the method of procedure in capital courts martial.[2] Another Member requested that the evidence in this particular case should be laid before the House.[3] The Under-Secretary of State for War replied that the proceedings at courts martial could not be shown to anyone without the consent of the accused; if the accused was dead such consent could not be given. However, he undertook to examine the papers himself and to disclose to the House so much of the real facts as was consistent with his duty and with the law.[4]

The next issue of *John Bull*, which appeared on 2 March, contained a sharp attack on the court martial system on account of the 'criminal callousness' brought to light in the case of Sub-Lieutenant D———. The unsigned article asserted that D—— had been granted no adequate facilities to prepare his defence; that he had only been informed of his conviction and his sentence a bare 12 hours before the time fixed for his execution; that he was allowed no right of appeal; and that the court's recommendation to mercy had been ignored. The writer, most probably Horatio Bottomley himself, demanded that 'the whole proceedings preliminary to and after the trial should form the subject of a special inquiry'.

The matter was raised again in the House of Commons on 6 March when the Under-Secretary of State for War was asked if he had any further statement to make about the case.[5] The Minister replied that his investigations had revealed that the recommendation to mercy had been duly considered by 'the various and many authorities' through which the court martial proceedings had passed before the sentence had been confirmed by the Commander-in-Chief. In answer to a supplementary question he said the facts published in *John Bull* had not been 'substantially correct'. The Minister declined to add anything more.

In the next issue of *John Bull* Horatio Bottomley announced triumphantly that the Law Officers were considering whether or not he should be prosecuted. It would have been no new experience for this 58-year-old journalist and financier to enter the dock at a criminal court. In 1893 he had successfully defended himself in a trial for conspiracy and in 1909 he had been acquitted on a charge of fraud. Having spent his early years in an orphanage, and subsequently worked as an errand boy, he had made a profit of over £3,000,000 by promoting companies before he reached the age of 45. He had sat in Parliament as a Liberal from 1906 until 1912 when he had applied for the Chiltern Hundreds. *John Bull*, which he had founded in 1906, was always published with the slogan on the front page 'Politics without Party – Criticism without Cant; Without Fear or Favour, Rancour or Rant'. The magazine had achieved more of a reputation for outspokenness than for reliability; it was widely read amongst servicemen and their families and claimed to have a weekly circulation of just under 2,000,000.

Bottomley recounted later[6] how he had been invited by Sir Reginald Brade, the Director of Personal Services at the War Office, to come round and discuss the 'misapprehensions and inaccuracies' in his recent article in order that he might be shown 'all the true facts of the case'. He visited Brade and during their two-hour discussion D———'s court martial file had been lying on a desk between them, but it was never opened as Sir Reginald explained that by the terms of the Army Act it could only be seen by the accused. Bottomley was told absolutely nothing about the trial. He wrote in *John Bull*, 'The interview has left me more convinced than ever of the justice of our charges against the present system.' He appeared to accept, however, Sir Reginald Brade's assurance that D—— had been in conference with his defending officer for four hours on the day before the court martial took place.

The execution of Sub-Lieutenant D—— was again ventilated in Parliament during a debate on the Consolidated Fund Bill on 14 March.[7] It was raised by Mr Pringle, a back-bencher, who stated that he was alluding to the case for the principal purpose of bringing about the reformation of the procedure at military courts martial. The exact details of the incident which had led to the charge in this instance were obscure, he said, as the only available information had come from the accused officer himself and at different times he had given 'somewhat disconnected accounts'. Mr Pringle had then gone on to repeat the version which had been related by Horatio Bottomley in *John Bull*, adding that the Prisoner's Friend had been appointed less than 48 hours before the trial and had only seen a summary of the prosecution evidence half-an-hour before he had gone into court. This officer had experienced great difficulty in obtaining coherent instructions from D——, said Mr Pringle, and he had been much impressed by the accused man's nervous condition. In consequence, he had decided that it would be inadvisable for D—— to offer any evidence on his own behalf.

The Under-Secretary for War was the next speaker in the debate. He said that he was not going to enter into a controversy about the facts of the case as they had been accurately stated by Mr Pringle. The executed officer had received orders to join his battalion which was heavily engaged in the front line. He had disappeared and two days later, after the battalion had been relieved, he was found in a village some way to the rear. He had been allocated for his defence an officer with 'distinguished legal qualifications' who had interviewed him from 11 a.m. until 3 p.m. either one day or two days before his trial. At that time D—— had been in possession of the summary of evidence against him and it was difficult to understand why he had not shown it to his defending officer until a short while before the commencement of the court martial. With regard to the recommendation to mercy on account of D——'s youth, such recommendations were 'almost invariably' made and were carefully considered before the confirmation of a death sentence. The minister continued, 'I can assure the House that both Lord French and Sir Douglas Haig are two of the most humane men who ever commanded great forces in the field.'

This was to be the last occasion on which the case of Sub-Lieutenant D—— was mentioned specifically in Parliament. It was referred to briefly by Horatio Bottomley in several subsequent issues of *John Bull* in the course of his campaign to ameliorate some of the harsher features of the court martial system.

A. P. Herbert's novel *The Secret Battle* was published in 1919. The story was told in the first person and began:

> I am going to write down some of the history of Harry Penrose because I do not think full justice has been done to him, and because there must be many other young men of his kind who flung themselves into the war at the beginning of it, and have gone out of it after many sufferings with the unjust and ignorant condemnation of their fellows.

Penrose, an exhibitioner at Oxford University, had been commissioned through the ranks and had been sent to Gallipoli with his battalion. He had proved to be a modest and courageous officer, but suffered from 'a curious distrust of his own capacity in the face of anything he had to do . . . his nervousness took the form of an intimate silent brooding over any ordeal that lay before him'. He soon became the battalion scouting officer because crawling about by himself under the noses of the Turks in no-man's-land made a special appeal to the romantic side of his nature. After many individual exploits he contracted severe dysentery, but he refused to report sick and remained in the line until he collapsed. As a result of his illness he was evacuated from the peninsula and sent back to England.

In 1916 Penrose had insisted on returning to his battalion which by then had been transferred to the Western Front. He was again appointed to his old position of scouting officer and used to go out night after night on lone reconnaissance patrols. Eventually – perhaps inevitably – his nerve had cracked. It had happened one night when the Germans had observed him close to their trenches and had opened an intensive fire on him with rifles, shells and grenades. He had told someone afterwards that he had 'simply sweated with funk'. The following evening his commanding officer had sent him to inspect a German outpost. Penrose had hidden in a shell-hole in no-man's-land unable to control his fear and had reported afterwards that he had been unable to find a gap in the enemy wire. A short while later he had been returned to England with a shrapnel wound in the chest.

When Penrose had recovered he was offered a posting to the War Office, which he had refused as he wanted to get back to active service. He had also declined to accept a safe job at the base in France. He had rejoined his battalion when it was in reserve and within hours of his arrival he was sent forward to the front line in charge of a wire-carrying party. On the way up they had come under heavy shellfire and had taken shelter in a dugout. Penrose's assistant-adjutant – in many ways his 'one and only enemy' – had found them there and had ordered him to bring his party out and to deliver the wire immediately. Penrose had replied that 'he'd see him damned first' as he intended to wait until the barrage had eased off. For this he was court-martialled, condemned to death and executed.

A. P. Herbert and Sub-Lieutenant D—— had served in different battalions in the Royal Naval Division and most probably had never known each other. According to Brigadier Basil Rackham, who was a friend and colleague of A. P. Herbert's at this period, *The Secret Battle*, although inspired by D——'s case, was intended to be entirely fictional.[8]

From November 1916 until April 1917 A. P. Herbert had been adjutant of his battalion with Basil Rackham as his assistant. 'During this time,' says Rackham, 'incensed by what he considered to be the injustice of the D—— case and, maybe, others, he often spoke of the possibility of writing a book about courts-martial.' He wished to emphasize in particular the inadequate presentation of defences, the bias of courts in favour of the prosecution, and the lack of consideration shown by the military authorities to men whose nerves had given out after long periods in action.[9]

13 November 1916, when D—— was alleged to have deserted, was a day of misfortune for the Royal Naval Division which was taking part in its first attack on the Western Front since it had joined the BEF during the previous May. The renewal of the offensive against the Ancre Heights by General Gough's Fifth Army was supposed to have opened several weeks earlier but had been delayed by the atrocious weather conditions. On the morning of 13 November although the ground was sufficiently hard for an infantry assault the whole area was shrouded in a dank and turbid fog which both concealed the advancing troops and added to the general confusion of the battlefield. The German resistance was obdurate and grim. All the British units involved were severely mauled and by noon D——'s battalion had been reduced to an effective strength of one officer and a few dozen men. By then an urgent appeal for reinforcements had been sent back to the base.

D——'s defending officer at his court martial might have had 'distinguished legal qualifications' but he seems to have had little skill or experience as a forensic advocate. In his cross-examination of the first prosecution witness, a lieutenant-commander who had been in charge of the rear headquarters of the battalion at the time, he elicited replies that must have considerably strengthened the prosecution case. The witness had admitted to holding a very poor opinion of D——'s capabilities as an officer, and had agreed that D—— had recently applied for a transfer to sea service on the ground that his very nervous temperament made him unfit for the firing line. Only two officers had been available when the request for immediate replacements had come through, said the commander, and he had felt a certain apprehension in sending forward D—— in response to it.

The other available officer at the rear battalion headquarters had been a lieutenant. He and D—— had reported to advance brigade headquarters and then set off into no-man's-land to search for their battalion, with which all contact had been lost. During the afternoon they had met up with a staff officer from their brigade who had just gathered up about 200 stragglers from various units in the Royal Naval Division. This officer, a sub-lieutenant, had trained with D—— in England and both men had been posted to France on the same draft. He was, says Brigadier Rackham, universally disliked.[10] The staff officer had told the lieutenant to take charge of the stragglers and to lead them back to the line. He ordered D—— to follow behind the party and to make sure that nobody dropped out. D—— had protested that the situation was so chaotic he thought he should return to brigade headquarters for fresh orders. After a brief argument he had disappeared and the staff officer had promptly reported him for refusing to obey a lawful order. The next time D—— had been seen was at a village behind the line two days later.

All this was given in evidence at the General Court Martial and was virtually unchallenged on behalf of D——. Indeed, the members of the court must have wondered what the defence was going to be as none had emerged from the cross-examination of the prosecution witnesses except, perhaps, a half-hearted suggestion that D—— had not been mentally in control of his actions on the day in question. When D—— was asked if he had anything to say in his defence he replied that he did not wish to give evidence or to call any witnesses.

In his closing address to the court the defending officer said that D—— was so highly neurotic he was unfit for service in the field. He went on to state that after refusing to accompany the stragglers on 13 November D—— had lost his way, but had reported to an officer at brigade headquarters on the following morning and had been told to wait around until his battalion was relieved from the line. Although it was permissible at that time for the accused at a court martial to decline to give evidence and then to put forward his substantive defence in a closing address, it cannot have created a very favourable impression when this procedure was adopted by an officer.[11]

The court sentenced D—— to death and recommended him to mercy on two grounds. Firstly, his youth and his inexperience of active operations. D—— had, in fact, joined the Royal Naval Division on being commissioned in June 1915, so he could not have served in the Antwerp expedition in 1914 as stated by Horatio Bottomley.

Secondly, because the prevailing conditions at the time of his desertion has been likely to seriously affect any young officer 'unless he had a strong character'.

D——'s divisional commander wished to see the sentence commuted. However, his corps and army commanders considered that it should be carried out. General Gough, a man of great personal courage and the only high-ranking officer to regularly visit the front line,[12] expressed the view that if a private soldier had behaved as D—— had done it was most probable he would have been shot.

On 14 January 1917 Haig's General Routine Orders carried an announcement of D——'s trial and conviction, ending with the sombre words, 'The sentence of the Court was "to suffer death by being shot". The sentence was duly carried out at 7.30 A.M. on the 5th January, 1917.'

On the last night before his execution D—— had written his final letter home.[13]

> Dearest Mother Mine,
>
>   I hope by now you will have heard the news. Dearest, I am leaving you now because He has willed it. You know all and you will have forgiven me all the past as a child. My sorrow tonight is for the trouble I have caused you and dad.
>
>   Please excuse any mistakes, but if it were not for the kind support of the Rev. —— who is with me tonight, I should not be able to write myself. I should like you to write to him, as he has been my friend.
>
>   I am leaving all my effects to you, dearest; will you give my little —— half the sum you have of mine?
>
>   Give dear Dad my love and wish him luck. I feel for you so much and I am sorry for bringing dishonour upon you all. Give —— my love. She will, I expect, understand, and give her back the presents, photos, cards, etc., she has sent me, poor girl.
>
>   So now, dearest Mother, I must close. May God bless and protect you all now and for ever more – Amen.

The chaplain of D——'s battalion wrote to his parents to tell them he had been with D—— until the moment of his death.[14] Afterwards, he said:

> I accompanied his body in an ambulance-car several miles away to a beautiful little cemetery, near a small town quite close to the sea, and here we buried him with the Church of England Service. A cross will soon be erected over his grave. Leave it to me, and I will see that it is done, before our hurried departure to another part of France.

Sub-Lieutenant D—— was not the first British officer, but the second to be executed during the war. On 14 December 1916, 12 days before D——'s court martial, an announcement appeared in Haig's General Routine Orders to the effect that an infantry subaltern had been tried by FGCM for desertion. The brief details were stated in a single sentence:

> The accused absented himself from the command of his platoon, while carrying out a relief of the front line, and remained absent till found behind the fighting area two days later.

He had been sentenced to death, the announcement continued, and 'The sentence was duly carried out at 7.25 A.M. on 10th December, 1916.'

Second-Lieutenant P—— had been 30 years old at the time of his execution. He had enlisted as a volunteer in 1914 and had joined a battalion of a North Country regiment on the Western Front in May 1916, at a time when they were preparing to move up to the Somme. After his first three days in action at the beginning of the Somme offensive he was knocked out by a clod of earth when an enemy shell exploded near him, and was sent back to the base with the diagnosis that he was suffering from shell-shock. P—— had spent 17 days in hospital and was transferred to a convalescent home in Dieppe on 25 July.

When P—— was admitted to the convalescent home it was noted that he was still in a shaky and nervous condition. In the middle of August he was examined by a consultant who found him unfit for duty at the front and recommended that he should be given a temporary posting to the base. Exactly a week later, on 26 August, he had appeared before a standing medical board at Etaples which had classified him as being fit for normal duties.

P—— had rejoined his battalion in September while they were undergoing a period of reorganization and rest. Shortly afterwards they were moved forward to a reserve position in the Somme and on 5 October they were suddenly ordered to relieve a unit in the front line, under cover of darkness that night. During the afternoon, as they were checking their weapons and equipment, P—— had complained to an officer in his company that he was feeling very unwell and was thinking of seeing a doctor. Around midnight, when the relief had been completed, he was found to be absent.

P—— had attended the regimental aid post of another battalion at ten o'clock the following morning and asked for some tablets for his rheumatism. Nothing more was then seen of him until he was arrested by a Military Policeman on 7 October in a very dazed condition some distance behind the line.

In an effort to prevent P—— from being court-martialled for

desertion his brigade commander had sent a note to the divisional commander on 17 October suggesting that he should be sent home for instructional or for administrative duties. He had only recently been treated for shell-shock, said the brigadier, and his nervous temperament made him a useless, if not a dangerous, officer when he went into action. But by then the wheels had already been set in motion and there was no turning back. The court martial took place on 21 November.

Second-Lieutenant P—— gave evidence at his trial, merely telling the court that since being affected by shell-shock he had suffered from fits of mental confusion. His battalion medical officer corroborated his statement and added that in times of stress he might well become so mentally confused that he would not be responsible for his actions. In the outcome P—— was sentenced to death without any recommendation to mercy.

P——'s commanding officer, and his brigade, divisional and corps commanders, were all in favour of the sentence being commuted. However, his army commander, the 59-year-old Sir Herbert Plumer, and the Commander-in-Chief disagreed with them. On 3 December P—— had appeared before a special medical board which had reported that although his mental powers were less than the average he was of sound mind and had been capable of appreciating the nature and quality of his offence.

Before the executions of both D—— and P—— the Adjutant-General was careful to point out to their commanding officers that under the Army Act an officer did not cease to be an officer even after sentence of death had been promulgated upon him, and that the condemned men must retain their badges of rank and their commissioned status up to the very end.

Notes

1. William Moore, *The Thin Yellow Line*.
2. Mr Morrell, House of Commons, Debate on Army Estimates, 20 February 1918.
3. Mr J. H. Thomas, ibid.
4. Mr Macpherson, ibid.
5. House of Commons, oral answers, 6 March 1918.
6. *John Bull*, 16 March 1918.
7. House of Commons, Consolidated Fund Bill, Third Reading, 14 March 1918.
8. Letter to the author dated 15 March 1980. Brigadier Rackham believes that A. P. Herbert was invited to be D——'s defending officer but declined.
9. Letter to the author dated 16 March 1980.
10. Letter to the author dated 16 March 1980.
11. A footnote in the 1914 *Manual of Military Law* stated: 'The accused . . . has the

privilege whether he has given evidence himself or not, of making statements in his address unsupported by evidence, and when those statements are in the personal knowledge of the accused, they must be dealt with as evidence, though not given on oath.'

12. Anthony Farrar-Hockley, *Goughie*.
13. Published in *John Bull*, 23 February 1918.
14. Also published in *John Bull*, 23 February 1918. Sub- Lieutenant D————'s body is buried at Le Crotoy Communal Cemetry in France. On the headstone is inscribed "If doing well ye suffer this is acceptable with God" 1 Epis Peter.

II

THE YEAR OF PASSCHENDAELE

A T A CONFERENCE between the Allied High Commands at the French General Headquarters on 15 November 1916, Sir Douglas Haig had stated that the BEF would be ready to resume the offensive on 1 February 1917, but that he would prefer to wait until the beginning of May when he would have received considerable reinforcements from England. The French were adamant that he should attack on the earlier date.

The total strength of the BEF at the end of 1916 was around 1,200,000 officers and men, organized into 56 infantry divisions. It was hoped to add a further nine divisions by the spring of 1917. The French Army was approximately twice as large as the British but it had already exhausted most of its possible reserves of manpower.

Although General Joffre was still the Commander-in-Chief of all the French armies on the Western Front the forthcoming operations had been entrusted to General Nivelle, the hope of the moment and newly-discovered prodigy. Nivelle abounded in optimism and his assessments and predictions were a constant solace to the despondent politicians in Paris. It was his belief that if the French were to launch a massive offensive at the beginning of 1917 they would be certain to achieve a total victory within a matter of a few weeks. He wanted the BEF to make a feint attack in the Arras sector in order to confuse the Germans and to draw off their reserves. There were many officers in the French and British High Commands who did not share Nivelle's confidence, but Haig eventually yielded to his enthusiasm and agreed that his plans should be adopted.

At the close of 1916 the fortunes of the Allies were at a low ebb. The British offensive in the Somme had achieved no major strategical gains and had resulted in losses to the BEF amounting to over 420,000 men. From the point of view of victory by attrition the ratio of British casualties to German had been in the region of three to two. The French Army had fought itself to a standstill and had neither the will nor the capacity to resume the attack. The Russian military machine was decomposing fast. Both in England and in France there was increasing talk of the possibility of a negotiated peace settlement.

As far as the BEF was concerned conscription had both eased the problem of manpower and lowered the quality of the reinforcements. Siegfried Sassoon commented:[1]

> The raw material to be trained was growing steadily worse. Most of those who came in now had joined the Army unwillingly and there was no reason why they should find military service tolerable. The war had become undisguisedly mechanical and inhuman. What in earlier days had been drafts of volunteers were now droves of victims.

A doctor who served as the medical officer to an infantry battalion on the Western Front described the winter of 1916–17 as a time of doubt and disillusionment for the troops. 'Men were weary, less certain of things,' he said; 'There was a feeling abroad that it was necessary to believe in something to carry on at all.'[2] To the intense annoyance of the officers and men of the BEF the newspapers at home were perpetually portraying their attitude towards the war as a spirit of crusading zeal. On his arrival in the Somme Norman Gladden looked around in vain for the laughing faces he had read about so often,[3] and Lord Moran, writing in his diary, alluded with cynical disbelief to the stories in the press of soldiers 'burning to get at the Hun' and of their reluctance to be relieved when they were involved in a battle. Perhaps these things did happen, he said, 'But there is nothing about those who find they are not equipped for the business, who falter and hang back. They are pushed back into the line and in their tale there is no room for rhetoric.' His own experience of troops returning from the front was that they looked tired and ill. 'The very gait of these men has lost its spring,' he observed. 'The sap has gone out of them. They are dried up.'[5]

During November and December 1916, and the first half of January 1917, the rain poured down on the Western Front almost continually and the whole area of the battlefield became a vast wilderness of churned-up mud patterned with rows of sodden and waterlogged trenches. Every formation which could be spared was withdrawn from the line to undergo a period of intensive training for the forthcoming offensive, but at the front the shelling never lessened; neither did the sniping, patrolling and raiding; nor the limited assaults.

For sensitive men in the opposing armies the experience was the same – the nihilism and the degradation of the way of life. A young German soldier wrote:[5]

> We are not youth any longer. We don't want to take the world by storm. We are fleeing. We fly from ourselves. From our life. We were eighteen and had begun to love life and the world; and we had to shoot it to pieces. The first bomb, the first explosion, burst in our hearts. We are cut off

from activity, from striving, from progress. We believe in such things no longer. We believe in the war.

Norman Gladden's experiences on joining the BEF towards the end of 1916 might or might not have been typical.[6] On arriving at the base depot at Etaples he and his draft were 'harangued' by the adjutant there on the austere and inflexible discipline they were about to encounter in the front line. This officer expounded graphically on the unpleasantness of Field Punishment Number One and informed them 'almost with fervour' that if they slept on sentry duty they would almost certainly be shot. When the draft was posted to a battalion, says Gladden, they were immediately made to feel that they had no rights of any sort. At every turn the 'old hands' proceeded to take advantage of them. They had difficulty in obtaining their proper share of the rations; they were detailed for all the most unpleasant working parties; and in the trenches they found themselves deprived of shelter from the weather.

Gladden complained, like so many others who wrote of their military service in the Great War, of the lack of information passed down to the troops. The secrecy was 'galling in the extreme to men with the average allotment of brain,' said Arthur Lambert,[7] and Edmund Blunden described the infantryman's knowledge of what was happening around him as being bounded by the skyline of his immediate orders.[8]

The morale of the BEF, fostered by the pride of regimental tradition, remained incredibly high. No doubt it would have been even higher if the officers and men in the trenches could have felt more confidence in the senior commanders, but the feeling was widespread that the distance of the generals from the battle zones kept them utterly out of touch with the holocaust at the front. Gladden considered it worthy of mention when he saw his brigadier in the forward firing line as he was normally 'a rare visitor to such places'.[9]

As far as the troops in the field were concerned a divisional or a corps commander was merely a name – an omniscience from whom directives would issue which seemed sometimes as callous as they were nonsensical. The uncaring attitude of some very senior officers was typified by the general in command of Siegfried Sassoon's division who forbade the wearing of steel helmets at the front as he thought it might weaken the fighting spirit of the men, and also prohibited the issue of a rum ration before the commencement of an attack.[10] The conditions of trench warfare and the wholesale casualties inflicted by shrapnel shells had made it essential for soldiers to have some form of protective covering for the head and steel helmets had come into use in the BEF during the first months of 1916. As for the rum issue, a doctor who had served as a medical officer in the Black Watch said later: 'If it hadn't been for the rum ration I do not think we should have won the war.'[11]

About the middle of January 1917 the bitter cold and the intermittent frosts on the Western Front had hardened the surface of the earth to such an extent that it was possible for a person to stumble over the irregular, pitted wastes without the certainty of sinking ankle- or knee-deep into a quagmire of mud. At this juncture Haig decided he could fulfil his promise to the French and open his offensive. The condition of the ground still precluded the customary pattern of assault with the infantry advancing line after line in open formation. For the preliminary attacks during that month and the next, waves of detached bombing parties worked their way forward into no-man's-land each carrying its own duckboards to lay across the worst of the morasses.

The operations of the BEF in January and February, though conducted on a very small scale, achieved some minor tactical successes. These availed them nothing, however, in regard to the forthcoming offensive as General Ludendorff, the director of strategy in the German High Command, had already decided to withdraw his troops from the Somme and to take up a new position on the Hindenburg Line running in an arc from Lens to Rheims. Ludendorff intended to reorganize his armies completely and to remain on the defensive until he had sufficient men and materials to strike a decisive blow at the Allied forces on the Western Front. The Germans commenced to evacuate their forward trenches on the Somme in the early hours of the morning on 12 March. They were allowed to complete their retirement without any serious interference, although at such a moment they might well have been caught off-balance.

In spite of the altered dispositions of the German armies on the left of the Allied line Nivelle and Haig decided to adhere to their original plan for a major offensive in April, with the British creating a diversion to the east of Arras and the French mounting a major onslaught in the district of Champagne.

Considering the conditions under which the BEF was serving during the winter months of 1916–17, the desertion rate was extremely low, but it was high enough to cause concern to some of the senior British officers. In recommending the execution of a deserter in early February a brigade commander wrote, 'Offences of this nature are now prevalent and ought to be dealt with severely to discourage others.' Most of the men who were shot at this time had gone absent whilst in reserve at a moment when their battalions had been warned to prepare for duty in the front line. Some deserters had already seen a considerable amount of active service: others had hardly been in the trenches at all. A Scottish private who deserted on 7 January whilst marching to the front had only joined his unit nine days previously.

It seemed to have become a convention in the Army for no one to plead 'guilty' to a capital charge no matter how overwhelming the evidence for the prosecution might be. A Yorkshire private was convicted of desertion on 19 October 1916. On 14 December, while he was in custody in the transport lines of his battalion awaiting promulgation, he was visited by an officer who told him he had been sentenced to death and the sentence had been commuted to a term of penal servitude which had been suspended. The reprieved soldier was ordered to report to his company in the trenches the following night. He never did so. A week later he was arrested by the Military Police attempting to make his way back to the area behind the lines. He was tried again on 11 January 1917 on a further charge of desertion. Whether or not he was represented by an officer on this occasion is not clear, but the president of the court noted on the record of the proceedings, 'The accused was given every opportunity of cross-examining the witnesses and making a statement in mitigation of punishment and calling witnesses in his defence. He declined to do so.' The outcome was inevitable, the private being executed early in February.

Some of the defences put forward to a charge of desertion were merely forlorn endeavours to avoid a sentence of death. A 22-year-old soldier who was posted to a battalion in the BEF in October 1916 went absent four times during the next three months before he was tried by court martial. He said in evidence that he had lost his head after receiving a letter from home telling him that his mother was not being properly looked after by his half-wit brother. Another private, who joined the BEF in December 1916 and deserted two months later, had been convicted 12 times of absence without leave while he was training in England and had absented himself yet again soon after he had landed at Le Havre. He informed the court that he was suffering from mental confusion at the time of his desertion as he had been so drunk the night before.

It might have been expected that the rigid standard of discipline of the pre-war regular soldiers would have made them less likely to commit serious military offences than the hastily-trained volunteers and conscripts now forming the main element of the BEF. In spite of the fact that the old peacetime army had been virtually obliterated the statistics of capital courts martial for this period show that a surprisingly high proportion of the executed men were regulars or reservists. Amongst the soldiers in this category three were separately tried for desertion during the first few weeks of March 1917. One of them was a 31-year-old private in a Durham regiment who, for a reason

which was never explained at his trial, had only gone into the front line
for the first time the previous month. He had absented himself from
the trenches and had been apprehended by the Military Police in Calais
a week later. He claimed in his defence that he had been suffering from
trench feet and bronchitis and considered himself to be unfit for duty.

Of the other two men, one was a regular and one a reservist. Their
cases had a common factor inasmuch as on being arrested they were
both wearing on their tunics the ribbons of decorations for gallantry
which they had never been awarded. It was usual for a deserter, like
any absconding fugitive, to seek the anonymity of the commonplace
rather than to indulge himself in a form of vainglorious display. The
regular soldier, a Scotsman, had enlisted in October 1913, at the age of
18. He had served in France for two years and had been slightly
wounded earlier in the campaign. He had deserted in October 1916
when he was a member of a tunnelling party in no-man's-land. Three
months later he was stopped by a Military Policeman in a town behind
the line with the ribbons of the DCM and the Legion of Honour on his
chest and four wound-stripes on his sleeve. The reservist was a
sergeant who had first joined the Army in 1906. He too had gone
absent in October 1916 and during November and December he had
cashed a number of cheques at French banks, always using a false name
and posing either as an officer or as a company sergeant-major. He was
arrested in Amiens in January 1917, wearing the ribbons of the VC,
the DCM and the MM. He said in evidence at his trial that he was
wounded in the head during a German air-raid when he had been
passing through Amiens off duty. He had then been taken to a French
hospital where he had been detained for treatment and had been unable
to contact his battalion. He was extremely vague in regard to the
location of the hospital and did not bring forward any witnesses to
corroborate his story. A fortnight after he had been convicted and
condemned to death he was examined by two doctors who had
discovered a small scar on the upper part of his scalp but who were
both agreed that this did not appear to be of very recent origin.

Although it has recently been stated[12] that in 1917 numerous
deserters were ekeing out an existence on the old battlefields on the
Somme and in the woods around Paris Plage to the south of Le
Touquet, it would seem that the provost services in the BEF were still
operating in a reasonably efficient manner and that it remained
exceptionally difficult for an absentee to preserve his liberty for any
considerable length of time. The men who eluded capture for the
longest periods had often been sheltered by French civilians. A regular
soldier in a Yorkshire regiment, who had been posted as 'missing' a
week before Christmas in 1914, was discovered by a gendarme at a
house in Hazebrouck on 1 December 1916. He had been living there

with a woman and one of her neighbours had disclosed his identity to the police. After an absence of nearly two years there was little to be said for him at his trial except to plead that he be given an opportunity to redeem himself in the field. He was duly condemned to death and his brigadier made the dispassionate comment, 'I can discover no redeeming feature in this case nor any reason why the sentence should not be carried out.'

Of the manifold difficulties facing a deserter who was endeavouring to merge himself with the French population behind the lines the greatest were the provision of money, food and clothing, as well as the paramount problem of communicating in a foreign tongue. Even if he was fortunate enough to find French people willing to shelter him in their home his presence was bound to become known to others in the vicinity. Many people whose friends and relations had been killed and wounded or were fighting at the front might resent the British absentee in their midst and might even be constrained to report his presence to the authorities. Sometimes denoucement came from closer at hand. A young gunner deserted on the Somme in July 1916, just after returning from home leave. He made his way south to a town in Provence where he befriended a prostitute and went to live with her. She betrayed him to the local police the following December after a quarrel and he was arrested at her house. He was executed by sentence of court martial on 3 February 1917.

Most deserters from the BEF still tried to get back to England because, despite the hazards of the journey, the British mainland seemed to offer more likelihood of a safe asylum. Very few absentees were managing to slip through the net at the transit ports. Two 20-year-old Kitchener volunteers who were executed together in March 1917 had been picked up by the Military Police in Folkestone just after they had successfully negotiated the Channel crossing. They were both members of the same battalion of a West Country regiment which they had joined in Gallipoli. Formerly they had been good soldiers and if they had had any special motive for deserting it was not revealed at their court martial as neither of them offered any explanation for their conduct.

The charge of desertion was then so simple to prove in terms of military law that once the necessary facts had been established there was little room for any possible defence. Many prisoners fell back on pleading loss of memory or insanity. A reservist from Lancashire who had re-enlisted on the outbreak of war and had gone absent in August 1916, was apprehended in Armentières three months later. He called witnesses at his trial to give evidence about his peculiar behaviour whilst serving in Egypt with his battalion during the previous year. Their testimony went no further than affirming that he had always liked to be alone and had sometimes gone off unaccountably at night to sleep by himself in the desert. After his conviction he was examined by a medical board which could find nothing to suggest that he might have been of unsound mind at the time of his desertion. In accordance with his sentence he was shot on 4 February 1917 at Poperinghe.

There can be no doubt that once a soldier had been condemned to death the opinions of his character as expressed by his commanding officer or his brigadier might be so damning that there would be small chance of his sentence being commuted. Their views were usually based on hearsay and were completely unknown to either the convicted man or to the officer who had defended him at his court martial. During the first three months of 1917 different commanding officers said in regard to condemned prisoners, 'He has always been a constant source of trouble', 'His character is worthless and is well-known in the battalion as such', and 'He has a very bad character and has caused endless trouble'. In two other cases the respective brigadiers commented, 'The accused is quite valueless from a fighting point-of-view' and 'He is a worthless soldier and a coward'. In civil trials any such appraisals would have had to be stated in open court and would have been subject to cross-examination by the defence.

One of the most unpleasant capital cases during this period concerned a private soldier who was charged both with desertion and theft. During an action in October 1916 the accused man was detailed to look after his platoon commander who had been mortally wounded. When the stretcher-bearers arrived they found him standing beside the dying officer with two watches, a wallet and a fountain pen in his hand. He had then disappeared and was apprehended at Etaples a few days afterwards. He contended at his trial that the platoon commander had asked him to take the articles and to give them in to his company headquarters. Before he could do so, he said, he had been hit by a piece of shrapnel and had been taken back for treatment. This story was not believed by the court and the private was sentenced to death.

Notes

1. Siegfried Sassoon, *Memoirs of an Infantry Officer*.
2. Lord Moran, *The Anatomy of Courage*.
3. Norman Gladden, *The Somme*.
4. Lord Moran, op. cit.
5. Erich Maria Remarque, *All Quiet on the Western Front*.
6. Norman Gladden, op. cit.
7. Arthur Lambert, *Over the Top*.
8. Edmund Blunden, *Undertones of War*.

9. Norman Gladden, op. cit.
10. Siegfried Sassoon, op. cit.
11. Lieutenant-Colonel J. S. Y. Rogers, evidence before the War Office Committee of Enquiry into Shell-Shock, 1920.
12. William Allison and John Fairley, *The Monocled Mutineer*.

NIVELLE'S FAILURE

O N 6 APRIL 1917 the United States of America formally proclaimed herself at war with Germany. Although the American armed forces were distant and ill-prepared and could offer no immediate assistance for the present, there was now a prospect of massive reinforcement for the Allies – provided they were able to maintain the struggle for at least another year. The proclamation from Washington was like a shout of encouragement from the river bank to a person in the grip of a swirling current.

The British opened their offensive at Arras on Easter Monday, 9 April. A very short while previously the surrounding countryside had been astir with the advent of an early spring, but the weather conditions that morning were reminiscent of the harshest winter months of the previous winter on the Somme. The troops advancing to the front for the first assault were saturated by squalls of rain, sleet or snow and the trenches in which they assembled were sometimes knee-deep in slush and mud.

The first six days of the Battle of Arras were very successful for the BEF, most of the initial objectives being taken without undue difficulty and the Canadian Corps achieving a singular victory with the capture of the dominating plateau of Vimy Ride. After that, however, the impetus was gradually lost and the battlefield reverted to its accustomed stagnation. Every yard of the barren, pitted ground was bitterly contested and the advancing troops suffered heavily each time they left the cover of their trenches. In accordance with his undertaking to General Nivelle, Haig persisted in the attack. He had no illusions about the difficulties which confronted the BEF; in the course of a memorandum to the War Cabinet he wrote:

> The enemy's fighting strength is not yet broken, and it is essential to realize that it can only be broken by hard and continual fighting. . . . The first step must always be to wear down ('soften' as it is said nowadays) the enemy's power of resistance until he is so weakened that he will not be able to withstand a decisive blow.

General Nivelle launched his great offensive in the middle of April. Within the first few days his sanguine forecasts were confuted and his hopes of victory disabused. All along the line the French infantry were forced to a halt with heavy losses. There was no triumphant break-through: no significant progress. On 26 April Haig was summoned to Paris to see the French War Minister who hinted to him that Nivelle's plans had gone awry and that he would soon be replaced as Commander-in-Chief by General Pétain. It seemed then that the 80,000 casualties the BEF had suffered in the diversionary battles during the month of April had been to no avail.

Unknown to the British politicians and General Staff the discipline of the French Army on the Western Front was in the process of breaking down completely. The mood of war-weariness and despondency which had overcome the French nation had now spread amongst her troops. The morale of the citizen-soldier hangs on a delicate balance; he requires a lasting sense of rationality and purpose; his commitment is never limitless nor confidence in his generals unbounded.

In spite of the magnitude of its losses the French Army was conscious of its lack of military achievement. The soldiers had lost most of their faith in their commanders and they had been contaminated by the circulation of subversive, treasonable literature. In addition, they had their well-justified complaints about the slow treatment of the wounded and the inadequacy of leave from the trenches.

The series of incidents which became known as the 'French Mutinies' began in April and persisted until the end of September. During this period there were demonstrations by soldiers against the continuance of the war; cases occurred of units refusing to go up to the line; acts of violence were committed against officers; and there was sabotage of stores and materials. Serious displays of mass ill-discipline took place on leave-trains with singing of revolutionary songs, the waving of red flags, wholesale drunkenness and attacks upon military policemen and railway employees.

At an inter-allied military conference in Paris on 4 and 5 May 1917, General Pétain, who had just been appointed Chief of the General Staff of the French Army, revealed to the British representatives the mutinous and demoralized condition of his troops. It was agreed that the principal offensive in the immediate future would have to be carried out by the BEF in Flanders with the French supporting them as vigorously as possible. Urging a united effort by both nations the British Prime Minister, Lloyd George, told the conference, 'The enemy must not be left in peace for one moment . . . we must go on hitting and hitting with all our strength until the Germans end, as they always do, by cracking.' By common consent the earlier view that the war could be won during 1917 was now abandoned and it was decided that the process of attrition should be continued until early in

1918 when the French and British survivors, with massive American support, would be able to strike a decisive blow against the weary and enfeebled remnants of the German western armies.

Britain's main concern at this juncture was the heavy losses of shipping in the Atlantic due to the activities of German submarines. Indeed, Admiral Jellicoe, the First Sea Lord, was continually warning the government that unless the Army could occupy in the near future the Belgian coastal strip containing the U-boat, destroyer and mine-layer bases the Navy would be powerless and the war would be lost. The British summer campaign in Flanders was designed to capture this area. On 12 May General Robertson, the Chief of the Imperial General Staff, sent a confidential despatch to Haig warning him that the Russians were on the verge of concluding a separate peace and that the unreliable state of the French Army might nullify their support for his offensive. Haig replied that in his opinion what he referred to as 'action of a wearing-down character' should still be carried out according to plan.

Between May and October 412 men in the French Army were sentenced to death for acts of ill-discipline and 55 were actually executed by firing squads. By a mixture of firmness and consideration General Pétain gradually improved the spirit and efficiency of his troops, but their reliability in battle remained in doubt. One of his most popular innovations was the granting of seven days, and later ten days, leave every four months to all soldiers on active service. This was far more generous than the leave allocation in the BEF and it considerably weakened the fighting strength of all French units at the front.

The first phase of the British operation to clear the Belgian coast was an assault on the high ground of the Messines Ridge. The opening of the attack was preceded by an immense artillery bombardment which hammered the German positions incessantly for nine days and nights. At dawn on 7 June 1917, 19 mines were exploded in the vicinity of the German forward trenches. A description of the scene by a British eye-witness is quoted in the Official History of the campaign:

> Great leaping streams of orange flame shot upwards, each like a huge volcano in itself, all along the front of attack followed by terrific explosions and dense masses of smoke and dust, which stood like great pillars towering into the sky, all illuminated by the fires below.

Directly after the explosions 80,000 troops, covered by a smoke-screen, advanced behind a creeping barrage to storm the German line. During the rest of the day the British consolidated their initial gains and successfully withstood all the counter-attacks which were launched against them by the enemy.

By 14 June the BEF had penetrated to a depth of between one and two miles into the German defences and at a cost of about 24,000 men the heights of Messines Ridge were in their hands. The next stage of the offensive, Haig told his army commanders, would be an advance across Flanders in the direction of Passchendaele.

As the details of the 'French Mutinies' leaked out there was a certain amount of uneasiness amongst the British commanders that the men of the BEF might react in a similar manner. The fact that this did not occur was partly due, perhaps, to the lack of unification between the two Allied armies and the consequent absence of contact between their soldiers.

The conduct of British courts martial in France was considerably improved at this time by the introduction of the CMO, the Court Martial Officer. Ever since the outbreak of war there had been constant allegations of acts of injustice committed by military tribunals at the front. It was the general impression of the peacetime lawyers who were serving in the Army for the duration that the court martial system left a great deal to be desired. Arthur Page, a barrister who had attended about 1,200 trials as a CMO, over 300 of the charges being capital, expressed the opinion in an article in *Blackwood's Magazine*[1] that nine out of every ten junior officers holding regular commissions were totally unfitted to sit as members of a court. In addition, he said, he had found that in the great majority of cases a regular officer who was acting as the president of a court martial wished to decide on the guilt or innocence of the accused without holding any preliminary discussion of the evidence. Page doubted whether many officers approached a trial with completely independent minds because, he wrote:[2]

> At the very outset one finds that the court is convened by a senior officer, usually a general, who by the form of the convening order states that 'Whereas it appears to me . . . that the persons named in the annexed schedule have committed the offences in the said schedule mentioned.'

On numerous occasions when a court martial had acquitted a prisoner, said Page, he had heard the members commenting ruefully that they would get into trouble for their decision. Even after the court had recorded a conviction, he continued, their discretion was often restricted when it came to passing sentence, as many senior commanders had circulated lists showing the sort of punishment they deemed appropriate for various offences.

Another barrister, Gerald Hurst, who had also been a CMO in France, writing in the *Contemporary Review* after the war, gave a specific instance of a divisional staff requiring the president of a court martial 'to furnish in writing a full explanation of his conduct in allowing an acquittal to take place'.[3]

In September 1916, 43 CMOs were appointed in the home command, all being temporary officers who belonged to the legal profession. The innovation was an immediate success and the system was expanded. Early in 1917 a CMO was allocated to every corps in the BEF. It was his duty to attend as many FGCMs as he could, though it was not always possible for him to be present at every capital trial in his corps area. He would sit as an additional member of the court – not as its president – and would give his advice on points of law and procedure. Apart from this special function he would vote in the ordinary way on the question of guilt and innocence and in the determination of sentence.

Arthur Page said it was his usual experience that the president of a court was profoundly relieved to have a CMO assisting him at the trial.[4] He had found that the majority of regular officers had 'a very wholesome fear of courts martial'. He described a typical FGCM in France at this time as taking place at a camp, nissen hut or dugout. 'A table with a blanket over it, and some upturned sugar boxes usually did service for court equipment.' He continued:

> I wish I could portray the scene as the drama unfolds. The dim light of a few sputtering candles throwing into relief the forms of the accused and his escort; the tired and drawn faces of the witnesses under their tin helmets; and the accused himself, apparently taking only a languid interest in the evidence as it accumulates against him.

According to Page the man on trial usually chose to be represented by his platoon or his company commander as the 'prisoner's friend', but when the death penalty was likely to be imposed he was defended, whenever possible, by an officer with pre-war legal training. Page paid tribute to the latitude which was always allowed to the defence at an FGCM and the efforts which were made to procure any witness or document he needed to support the prisoner's case.[5] Gerald Hurst also spoke highly of the standard of justice of trials in the BEF after the CMOs had been introduced. In his opinion:[6]

> No one who has often taken part in courts martial cases will question the fairness, courtesy, and patience which characterize trials. An accused is given the benefit of any doubt. If the proportion of acquittals is comparatively low, it is due to the care which is usually taken not to convene courts martial in the absence of a real prima facie case against the accused.

Nevertheless, there were certain features of trials on active service which must have been disturbing to a lawyer with experience of the civil courts. The proceedings, said Hurst,[7] were remote from outside scrutiny as although theoretically they were open to the public and the Press, in practice no spectators were ever present. Percy Winfield, who contributed an officially-authorized article on courts martial to the *Law Quarterly Review* in April 1918, remarked on two further characteristics which were both unfavourable to the accused.[8] Firstly, the members of the court were soldiers; they were not easily swayed by argument and had little time for rhetoric or oratory. Secondly, the prisoner's friend was an officer even more than an advocate and he was usually influenced by 'an unconscious bias in favour of discipline'.

Winfield suggested one reform to bring courts martial into line with civil practice. He said:

The accused, if an officer, is allowed a seat; if of any other rank, only when the court think proper. It is hard to see how discipline could be injured if this was made a matter of right for all ranks.

Even after the 1914–18 war one of the English High Court judges, Mr Justice Horridge, would not allow a prisoner to be seated at assizes unless there were special circumstances or the trial was likely to continue for a long time. A clerk of assize for the Midland Circuit has told how at Derby in 1922 Horridge refused an application by the famous Irish counsel Maurice Healy that his client should be permitted to sit down in the dock while the trial was in progress.[9]

When a prisoner in the BEF was convicted of desertion at this stage of the war it did not make any difference to his ultimate sentence whether he was a regular, a reservist, a conscript or a volunteer. As far as the senior officers were concerned there was a general standard of discipline and a general standard of military conduct which were applicable to every soldier whatever his mode of enlistment. Two volunteers were tried by court martial in early June 1917, and both were executed during the first week of July. One of them, a married private from Surrey, had joined up in November 1914. He had never settled down in the Army and had been awarded 84 days' Field Punishment Number One for desertion in March 1916. In an attack on 3 May 1917 he was overcome with terror and asked his platoon sergeant for permission to report sick. In spite of the fact that his request was refused he went back to the regimental aid post where he told his medical officer that his nerves had given out and he was unable to stick it any longer. The doctor examined him and ordered him to return to the trenches. The following day he was arrested in Arras by a military policeman who said at the subsequent trial that the prisoner had been wandering in the street in a dazed condition and had seemed to be unable to give a satisfactory account of himself. The other volunteer, a Londoner, had been in constant trouble since he had enlisted in May 1915; he was actually under a suspended sentence of 15 years' penal servitude for desertion when he absented himself again in April 1917. He had only remained at liberty for two days and he told the members of the court that his time as a soldier had been a perpetual misery to him.

A 21-year-old Scottish private who was executed in June 1917 must have been one of the earliest conscripts as his date of enlistment was in the middle of February 1916. He deserted from the trenches when his battalion was preparing to attack and surrendered himself to a rear unit five days later admitting that he was an absentee. He stated in his defence that at the moment he left the front line he had been unable to control his behaviour. In supporting the confirmation of the death sentence the man's brigade commander wrote:

> It may be pleaded that this man is young but I fancy there must have been a good many still younger who did their duty like men. This appears to be a clear case of shirking going over the parapet.

A Welsh reservist, court-martialled for desertion in April 1917, had originally joined the Army in 1904 and had been recalled to the colours on the outbreak of war. Like so many other members of the reserve he had found himself in France within a matter of days of reporting for duty. He had taken part in the retreat from Mons and in the bitter fighting throughout the following autumn and winter. During 1915 he was twice wounded and twice returned to the trenches after convalescence. He had deserted at the end of December 1916, when his battalion was resting from the line, and he had been arrested in a back area in March 1917. Pleading for his life at his trial he told the court of his record of service and added that at the time of his offence he had been so overburdened with family troubles that he had not known what he was doing. He was condemned to death and was shot at dawn on 15 May 1917.

A 20-year-old regular soldier from Warwickshire was executed four days later. He had enlisted in January 1914, at the age of 17. A French woman, giving evidence for the prosecution at his court martial, said he had come to live in a hut at the back of her house during the summer of 1916. Although he had always worn British Army uniform her suspicions had not been aroused at first and she had supplied him regularly with food. A few months later, however, she and her husband had become dubious about him and the following November they had reported their misgivings to the police. After the soldier had been apprehended by the Town Major it was discovered that he had gone absent from his battalion at the beginning of the previous July when they had been moving up to take part in an attack on the Somme.

The officers on an FGCM in France had usually seen a good deal of active service and, in general, they formed neither a sentimental nor a compassionate tribunal when dealing with those who appeared to have evaded their duty. A young conscript who was condemned to death at the end of May 1917 had deserted during his first spell of service in the front line. He had committed the same offence a few months before when his draft was in the base area and he was under a suspended sentence of five years' penal servitude. On the other hand, the court had been told that at the time of his second desertion his brother had just been killed in action and he had been informed that his mother was ill. He was executed soon after his nineteenth birthday. Mere youthfulness was rarely considered to be a ground for mitigating a death sentence and many of the men who were shot by firing squads were in their late teens or their early twenties. Further, a soldier's concern for his close relations at home was regarded as a natural hazard of life at the front. An Irish private, executed in June 1917, had received news shortly before his desertion of the illness of his child. He had tried to obtain leave but had failed owing to the exigencies of the manpower situation.

In those days military justice in the field was applied in terms of a simplistic philosophy. Either a soldier was dependable or he was a funk; either he performed his duties at the front or he shirked them. It was only in after years that medical men sought to study and to analyse the emotions of courage and cowardice in the context of modern warfare. Lord Moran has written:[10]

> When a soldier's resistance to fear has been lowered by sickness or by a wound the balance has been tilted against him and his control is in jeopardy at any rate for a time. The wounded soldier has just visualized danger in a new and very personal way.

Again and again during the 1914–18 war men charged with desertion were claiming that when they returned to the front after recovering from wounds they had found their nerves completely shattered. Such a plea was put forward by a private who was executed in July 1917. He had been a regular soldier before the war and had landed in France with the original expeditionary force. He was wounded a month later and was left lying out in the open for five days and five nights without attention and unable to walk. Since then, he said, he had never again been the same man and he was always terrified when he came under fire. Another recurrent plea advanced by deserters was that their endurance and their fortitude had gradually been sapped by the endless fighting. This was never accepted as a valid defence, but according to Lord Moran:[11]

> Courage is will-power, whereof no man has an unlimited stock; and when in war it is used up, he is finished. . . . His will is perhaps almost destroyed by intensive shelling, or by a bloody battle, or it is gradually used up by monotony, by exposure, by the loss of support of the staunchest spirits on whom he had come to depend, by physical exhaustion, by a wrong attitude to danger, to casualties, to war, to death itself.

Moran's opinions were based upon two-and-a-half years' experience as a regimental medical officer with an infantry battalion in the BEF.

Notes

1. *Blackwood's Magazine*, June 1919, p. 791.
2. Ib.
3. Gerald B. Hurst, 'The Administration of Military Law', in *Contemporary Review*, 1919, p. 459.
4. Op. cit.
5. Ib.
6. Op. cit.
7. Ib.
8. Percy H. Winfield, 'Courts-Martial from the Lawyer's Point of View' in *Law Quarterly Review*, No. CXXXIV, April 1918.
9. *Stage and Bar*, recollections of George Pleydell Bancroft.
10. Lord Moran, *The Anatomy of Courage*.
11. Ib.

13
FLANDERS

D URING THE SUMMER of 1917 control of British war policy was handed over to a Cabinet Committee of five members headed by the Prime Minister. Towards the end of June Sir Douglas Haig was summoned to London in order to explain to them his proposals for an offensive in Flanders.

With ebullient optimism Haig outlined his plan to capture the German submarine bases at Ostend and Zeebrugge and to close the ship canal at Bruges. Lloyd George remained sceptical, pointing out that the French armies were not yet in a condition to lend any substantial assistance and that Pétain had already stated his opinion that for the remainder of the year the Allies should devote their efforts to 'wearing down the enemy with a punch here and a punch there' rather than embarking upon any large-scale attacks. Haig replied by warming to his theme that the German Army was now in desperate straits; he committed himself to the view that if the fighting could be sustained at its present intensity for another six months the Germans would be at the end of their available manpower. The lack of support from the French did not concern him as he visualized his scheme as an entirely British operation.

At this stage Admiral Jellicoe, the First Sea Lord, intervened in the discussion to say that if the enemy were not dislodged from the Belgian coastline by the end of the year Britain would be unable to continue the war owing to lack of shipping. This was a powerful argument in favour of the Flanders operation, but the majority of the committee remained unconvinced and the meeting concluded without a definite decision being taken. It is now known that Jellicoe's assessment of the situation was faulty as the main U-boat campaign was, in fact, being conducted from ports in Germany.

Eventually, towards the end of July, the Cabinet's War Committee informed Haig that he could proceed with his plans. Thus began the Third Battle of Ypres, of which Liddell Hart has said, 'It is symbolical of its course and its issue that it is commonly spoken of by the title of "Passchendaele", which in reality was merely the last scene of the gloomiest drama of British military history.'[1]

The offensive was to take place over an area of reclaimed marshland in which the fields of soggy earth, still subject to constant flooding, were mainly used for pasturage as they were too wet for cultivation. During a ten-day preliminary bombardment a great many of the dykes were destroyed and the soil became undrainable.

On 31 July ten infantry divisions attacked on an eleven-mile front. By nightfall they had made a general advance of about 3,000 yards at a cost of over 31,000 casualties. The outlook for the immediate future seemed bleak as the Germans were consolidating new positions and torrential rain was converting the ground into a quagmire. Although General Gough, whose Fifth Army had been involved in some of the hardest fighting, advised that the operation should be discontinued, Haig was determined that the BEF should keep on pressing forward. In a mood of stubborn confidence he summarized the initial results to the War Cabinet as 'highly satisfactory and the losses slight for such a great battle'. It was not the first time in their war-torn history that the lowlands of Flanders were destined to become the graveyard of a military endeavour.

The German defensive system in Flanders consisted of sparsely-manned forward trenches supported by a network of machine gun posts in concrete pillboxes; behind these reserves of infantry waited in readiness to counter-attack. The BEF was now faced with the added barrier of a broad mud-swamp. Throughout the month of August they continued to attack, making little headway against the German positions. Edwin Vaughan, a young infantry officer, described in his diary the events of a day when his division was repulsed with heavy losses.[2] In the late evening Vaughan was ordered to report to his brigade headquarters and as he made his way back across the battle-ground in a heavy downpour of rain, he said:

> From the darkness on all sides came the groans and wails of wounded men; faint, long, sobbing moans of agony, and despairing shrieks. It was only too obvious that dozens of men with serious wounds must have crawled for safety into new shell-holes, and now the water was rising about them and, powerless to move, they were slowly drowning.

Before long the cries of the wounded men had much diminished, Vaughan continued, 'The reason was only too apparent, for the water was right over the tops of the shell-holes'.

On 4 September Haig was called back to London for another conference. By then the Flanders offensive had lasted just over four weeks and the British losses had already amounted to a total of more than 68,000 officers and men. Lloyd George suggested to Haig that he should husband his resources for a while and start the onslaught afresh in 1918 when the French and American Armies would be in a position to share some of the burden. Haig, whilst admitting that adverse weather conditions might bring the fighting in Flanders to a halt, reiterated his faith in the outcome of the operations. The War Cabinet were unconvinced but they yielded to the tenacity of his views.

In the first three weeks of September the battlefield was dried out by a succession of fresh and windy days. On 20 September, under cover of an early-morning mist and a massive artillery barrage, British and Australian troops resumed the attack on a front four miles wide. They managed to capture the majority of their objectives and to withstand the ferocity of the German counter-attacks which were instantly levelled against them. In the fighting over the next two weeks the First and Third Armies seized possession of a strategically important ridge to the east of Ypres. But presently the rain had started again and the whole area was once more a morass. If Haig had decided to call a halt at that stage his Flanders campaign might have been considered a modest, though a costly, success. As it was he resolved to continue the offensive into the autumn with a sustained thrust in the general direction of Passchendaele.

During the early part of September 1917, Horatio Bottomley was allowed to make an officially-guided tour of the British sector on the Western Front. Later he set out his impressions of his visit in a series of articles in *John Bull*. Obviously he was deeply impressed by the predictions and assurances conveyed to him by Sir Douglas Haig for soon after returning to England he wrote,[3] 'The war is won. Germany is beaten. . . . From Field Marshal Commander-in-Chief, right down to the rawest Tommy in the trenches, there is but one spirit – that of absolute optimism and confidence.' In less euphoric style he told of his conversations with the troops in the trenches. Their six principal complaints, he said, related to leave, pay, field punishment, military policing, short rations, and 'cushy posts at the back which might be filled by wounded officers and others – thus releasing able men for the trenches'.[4]

The last-mentioned grievance arose out of the callousness and inefficiency of so many of those employed on the staff. Often during a battle staff officers were reluctant to go forward and see for themselves what was happening in order to send back accurate information to their headquarters. As a result the higher commands were sometimes completely out of touch with the situation in the field. According to the Official History of the war:

> Again and again battalions report that orders to attack reached them so late that there was only just time to hustle their companies forward behind the barrage, furnished with the barest verbal instructions. In a few cases the orders actually arrived after Zero hour.

The aversion felt for staff officers and the contempt with which they were regarded by the men at the front are apparent from the literature of the period. Siegfried Sassoon has ensured a derisive immortality for the 'scarlet majors at the base', and the opening stanza of his less-known, but equally scornful war poem 'The General' seems also to exemplify the profound resentment of the fighting soldier:

> 'Good-morning; good-morning!' the General said
> When we met him last week on our way to the line.
> Now the soldiers he smiled at are most of 'em dead,
> And we're cursing his staff for incompetent swine.

Headquarters staffs and the men in the line lived in two disparate worlds and neither had a true conception of the lifestyle of the other. The infantry, whilst in action, were continually infuriated by the inept and often fatuous messages they received from the rear. 'Division could always be trusted', wrote Robert Graves,[5] 'to send a warning about verdigris or vermorial-sprayers or keeping pets out of the trenches, or some other triviality exactly when an attack was in progress.' At times the insensitive directives emanating from some distant headquarters could cause immeasurable suffering to soldiers in action. John Glubb, who was then a junior officer in the Royal Engineers but in the course of time was to become a general, has told[6] how during the coldest months of the winter of 1916–17 the men in his sector of the front were allowed no fuel for fires and were forbidden to gather up the shell-shattered branches from a nearby wood. 'This was a most inhuman order,' he wrote, 'doubtless issued by some Q authority in a comfortable office at the base. The troops were perpetually wet through and could never get warm or dry. To be constantly cold is terribly depressing to morale.' The arrogance of staff officers on a personal level served to increase their unpopularity. They were always, said Sassoon, 'so damned well-dressed and superior'.[7]

The indifference of some of the generals with regard to the sensibilities of the men they commanded enlarged the chasm between the trenches and the rear still more. Usually the combat formations only came into direct contact with a very senior officer when they had been withdrawn from the line to reorganize and rest.[8] Huntley Gordon, a subaltern with a regular commission, found that 'the brasshats seem to do nothing but criticize'.[9] On one occasion when John Glubb's regiment was recuperating from a particularly arduous spell in action their divisional commander announced that he was coming to inspect them on the following morning. Elaborate preparations were commenced immediately and the men stayed up half the night cleaning and burnishing. At the time fixed for the inspection the general had not arrived. Glubb continued:[10]

We waited on parade for two hours in the rain and then received a signal postponing it until next day. The next night and morning the same thing was repeated. We were completely fed up.

Horatio Bottomley's assertion in *John Bull* that he had noticed a buoyant optimism among the soldiers in the trenches diverges significantly from the mood of resignation bordering on fatalism which underlies so much of the writing of those who were actually involved in the battle. It is true that in their works there is no prospect of submission, no lessened aspiration for eventual victory. There is instead a scarcely-voiced belief that Britain would ultimately triumph in spite of her generals and her politicians; that the patterns of her recent history would be re-enacted once again.

Stephen Graham had admitted[11] that before being conscripted into the Scots Guards during the early months of 1917 he still had visionary notions of a patriot's transcendent obligation to his country in time of war. 'It seemed that in putting on the King's uniform one had put on an ideal', he wrote. 'But all of us soon learned that the uniform betokened hard duty and bondage, a durance such as that of a slave or prisoner.' Most of the duration-soldiers were resentful of the excesses of military discipline within a system which remained 'in horrible ignorance that the civilian army was brain and nerve as well as bone and muscle'.[12]

The essential character of the rational soldier is seldom defiled by the scenes of the battlefield. Compassion may be nurtured on enforced brutality, and constant fear can sometimes beget a deepened sense of humility. Towards the end of the war Siegfried Sassoon reflected on 'the patience and simple decency' of the men in the company he commanded.[13] 'The greatest number of the soldiers had become indifferent to the horror of death,' said Stephen Graham, 'and even more intensely alive than before of the horror of dying themselves.'[14] On the other side of no-man's-land the troops were undergoing a similar experience. A German soldier wrote,

We count the weeks no more. . . . Our life alternates between billets and the front. We have grown accustomed to it. War is a cause of death like cancer and tuberculosis, like influenza and dysentery. The deaths are merely more frequent, more varied and terrible.[15]

There was little animosity on a personal level between the opposing forces in the forward areas. Lord Moran has criticized the faulty psychology of the British generals who tried to goad their troops 'to the required pitch of ferocity' by stressing the depravity of the enemy. The BEF had nothing against the German soldier, said Moran; 'they followed the same craft; he was only doing his job just the same as they were'.[16] Others have expressed the same view. Huntley Gordon treated the routine atrocity stories with disbelief as coming from the world of Grimms' fairy tales,[17] and in Graham's opinion the majority of British soldiers retained a sneaking admiration for the fighting qualities of the German Army.[18]

The mutual respect of the adversaries and the common bondage of their tribulations in no way diminished the ferocity with which they fought each other. Knives, bayonets, rifle-butts, machetes and pick-axe handles were used by both sides in close-quarter combat. For a time in Flanders the Germans discarded their bayonets before going into the attack and armed themselves only with spades and bombs. Erich Maria Remarque has written:[19]

> The sharpened spade is a more handy and many-sided weapon; not only can it be used for jabbing a man under the chin, but it is much better for striking with because of its greater weight; and if one hits between the neck and shoulder it easily cleaves down as far as the chest.

On the Western Front in July 1917 the German Army first employed mustard gas as a weapon of warfare. This yellow-coloured liquid could burn through clothing and bodily tissues, and caused appalling blisters on the flesh. Its effects were particularly harmful to the eyes and the respiratory tract.

In general, the soldiers of all the nations involved in the fighting in France observed the tenets of the Geneva Convention. It was natural that there should be exceptions, but these were very rare. After a British attack in Flanders Norman Gladden was sickened to see two privates in his company sniping at German prisoners coming in to surrender. Both these men, said Gladden, were 'normal, kindly fellows in ordinary times, loving fathers of families'.[20] According to Remarque if the Allies found a German soldier in possession of a 'saw' bayonet, with a blade along one side and a serrated edge along the other, they killed him at once.[21]

The mutiny at the Etaples base in September 1917 bore little resemblance either in magnitude or in design to the French Army mutinies which had taken place during the previous year. From the information at present available it would seem that the trouble at Etaples was inspired neither by political nor by anti-war motives but was in essence no more than a demonstration against the conditions at this particular camp. It is more than probable, however, that subversive elements contributed to the disorders.

There was no substantial group in England at that time which favoured a negotiated peace with Germany. The Union of Democratic

Control had been founded in the autumn of 1914 to voice the opinions of those who had opposed entry into the war and drew its support from a small band of left-wing politicians and middle-class intellectuals. Both the Independent Labour Party and the Marxist British Socialist Movement desired an immediate armistice as part of their long-term strategy and supported the plans for a general peace which were being propagated by the Bolsheviks in Russia. These two organizations held a joint convention at Leeds in June 1917 to inaugurate a British revolution; it was attended by over 1,100 delegates who called for the ending of the war and for the institution of workers' and soldiers' councils to co-ordinate seditious activities. Although such resolutions and the doctrines which underlay them were not treated very seriously they might well have influenced some of the soldiers who were on leave or were stationed in England.

The base at Etaples was virtually a reception unit for drafts which had just arrived from the United Kingdom in transit for the Western Front. The troops generally spent two weeks there undergoing their final indoctrination for the trenches on training grounds known as the 'Bull Ring'. They were accommodated, whatever the weather, in canvas tents; the routine was hard and the amenities were appalling. Norman Gladden, who passed through the base during the summer of 1916, has said that the rations were poor and the meals were served in discomfort and squalor. 'Tables were usually covered with filth from the previous sittings,' he wrote, 'and the atmosphere stank of stale food and crowded humanity.'[22]

The camp was situated on a hill behind the town of Etaples, which was permanently out of bounds to the inmates with the exception of the resident staff. Apart from the canteens and the camp cinema no recreational facilities were provided for the troops who, in any case, had very little time to themselves. Perhaps the harsh regime and the wretched living conditions were deliberately designed as a preparation for the terrible environment of the front line.

The duration-soldiers of the 1914–18 war believed that there was an undefined official policy to crush the individual temperament of the recruit as a means of enforcing his compliance with military discipline. When Stephen Graham first reported to his depot, someone told him, 'The great process of bullying and intimidation has set in. They try to break you at the beginning and take all your pride out of you.'[23] And Gladden said of the officers and NCOs on the training staff at Etaples, 'Their manner, with a few exceptions, was immoderate and irascible; their aim no doubt was to break us in the shortest possible time.'[24]

The only direct means of access to the town of Etaples from the camp was either across a railway bridge or across a bridge over the River Canche, both of which were guarded night and day by the

Military Police. The 'Bull Ring Mutiny', as it has been called, broke out on Sunday, 9 September 1917. Early in the afternoon the police on the Canche bridge arrested a gunner in the New Zealand Artillery for a reason which is unknown, but they released him again a short time later. An angry crowd of soldiers, swollen by curious onlookers, gathered around the bridge refusing to believe that the New Zealander had really been freed. Gradually their attitude became more menacing; not only were stones and other missiles hurled at the police but attempts were made to storm a guard-hut nearby. At one stage a private in the Military Police, over-reacting to the situation, drew his revolver and fired a few shots over the heads of the men nearest to him. Unfortunately a corporal in the Gordon Highlanders standing on the outskirts of the throng, but playing no part in the violence, was hit in the head by a bullet and died soon after his admittance to hospital.[25] Another of the bullets struck and wounded a French woman in an adjoining street.

In the evening the disorders at the bridge developed into a riot. The police had lost control and were withdrawn, their places being taken by a hastily-improvised picket consisting of an officer and 50 men. These were soon reinforced by an assorted force of another 200 officers and men from the base. In spite of appeals from the captain in charge the mutineers rushed the bridge, barged through the picket and swarmed into the town, where some of them raided the offices of the base commandant. For the next hour or two officers toured the streets of Etaples urging the men to return to their quarters immediately. Most of them complied; by about 10 p.m. all were back in the camp and the atmosphere seemed to have quietened down. The feeling among the mutineers that day, the base commandant recorded in his War Diary, had only been directed at the Military Police and the officers had been treated respectfully.[26]

Corporal S——, who had been arrested on the Sunday evening, was tried for mutiny on the following day by a court consisting of two majors and a captain. This was one of the most hastily convened courts martial of the war, which probably reflects the serious view the base commandant was then taking of the incident. S——, a 30-year-old regular soldier in a Northumberland regiment, had served in the Army for eight years and had been in France since November 1915. He was a married man with two young children. The case against him was very strong. At about 9.15 p.m. the bridge across the Canche had been guarded by a mixed picket of British and Canadian troops, only some of whom were armed, when a crowd about 70 or 80 strong was seen approaching from the direction of the camp. It is significant that besides carrying notice boards which had been torn from their sockets a number of the oncoming throng were waving improvised red flags.

This was the party which had rushed the bridge and broken through to the town. Apparently little effort was made to resist them and the captain in charge of the picket said that he had considered his men to be utterly unreliable.

Fearing a recurrence of the incident the captain told his four officers to arrange the members of the picket in regimental groups under their own NCOs. When this had been done he spoke to all men calling on them to perform their duty. At this stage Corporal S——, who was one of the mob which had forced its way across the bridge, returned and started urging the picket to join in the mutiny. He was reported to have said, 'Don't listen to the bloody officer. What you want to do with that bugger is to tie a rope round his neck with a stone attached to it and throw him into the river'. The captain, doubting his ability to effect an arrest at that moment, ordered the corporal to move away. S—— at first refused to do so but he eventually wandered off. A sergeant and four privates, who were all considered to be dependable, were then detailed to take S—— into custody if he should return to the bridge. A short while later S—— did in fact come back and he was promptly apprehended, still shouting obscenities at the captain.

Corporal S—— did not challenge any of the prosecution evidence. His defence was simply that he had been very drunk when the episode had occurred. All the witnesses except one, however, maintained that he had appeared to be perfectly sober. He was condemned to death and was shot on 4 October.

At the same time as Corporal S——'s court martial was taking place, a Board of Enquiry consisting of senior officers unconnected with the base was commencing an investigation into the events of the previous day. Meanwhile training at Etaples was continued normally and drafts arrived and departed according to prearranged schedules. When parades had finished on the Monday afternoon a party of men from the camp went past the picket on the Canche bridge and held protest meetings in the town. Others demonstrated outside the detention centre and the railway station but they dispersed peacefully when they were addressed by officers. On the Tuesday morning the Provost Marshal of the BEF arrived in Etaples accompanied by a colonel from the Adjutant-General's staff to examine the gravity of the situation. The base commandant appealed to them for reinforcements from outside; in particular he asked for units of cavalry. During the afternoon he was informed by GHQ that it had been decided to send him 800 officers and men from the 1st Battalion, the Honourable Artillery Company, for temporary policing duties. That evening the picket again failed to stop troops from the camp from getting into Etaples. There were further demonstrations in the town and five men were arrested.

On Wednesday 12 September, the fourth day of the disorders, the mutiny passed beyond the control of the base commandant and his staff. All troops had been confined to the camp until further orders, but in spite of this at three o'clock in the afternoon about a thousand men marched out under their chosen leaders, crossed the bridges unhindered, and entered the town. After holding a mass demonstration there they marched back to the base. During the evening the advance party from the HAC arrived at Etaples and hurriedly took up their posts. Staff officers at GHQ, who were keeping in close contact by telephone, viewed these developments with increasing concern. As an additional precaution the 19th Hussars and four machine gun sections stationed in a nearby town were placed on an immediate alert.

On Thursday 13 September the remainder of the HAC contingent reached the base, and the Hussars and machine gunners stood in readiness to move in if necessary. By this time GHQ were treating the Bull Ring Mutiny as a matter of topmost importance. Two experienced and war-hardened infantry battalions were detached from their division to be entrained for Etaples and the base commandant was informed that an entire infantry brigade would also be at his disposal. Inside the camp all ammunition was withdrawn from the troops. That evening 200 men broke bounds but they were repulsed at the Canche bridge by a picket from the HAC armed with entrenching-tool handles. In the close-quarter fighting two of the mutineers were slightly injured.

Friday 14 September was the last day of the disorders. With the Military Police, the HAC and the two battalions from the front manning strongpoints and sending out constant patrols, the inmates of the camp remained quiescent during the morning. In the afternoon 60 men managed to enter Etaples but they were soon rounded up and placed under arrest. At that point the mutiny ended just as suddenly and capriciously as it had begun. The following day Etaples was thrown open to all the soldiers who were temporarily stationed at the base, and GHQ was satisfied that the whole incident was over.

Gill and Dallas in their balanced study of the mutiny[27] have pointed out that apart from the base commandant's War Diary, no official documents from the archives which might throw any further light on the Etaples disorders are at present open to the public. They quote the retrospective opinion of the camp adjutant at the time that the chief cause of discontent was that men who had already done so much service at the front were made to undergo the same strenuous training as the new drafts freshly arrived from home. Also, that the usual regimental links between officers and men had been disrupted by the arrangements at the base.

A book has recently been published which purports to reveal some startling new facts about the Bull Ring Mutiny.[28] These are based on the misting memories of several men who may or may not have actually been participants but whose reminiscences have obviously been interspersed with a mass of rumour, hearsay and exaggeration. Amongst their other discernible inaccuracies the authors suggest that three men were court-martialled and shot for taking part in the mutiny. Corporal S——, in fact, was the only soldier who was executed on any charge arising out of the Etaples disorders.

Notes

1. B. H. Liddell Hart, *History of The First World War*.
2. *Some Desperate Glory*, the diary of Edwin Campion Vaughan.
3. *John Bull*, 22 September 1917.
4. *John Bull*, 6 October 1917.
5. Robert Graves, *Goodbye to All That*.
6. John Glubb, *Into Battle*.
7. Siegfried Sassoon, *Sherston's Progress*.
8. During two-and-a-half years with a battalion in the line the highest-ranking officer Lord Moran came across was his divisional commander whom he only knew by sight. Lord Moran, *The Anatomy of Courage*.
9. Huntley Gordon, *The Unreturning Army*.
10. John Glubb, op. cit.
11. Stephen Graham, *A Private in the Guards*.
12. Arthur Lambert, *Over the Top*.
13. Siegfried Sassoon, *Sherston's Progress*.
14. Stephen Graham, op. cit.
15. Erich Maria Remarque, *All Quiet on the Western Front*.
16. Lord Moran, *The Anatomy of Courage*.
17. Huntley Gordon, op. cit.
18. Stephen Graham, op. cit.
19. Erich Maria Remarque, op. cit.
20. Norman Gladden, *Ypres 1917*.
21. Erich Maria Remarque, op. cit.
22. Norman Gladden, *The Somme 1916*.
23. Stephen Graham, op. cit.
24. Norman Gladden, op. cit.
25. The Military Policeman concerned was later court-martialled and convicted of manslaughter. He was sentenced to one year's imprisonment.
26. My account of the mutiny is largely taken from an article, 'Mutiny at Etaples base in 1917', by Douglas Gill and Gloden Dallas, published in *Past and Present*, No. 69, November 1975.
27. Op. cit.
28. William Allison and John Fairly, *The Monocled Mutineer*.

14

THE RENEWAL OF
PARLIAMENTARY ATTENTION

QUESTIONS MAY BE asked in Parliament with the sole object of embarrassing the government of the day or they may be asked in a genuine attempt to elicit information. It is sometimes difficult to be absolutely sure which of these two alternatives the questioner has in mind.

Very few people doubted the sincerity of Philip Snowden,[1] who revived the matter of capital courts martial in the House of Commons during the autumn of 1917.[2] Snowden, who was then in the early fifties, was the leader of the Independent Labour Party. At the age of 27 a cycling accident had affected his spinal cord and had left him a chronic cripple. He had always been bitterly opposed to the war and had constantly espoused the cause of the conscientious objectors. At Question Time on 31 October Snowden asked Mr Macpherson, the Under-Secretary of State for War, whether he would amend the Army Act so as to provide that all offences against military discipline would be tried by a judge and a jury of soldiers; whether he would grant facilities for the relatives of executed soldiers to examine the records of their courts martial 'with a view of securing a revision of the sentences and the clearing of the reputations of the executed men'; and whether he would recommend to the Army Council that death sentences for infractions of discipline should not be passed upon soldiers engaged in defending their country. Mr Macpherson answered, 'The reply in each case is in the negative.' Snowden then asked if it was right that men should be condemned to death by the members of courts who had no experience of weighing up evidence. The Minister replied that all his investigations had led him to believe that 'trial by court martial is one of the fairest'.

There were a series of supplementary questions with regard to the adequacy of the confirmation procedure for capital sentences and the inadvisability of returning shell-shocked men to service in the front line. A Member mentioned for the second time the name of an Irish soldier who, he alleged, had been executed 'under cruel circumstances'.[3] The Minister said that he was not aware of the details of this particular case, but he added an assurance that when any death sentence is passed 'the most careful and thorough investigation is made'.

Philip Snowden rose again to ask the Minister if he would enquire into the case of a 21-year-old private in the Royal Scots Fusiliers – he gave the man's number and named his battalion – who had been shot the previous August for desertion. According to Snowden this soldier had been invalided home suffering from severe shell-shock; he had then returned to France 'completely nerve-shattered' and had deserted on his way to the trenches after a shell had landed very close to him. Mr Macpherson in reply said that he was not prepared to interfere with the discretion of the Commander-in-Chief who only confirmed a sentence of death after giving his fullest consideration to the facts.

From the particulars revealed by Snowden it is possible to identify the case to which he was alluding. The accused soldier, a special reservist, had been posted to France within a few weeks of the outbreak of war. He was injured in December 1914 when his dugout received a direct hit and had been sent back to England suffering from shell-shock. It is not clear how long his treatment lasted as no medical evidence whatsoever was given at his trial. At some stage, however, he was adjudged to have recovered sufficiently to rejoin the BEF. He went absent on 25 July 1917 when his battalion had been warned for duty in the trenches and he was apprehended a few days later. During the following week an enemy shell had burst just outside the guard-tent in which he was detained awaiting court martial and in the resulting confusion he had made good his escape. He was rearrested at a back line examination post on 3 August. At his trial he claimed that he had been an inmate of a lunatic asylum in Scotland from 1908 until 1912 and had deserted because he always became upset by enemy gunfire. He was executed at the end of August.

At Question Time on 6 November Philip Snowden asked the Under-Secretary for War to enquire into the case of a 19-year-old private in the 1/5th Lincolnshire Regiment who had recently deserted soon after going on the top twice and who, at the time of his offence, had been undergoing Field Punishment Number One for two hours a day at a place exposed to enemy shellfire.[4] Snowden implored the Minister to prevent this soldier being condemned to death and executed on account of his youth and his past fighting record. Mr Macpherson replied that it was impossible for him to attempt to interfere with the course of military justice, but any extenuating circumstances would certainly be taken into consideration by the members of the court martial and if a death sentence was passed they would be reconsidered by the confirming authorities. In fact no soldier in the 1/5th Lincolnshire Regiment was executed either in 1917 or in

1918 so it is apparent that if this man was convicted he must have been punished in some other way.

In answer to another questioner the Minister stated that he was extremely doubtful if troops ever had to undergo field punishment under enemy shellfire. However, he gave an undertaking to look into the matter.

Courts martial and death sentences in the field were the subject of more questions in the House during the following week.[5] Major Davies, a back-bencher, expressed his concern at the lack of a proper system for ensuring that defending officers had sufficient training and experience. He went on to suggest that anyone court-martialled on active service should have the right to be represented by an officer with legal qualifications. The Under-Secretary declined even to consider a proposal which would undoubtedly have required a certain amount of organization in an already fully-preoccupied army and would probably have been anathema to a number of its senior commanders.

Mr King, a Labour Member, then asked whether the names of soldiers who had been executed by sentence of court martial were published in ordinary casualty lists or if their dependents were informed of the actual manner of their deaths. The Minister said that the relatives were always told the true facts. Another Member asserted that the information was conveyed to them 'by a very brutal letter' and urged that for the future the name of every executed man should be published in a routine casualty list. That, said Mr Macpherson, would be stating a falsehood, and in any event, the official notification to the next-of-kin was by means of a polite letter telling them what was of necessity a brutal fact.

On 26 November 1917 Andrew Bonar Law, the Chancellor of the Exchequer and Leader of the House, made a short statement regarding military executions.[6] He said:

> It has been arranged that in the future the communications made to the dependents of the soldiers shot at the front should merely state that they have died on service.

He added that it was still being considered whether or not the immediate relations of executed men should be eligible for pensions.

Two days later the President of the Board of Local Government denied a suggestion that some Boards of Guardians were refusing to grant Poor Law relief to the dependents of soldiers who had been shot by sentence of court martial.[7] If pensions were granted to these people instead of ordinary relief, he said, it would be putting them on exactly the same footing as the widows and children of the men who had died honourably in the service of their country. He refused to accept an allegation made in a supplementary question that some men had been executed shortly after being treated in hospital for shell-shock.

On 3 December Philip Snowden asked the Under-Secretary of State for War if he was aware that when a soldier was condemned to death and executed 'without colour of jurisdiction or in excess of authority' the relations of the deceased man could bring a criminal prosecution, not only against the members of the court, but also against the Commander-in-Chief who had confirmed the sentence.[8] He maintained that some such prosecutions were under contemplation but that the Army Council was refusing to allow the relatives concerned to inspect the records of the courts martial. Mr Macpherson said the question raised difficult points of law upon which he would prefer not to comment. He went on, 'The proper and constitutional remedy of any relative who wishes a review of the proceedings is to petition His Majesty.' Mr Snowden then stated that 25 death sentences had been confirmed by Sir Douglas Haig in a part of the month of October and out of all those cases only one prisoner had had the benefit of a defending officer. Mr Macpherson did not agree with either of these figures and stressed the 'careful reviews' to which a sentence was subjected by 'variously qualified officers' before it was placed before the Commander-in-Chief. There the matter was left. Mr Snowden's estimate in relation to confirmation of sentences would appear to have been an exaggeration as the records show that a total of 18 British soldiers were executed in France during the whole of the month of October 1917.

Philip Snowden drew the Under-Secretary's attention to another capital case on 12 December and suggested it should be reviewed to consider whether a miscarriage of justice had occurred.[9] The executed soldier was a private in the West Yorkshire Regiment, Mr Snowden said, who had enlisted in October 1914 and who was invalided home from the Dardanelles, 'wounded and frostbitten'. He had then been posted to the BEF and after severe fighting on the Somme had been admitted to hospital suffering from shell-shock. He was again returned to the line, 'shattered in health', and had been shot for desertion on 4 November 1916. Mr Macpherson replied that the decisions of all courts martial in the BEF were scrutinized by the Judge Advocate General in France with regard to the legality of both the findings and the sentences and he was not prepared to have them subjected to further re-examination.

The case referred to by Snowden concerned a married volunteer with three children who was 32 at the time of his execution. It was quite true that he had served at Gallipoli and had been returned to England suffering from frostbite, but it does not appear that he was wounded in the campaign. After he had recovered from his ailment he was posted to France and at the beginning of July 1916 he had been buried when a German shell had landed very close to his trench. It is not clear whether he was injured or was merely shocked; however, he was detained at a base hospital for a short time before being sent back to his battalion. On 28 August he had been sentenced to a period of field punishment for being absent without leave and he had still been undergoing this sentence at the time of his desertion from the front line on 12 September. He had remained at liberty for about a month before he was arrested by the Military Police at Boulogne, dressed in uniform but wearing no badges of identification. Two days after his court martial, at the instigation of his brigadier who was worried about his mental stability, the condemned man was examined by a doctor who found that his condition was perfectly normal. There seem to be no grounds for the suggestion that he was wrongfully convicted of deserting; none the less, it is rather surprising that the general commanding his division should have felt justified, on the scant evidence available to him, of advancing the proposition, 'The accused is evidently a worthless soldier with no heart for fighting.' With such a comment before him it is small wonder that Sir Douglas Haig saw fit to confirm the death sentence.

On 14 December Mr Macpherson told the House he was in communication with the Commanders-in-Chief of British armies overseas regarding a proposal that in every capital court martial the prisoner should be assisted either by an officer or by one of his own comrades.[10] When the Minister was asked if he would ensure that no soldier was executed who had been seriously wounded or invalided with shell-shock he stated that he was not in a position to give effect to this suggestion.

A Conservative back-bencher, General M'Calmont, then enquired:

Is it not a universal practice for a most complete and exhaustive report to be called for in every case after a death sentence has been awarded, and that, under those circumstances, it is practically impossible for any man to be executed who has suffered from shell-shock, because the fact that he has so suffered is certian to be included in the report?

Mr Macpherson replied:

I am assured of all these facts, and in the cases personally brought to my notice the Court had given them most careful consideration.

No doubt it was extremely difficult at that time for the majority of Ministers and Members of Parliament to visualize the proceedings of a court martial in the field: the stilted brevity of the evidence, the haphazard presentation of the defence, and the perfunctory enquiries which were usually made into the character and record of a convicted soldier. Even the officers who reported after a sentence of death had been passed rarely requested additional information with regard to the condemned man's background or his state of health. Mr Macpherson's answer to General M'Calmont was, to put it at its highest, both inaccurate and misleading.

During the week before Christmas in 1917 Mr Macpherson confirmed that when a soldier had been shot for cowardice it was customary to make a general announcement on parade revealing his number, his name and his unit.[11] The Minister refused to have the practice discontinued and he declined to accept a suggestion that it might be kinder to the relatives of the executed man to inform them directly of what had taken place rather than to run the risk of their finding out through gossip and rumour. He was pressed again for reassurance that when a prisoner on trial had suffered from shell-shock the fact was always disclosed. Mr Macpherson who, not for the first time, was grossly misinformed by his advisers, emphatically declared that he had never come across a single case 'where any soldier has been executed without being examined, before trial and before sentence, by a medical officer'.

The concern felt by some Members of Parliament regarding the deleterious effects of battle strain on the troops in the front line was not shared by the military hierarchy, who still thought that a soldier whose nerves had cracked must be a 'funk' or a 'shirker'. Siegfried Sassoon has written:[12]

> In the eyes of the War Office a man was either wounded or well unless he had some officially authorized disease. Damage on the mind did not count as illness. If 'war neuroses' were indiscriminately encouraged half the expeditionary force might go sick with a touch of neurasthenia.

A consultant who had been on the staff of an army neurological hospital in Scotland in 1917 told Sassoon how their local Director of Medical Services had openly asserted that he had never in the past, and would never in the future, believe in the existence of such a thing as shell-shock.[13]

Out of the 32 soldiers who were tried and executed for desertion between 20 July and 11 October 1917, only three appear to have undergone any form of medical examination in connection with their courts martial or their sentences. The first was a private in a Scottish Pioneer battalion who had never served in the line. He had joined his unit in Flanders in January 1917 when they were resting, and two weeks later had been sent to a field ambulance hospital where he was detained for a week. On leaving the hospital he had disappeared and had remained at large until he was apprehended in a back area the following August. Two days before his trial he was seen by a doctor who certified him as 'fit and able to undergo imprisonment with or without hard labour'. The second man, an infantry private, had deserted from the assembly positions just prior to an attack. He had stated at his court martial that his sister had drowned herself 12 years previously and that he had doubts about his own sanity. His conduct sheet revealed that he had been sentenced to a year's imprisonment in July 1916, during the Battle of the Somme, for attempting to commit suicide by cutting his throat with a razor. After his conviction for desertion he was examined by a captain in the RAMC who reported that he was both mentally and physically normal. The third soldier, a private in a Kentish regiment, had been accepted as a volunteer in December 1914, but had been categorized as unfit for service overseas because of his nervous disposition. In spite of this, however, he had been posted to a battalion at the front during the summer of 1916 when the manpower situation was becoming desperate. He had deserted in August 1917 when, as he said in his defence, he had been unable to stand the strain of shellfire any longer. On the day of his trial he was certified by his regimental doctor as being 'medically fit'.

The members of an FGCM usually saw no documents relating to a prisoner they had convicted other than his conduct sheet and his personal pay book. For the rest they were obliged to rely upon the defence evidence and the statement in mitigation to acquaint them with any matters which might dispose them to pass a more compassionate sentence. Even if some factor came to light which merited further enquiries, under the circumstances of active service any detailed investigations were extremely difficult, if not impossible. The proceedings were essentially of a summary nature and a court was rarely reconvened for a second time. During the last two years of the war a lot of men on trial for cowardice and desertion claimed to have been treated in hospital for shell-shock. The corroborative medical records were never to hand, and even if they had been, 'shell-shock' was so nebulous a term that they would probably have disclosed a wide range of neurasthenic conditions considerably varying in symptoms and severity, the prognoses for which were extremely vague.

There can be little doubt that many soldiers were executed without any attempt being made to assess the degree of responsibility they might have had for their own behaviour at the time of their offences. A number of disquieting cases occurred even during the brief period under consideration. A reservist from Lincolnshire, who had originally enlisted in 1904 and had arrived in France with the initial expeditionary force, said in his defence that his nerves had been completely shattered by his long spell in action. He had been wounded in November 1914, and again in July 1916, and had deserted from the trenches during the summer of 1917. A Scottish soldier who had served in the BEF without fault for 26 months reported sick with nervous exhaustion at the beginning of the Flanders offensive. He was ordered back to duty and went absent a few weeks later. A deserter from a British colonial regiment was described as willing, well behaved and of a higher standard of intelligence than the remainder of his platoon. He gave evidence that he was troubled with his head and he could not stand the sound of guns.

In Lord Moran's opinion shell-shock could be a genuine condition. 'There were some men of stout heart,' he wrote, 'who were brought to that plight by the blast of a shell which damaged their brains. These men had come out of some rending explosion with their skins intact but with dishevelled minds.'[14] He had found that his views were not universally shared by his medical colleagues in France. On one occasion Moran was taken for a drive in the car of another doctor who stopped outside a casualty clearing station and told him, 'There's a fellow here who ran away from the trenches. They are going to shoot him and they want me to say if he's responsible. I shan't be long'.[15]

Certain of the troops who committed acts of cowardice 'were plainly worthless fellows', said Lord Moran, but the nervous systems of others had been scarred by months of warfare.[16] Nevertheless, long service at the front was by itself rarely regarded as a relevant ground for commuting a death sentence.

A sergeant in a Worcestershire regiment, executed for desertion in August 1917 at the age of 23 had enlisted in 1912 and had served in France for three years. When his company was advancing to take up position in a forward trench they had come under a heavy bombardment and he and a number of other men had sheltered in a concrete dugout. The advance was later resumed but the sergeant had remained in the dugout and had reported back two days afterwards with the explanation that he had lost his way. On the face of it his behaviour had been inexplicable as he was described as a very good soldier who had been engaged in every action in which his battalion had fought between September 1914 and September 1915. This was the sort of case which would have merited some probing into the accused man's mental state.

Apart from shell-shock, altogether little or no consideration was given to the possible effects of battle strain upon a deserter's behaviour when deciding whether or not he should be shot for his offence. A soldier from West Yorkshire, executed on 30 August, had enlisted voluntarily in April 1915. Immediately he had completed his basic training he was sent to the Dardanelles and had taken part in the final evacuation from the Gallipoli peninsula. He had been posted to France during the Battle of the Somme and had sustained a shrapnel wound in mid-September 1916. Having returned to his battalion at the beginning of 1917 he had deserted five months later when they were about to commence a tour of duty in the front line. Another volunteer who had also been wounded the previous year in the Somme was executed on 27 October. He was 33 at the time of his death and had been employed as a gentleman's servant before the war. After seven months' active service with a Cheshire regiment he had received wounds to both legs in July 1916. When he rejoined the BEF in February 1917, he said in his defence, he had found that his nerves were beyond his control and he had deserted the following May from a training area where his brigade was practising for an attack.

Three more volunteers, all of whom had seen substantial service in the line, were executed for desertion during the month of October 1917. One of them, a private from Northumberland, said at his trial that he had been in France for 20 months without leave and was suffering from acute depression. Another, a 27-year-old Irishman, stated that he had felt ill and cold on the day he committed his offence and that he had served with the BEF for a continuous period of eight months. The third was a Welsh stretcher-bearer who had deserted after helping to carry a wounded man to a forward dressing station. His company commander said that he had been with the battalion ever since they landed in France and hitherto had proved himself a good soldier.

In the ethos of a war of attrition desertion became a particularly heinous crime. Since numerical superiority was considered as being almost of equal importance with the ordinary skills of the battlefield, half-trained British soldiers were sent into action in their masses. There was no process, however, for weeding out the men who lacked the will, the temperament or the physical ability to endure the life at the front. One such soldier was executed in October 1917. He was a married man of 42 with seven children and had enlisted as a volunteer in a Northumberland regiment during January 1915. Whilst training in England he had acquired a reputation as a persistent deserter and had been convicted three times by courts martial in France, once for desertion and twice for absence without leave. Finally, he had disappeared from the support line in September 1917 and after several days had been found hiding in a cellar, weak and hungry. He gave as his reason for his last offence that he was worried about his wife who had not written to him; also, that his spirits had sunk so low he had had no thought other than to get away from it all.

Notes

1. Philip Snowden (1864–1937), son of a Yorkshire weaver, became Chancellor of the Exchequer in the Labour governments of 1924 and 1929. He was created a viscount in 1932 on his retirement from active politics.
2. House of Commons, oral answers, 31 October 1917.
3. He had already referred to the matter in January 1916 (see pp. 65–6).
4. House of Commons, oral answers, 6 November 1917.
5. House of Commons, oral answers, 13 November 1917.
6. House of Commons, oral answers, 26 November 1917.
7. House of Commons, oral answers, 28 November 1917.
8. House of Commons, written answers, 3 December 1917.
9. House of Commons, oral answers, 12 December 1917.
10. House of Commons, oral answers, 14 December 1917.
11. House of Commons, oral answers, 18 December 1917.
12. Siegfried Sassoon, *Sherston's Progress.*
13. Ib.
14. Lord Moran, *The Anatomy of Courage.*
15. Ib.
16. Ib.

THE CLOSE OF THE FLANDERS OFFENSIVE

D URING THE EARLY part of October 1917 the battle front at Passchendaele had become a desolate waste of mud and water. 'In all that vast wilderness of slime,' says the Official History, 'hardly tree, hedge, wall or building could be seen.' Shells, ammunition and supplies were lugged forward by soldiers, mules and pack-horses along the narrow duckboard tracks traversing the area behind the trenches. Any animal which stumbled off the slippery planks could be immersed completely in the swamps on either side.

In spite of these terrible conditions Haig obstinately persisted with his foredoomed offensive. He was encouraged by the British Prime Minister, Lloyd George, who still believed that the German Army was on the verge of disintegration. On 12 October, against the advice of General Gough, the attack was resumed and the infantry advanced in close formation across the quagmire, only to be driven back again almost to their starting line. During the ensuing weeks assault followed assault with little ground being gained and with most of the available British reserves being dissipated in the struggle. Ultimately, on 4 November, Haig achieved his hollow triumph when his weary troops entered the tactically valueless bombed-out shell of the village of Passchendaele. At this point, with his soldiers near to exhaustion, the Commander-in-Chief decided to bring the Flanders campaign to a close. Since the beginning of August the BEF had suffered close on 238,000 casualties in the fighting; they had made no appreciable gains and their prime objective, the Flemish coast, remained firmly in enemy hands. 'So fruitless in its results, so depressing in its direction was this 1917 offensive,' wrote Liddell Hart, 'that "Passchendaele" has come to be, like Walcheren a century before, a synonym for military failure – a name black-bordered in the records of the British Army.'[1]

Haig had not finished his offensive operations for the year. He now turned his attention to the drier undulating downland at the southern end of the British sector where the Germans had retired to the comparative comfort and security of their prepared positions on the Hindenburg Line. Early in the morning on 20 November five divisions from the Third Army, led by 300 tanks and supported by 1,000 guns, went into the attack on a four-mile front to the west of the town of Cambrai. Owing to a thick ground mist and the absence of the usual preliminary bombardment, the Germans were taken completely by surprise; their outposts were overrun and their main defensive strategy thrown into confusion. By the end of the day the British had created a salient three to four miles deep and Ludendorff was contemplating a general withdrawal from the area.

The news of the British advance on the opening day of the Battle of Cambrai set off a wave of rejoicing in England where a war-weary people were avid for the scent of victory. It was as though the German Army had been routed. Church bells were pealed and messages of congratulation were sent to the Commander-in-Chief from both the King and the Lord Mayor of London.

But it was all too premature. On 21 November the tide of fortune changed and the British forces could make no headway against the German reinforcements which had been rushed to man the perimeter of the salient. The Official History blames bad generalship for the failure of the Third Army to exploit its successes of the previous day. The attacks were lacking in co-ordination; inadequate use was made of artillery; and worn-out troops remained in action two long without relief. The battle continued for another nine days with no substantial gains by either side. Gradually the weather was deteriorating; on 26 November snow fell continuously all day; on 27 November there was a bitter-cold wind and drizzling rain. It was a presage of the winter ahead. By then Haig must have realized that there was no more chance of a breakthrough at Cambrai than there had been at Passchendaele.

On 30 November the Germans struck back. After a heavy barrage of gas and high-explosive shells their infantry, armed in some cases with portable flame-throwers, assailed the flanks of the salient while low-flying aircraft raked the British trenches with machine gun fire. A further attack of equal intensity occurred on the next day. The salient had now become a worthless liability and early in December Haig decided to pull back his exposed divisions in order to rectify the British line for the winter. At the termination of the Cambrai offensive no ground had been won and no ground lost; in its abortive effort the Third Army had sustained casualties of over 44,000 officers and men.

As 1917 drew to a close the immediate prospects for the Allies seemed gloomy in the extreme and the vision of outright victory had receded into a dimmed obscurity. At the start of the year the Russian armies on the Eastern Front had been flagging. In March, after the revolution in St Petersburg, the proclamation of a provisional government and the abdication of the Tsar, they virtually desisted from any further offensive action.

In May 1917 Sir William Robertson submitted a memorandum to the War Cabinet on the Russian military potential for the future. He stated:

> It is folly to suppose that an army without discipline and efficient services of maintenance can have any fighting value worthy of the name. . . . We should be prepared for the worst, namely that the Central Powers will be free to concentrate their forces against the remaining enemies. It must be assumed that the whole German Army on the Eastern Front will be available for operations in the West.

Robertson went on to advocate that in the event of Russia concluding a separate peace Britain should assemble all her available forces on the Western Front for the vital tasks of defending the Channel ports and averting a French collapse. During the summer months the Germans transferred ten of their battle-tested divisions to the west and plans were put in hand to turn over all the resources of the German railway system to the transportation of the bulk of the Eastern Army to France with the utmost rapidity. In November the Bolsheviks seized power in Russia and immediately requested an armistice from the Central Powers. All hostilities ceased on the Eastern Front during the first week of December, which left the Germans with a massive reserve of more than 80 inactive divisions.

It was clear that as more and more American formations took the field the balance of manpower on the Western Front would swing back in favour of the Allies; the primal question was whether they would be able to hold out sufficiently long to reap this advantage. In the summer of 1917 General Pershing, the American Commander-in-Chief, was urging his government to send at least a million men to France by the end of the following spring, but in all the circumstances this was going to prove a considerable undertaking and in fact only four trained American divisions had reached France by the beginning of December.

Haig doubted the ability of the French Army to withstand an all-out German offensive, in spite of the progress achieved by General Pétain in restoring its morale. To add to her problems France had now conscripted nearly every available man of military age who was fit for service and could no longer fully replenish the wastage of the battle-field. The efficacy of Franco-British co-operation on the Western Front was bedevilled by the personal mistrust, bordering upon enmity, which existed between Haig and Pétain, each of whom suspected the other of placing his national interests before the unity of the *entente*.

Britain and France had difficulty in agreeing a common strategic policy to meet the implications of the altered situation. Early in

October Haig submitted his personal views to the War Cabinet. He had asked for all his divisions to be brought up to full fighting strength and had continued:

> Success on the Western Front is the only alternative to an unsatisfactory peace. . . . [An] indispensable condition of decisive success on the Western Front is that the War Cabinet should have a firm faith in its possibility and should resolve finally and unreservedly to concentrate our resources on it, and at once.

The French government, supported by their General Staff, were opposed to the Allies taking any aggressive action on the Western Front for the present and wished to rely on economic warfare until the Americans had built up a sufficiently powerful army to sustain a major offensive. Pétain was continually stressing his lack of reserves and complaining that the BEF was holding too small a sector of the line. At the end of October he had told Haig bluntly that he could not even discuss a joint plan for the following year until some form of readjustment had taken place which enabled him to shorten his front and to build up his reserves. The War Cabinet in London had consented in principle to an extension of the British sector but had left it to the two Commanders-in-Chief to work out the details.

On 24 October disaster had befallen the Italian Army in the Julian Alps to the north of the Adriatic Sea when a surprise attack by the Austrians and Germans had broken through their line at Caporetto. For a moment Italy was in danger of complete collapse as her forces had reeled back with heavy losses. Six French and five British divisions had been rushed down from the Western Front and with their assistance the onslaught had been stemmed.

One of the adverse consequences of Caporetto was a serious diminution in the strength of the BEF at a time when manpower shortage was a crucial problem. To increase Haig's dificulties in this respect he had been notified by the War Office that the total number of reinforcements he could hope to receive during 1918 would fall considerably short of his requirements.

It might have been expected in the fourth year of the war that the courts martial on the Western Front would reveal some altered patterns of behaviour or a different outlook on the part of the accused men, but in reality the substance of the trials remained the same. Most desertions still took place from units in the forward and support trenches, or from battalions when they were resting and had just been warned for duty in the line. For nearly all deserters there must have been a desperate moment of decision – a moment of choice between the frenzied terrors of the battlefield and the role of a pariah, solitary, hunted and virtually foredoomed to ultimate capture and retribution. It would seem that the offence was seldom preconceived or planned and was often committed in a state of mental turmoil.

It is difficult to determine in any one case what factors, apart from fear and fatigue, eventually precipitated a desertion. During the autumn of 1917 several executed soldiers had pleaded that paucity of leave or the toll the war had taken on their own immediate families had undermined their stability. In mid-December Haig told the War Office that leave was a matter of urgency for his troops. 'They have earned it,' he said, 'and it is a valuable means of keeping them in good heart.' During the previous month the period of home leave allowable to the BEF had been increased from ten days to 14 days every 15 months.

A regular soldier in a Staffordshire regiment was executed for desertion on 6 November after serving in France for three years. He had enlisted originally for a term of six years and if it had not been for the war he would have been due for discharge in August 1916. He felt that he had been unfairly treated because, by some incongruity of thought, he believed that he was entitled to a month's leave on the date when his engagement would have terminated. Although this was the third occasion on which he had deserted, his platoon commander still spoke very highly of his qualities and his efficiency. An Irish private who was executed on the same day claimed that he had not been home on leave since December 1914. During the first few weeks of the war he had volunteered for an infantry regiment in his native Belfast and he had been sent to the Dardanelles in 1915. After the evacuation from Gallipoli he went to Salonika until the early spring of 1917 when his battalion was transferred to the Western Front. He claimed that two of his brothers had been killed in France and one had been lost at sea, but that his application for compassionate leave in order to comfort his parents had been refused. He had two previous convictions for desertion and was subject to a suspended sentence of seven years' penal servitude. A similar reason for deserting was put forward by a soldier in a Rifle regiment who was shot at the end of October. He had not been granted leave, he said, after both his brothers had been killed in the Somme and his sister had begged him to return home.

The youngest deserter to be executed during the closing months of 1917 was a youth of 19 from Kent. He had managed to enlist at the age of 16 amid the inebriative atmosphere which followed the outbreak of the war. However, his early ardour and his visions of glory had soon perished in the holocaust of the Western Front. During his two years in France prior to his final trial he had been court-martialled three times, twice for desertion and once for cowardice. On two occasions he had been sentenced to death and he was already under the shadow of three suspended sentences of imprisonment. Three other very young deserters – they were all 20 – were shot around this time, one in October and two in November.

No doubt domestic worries, and also homesickness, preyed on the minds of soldiers in the trenches. A private from South Wales, who had joined the regular Army in February 1914, was sent to France in September 1915, five days after his marriage. He deserted in August 1917 while he was serving as a brigade runner in the front line. A week later he was arrested in Calais by a lance-corporal of the Military Police who found him wearing uniform without shoulder or cap badges. At first the Welshman had given a false name and pretended that he was on the staff of a camp at Boulogne. After 24 hours in custody he had revealed his true identity. At his court martial he stated that he was uneasy about his wife but he did not explain the source of his anxiety. He was shot on 22 November.

A number of men who had lost their nerve in Flanders and at Passchendaele were sentenced to death and executed during the autumn of 1917. A soldier from Yorkshire with four years' regular service had broken down in the trenches under a heavy artillery barrage. He had told his platoon commander he could stand no more and the officer had sent him back to the regimental aid post. Shell-shock, however, was still a suspect complaint. The doctor had examined him, given him some medicine and told him to return to duty. Instead of obeying, the Yorkshireman had made his way to a town behind the line where he had remained unrecognized for two months until he was arrested by the Military Police for stealing a wallet from a French civilian whom he had just met in a local estaminet. Shell-shock was also pleaded unsuccessfully by a Londoner, a volunteer from 1915, who had deserted at the end of November. His battalion had been moving up from the support trenches to reinforce a part of the line which was being attacked by German infantry when he had fallen out without permission and sat down at the side of the road. He had resisted all efforts to make him rejoin his platoon, protesting that he could not go on as he was sick with fear. This man was court-martialled 12 days before Christmas; he was informed that he had been sentenced to death on the day after Boxing Day and he was executed on 28 December.

It was unusual so late in the war for a soldier on a capital charge to be undefended at his court martial. A private in a Yorkshire regiment, tried for desertion on 27 November, had no defending officer. He had joined up as a volunteer in September 1914 and had first been sent to Egypt and thence to France in April 1916. He maintained that he had been buried by a shell-burst the following September and had been invalided home with heart failure and nerves. When he returned to the Western Front, he said, he found that he shook from head to foot whenever he went into the trenches. Not unnaturally, the court expressed a desire to hear some medical evidence about the man but as none was available they did not pursue the matter and proceeded to sentence him to death. He, too, was shot on 28 December.

A soldier who refused to go up to the front must have realized that he ran a very grave risk of being executed, for disobedience in itself was a capital offence. On 26 October a battalion of a London regiment which was in reserve in the Passchendaele sector had received orders to advance forthwith and to take up position in the line. While the rest of his company was falling in ready to move off Private S declined to leave his dugout. Both the adjutant and the regimental sergeant-major were called to the scene and they found S sitting on the ground with his rifle and equipment at his side. They told him repeatedly to go on parade and warned him of the consequences of his continued refusal, but he would neither move nor reply and eventually he was placed under close arrest. S was court-martialled in November for 'disobeying an order in such a manner as to show wilful defiance of authority'. It came out at his trial that he had been called up in February 1916, soon after the introduction of conscription. He was posted to France in January 1917 and had been a company stretcher-bearer during the heavy fighting in the spring and summer. He had borne a very good military character and had always carried out his duties in a satisfactory manner until the middle of August when he was awarded three months' Field Punishment Number One by his commanding officer for disobedience of an order. S told the court that he had seen so many terrible sights on the Western Front that they had affected his mind and he was no longer accountable for his behaviour. A captain in the RAMC gave evidence that he had spoken to S for ten minutes and had found no sign of mental deficiency or mental derangement. S was sentenced to death and he was shot two weeks before Christmas.

A court martial in December demonstrated yet again the difficulty of turning a vagrant into a soldier. Private H was conscripted into a Lancashire regiment in September 1916, at the age of 26. He had left school when he was 13 and had never had any regular employment, although he had worked occasionally as a boiler-cleaner. He had had many convictions in civil courts, principally for minor thefts, drunkenness, assaults and vagrancy offences. He had also spent a short period in a lunatic asylum. During his military training in England he had been in frequent trouble and immediately after his arrival in France at the beginning of August 1917 he was given 21 days' Field Punishment Number One for being found out of bounds. While he was still serving this sentence he was posted to a battalion which was then in reserve. In the early hours of the morning on 1 September, during Private H's first tour of duty in the line, his battalion has been subjected to a gas attack. When it was over he had disappeared, leaving his rifle behind him, and he had remained absent for the next eight days. He was charged, not with desertion, but with 'leaving his post without orders from his superior officer'. His defence was that he had been lying about all night in the cold and had wandered off in search of a town where he could get warm. He had added that he was without friends in the regiment, he had had no pay for a long time, and he had been kept in handcuffs for the past six or seven months.

Although the court sentenced H to death they had added a note to the proceedings suggesting that in view of his very low mentality a proper medical report on him might be desirable. Accordingly, H was sent under escort to a military hospital in Boulogne where he was examined by a specialist in mental illness. The doctor reported that H was dull, morose and reluctant to answer any questions; he was responsible for his actions but he was below average intelligence and he exhibited all the attributes of a 'criminal degenerate'. Before this assessment was compiled the hospital had received information from England that in May 1914 the medical officer at a prison in Cheshire had certified H as being mentally deficient.

The recommendations as to whether H's sentence should be confirmed or commuted were all in favour of execution. His commanding officer stated that his behaviour had shown a complete lack of manly characteristics. The corps commander observed that he seemed a thoroughly bad soldier in every way, and the army commander, in urging that the sentence be carried out, was anxious to emphasize that he had been careful not to allow H's general worthlessness to sway his judgment. H was shot at dawn on 13 February 1918.

The cumulative effect of a series of adverse opinions from his subordinate commanders upon the mind of the Commander-in-Chief, when making the ultimate decision, must have been considerable. In most cases these recommendations abounded in hearsay and speculation. When a deserter from Devon was sentenced to death in November 1917, his colonel had commented that the man had been a constant source of annoyance and was absolutely untrustworthy both in fighting and in everyday work. The brigadier for his part expanded on this view. The example of such a soldier, he said, must be a dangerous influence on the fighting qualities of all those with whom he came into contact.

When making his recommendation, it was difficult for a senior officer to know for certain what factors might be considered irrelevant by those above him in the chain of command. In February 1918 the GOC of the 15th (Scottish) Division advocated the commutation of a death sentence on a deserter with a good fighting record on the ground that his execution would cast a shadow on the reputation of the famous regiment to which he belonged. This elicited a stern rebuke from the adjutant-general who wrote:

> The G.O.C. 15th Division should be reminded that the commutation of a sentence for an offence which has been deliberately committed tends to stultify action in subsequent cases of a like nature. In making his recommendation in the particular case under remark, the G.O.C. 15th Division appears to have entirely overlooked the larger question and confined himself to a very narrow view of the general requirements of military discipline. . . . [He] was entirely wrong to introduce a factor (i.e. upholding the honour of the regiment) which affects the whole of his division and not merely one particular unit of it.

All through the shortened, rainswept days of December the BEF was occupied in building a new defence position in depth to withstand the anticipated German offensive, which was expected to coincide with the first break in the winter weather. So as to rest the maximum number of his troops Haig had ordered a damping down of all activities at the Front which might provoke retaliation. In consequence the guns fired less frequently, patrolling was more restrained and trench raids were only carried out from tactical necessity.

A cloud of foreboding overhung the British Lines – a mood of resignation and despair. Edmund Blunden, an infantry officer, thought back on all the casualties of 1917, the wasted efforts and the growing intensity and sweep of destructive forces. 'We should all die,' he reflected gloomily, 'presumably round Ypres.'[2]

The same spirit of desperation pervades Siegfried Sassoon's poem 'Attack', with his sombre image of 'Lines of grey, muttering faces, masked with fear' as soldiers leave their trenches to go over the top, and the final couplet:

> And hope, with furtive eyes and grappling fists,
> Flounders in the mud. O Jesus, make it stop!

Notes

1. B. H. Liddell Hart, *History of The First World War*.
2. Edmund Blunden, *Undertones of War*.

16

THE YEAR OF THE ARMISTICE

B Y THE END of January 1918 the progress made by the BEF in constructing their new defence line was far from satisfactory. The Germans were constantly harassing the work being done in the forward localities with raids and mortar fire; completion of support positions and communication trenches was hampered by lack of labour; and the energy of the troops had been sapped by the severe conditions of the winter, the bitter cold and the deeply-frozen earth.

Haig had informed the War Office that he would need 615,000 extra men for the operations of the coming year; he was told he could expect little more than 100,000, most of them being 18-year-old conscripts seeing active service for the first time. Undoubtedly a greater number of reinforcements would have been available, but the Cabinet were afraid that if Haig was sent his full requirement he might fritter away their lives with a new programme of costly and ineffectual attacks.

At that time the BEF was organized into 63 divisions and had a numerical strength of just over a million men. The French had a total of 99 divisions on the Western Front, but as their soldiers continued to be granted leave every four months the individual units were invariably below establishment. The Germans now had a superiority both in manpower and in artillery over the Allies. Moreover, they had been able to replace in their front-line formations all men who were more than 35 years of age. The transfer of troops from the Russian Front was proceeding steadily and by March the German Army in the west numbered 187 divisions.

All the intelligence reports which were being received by the Allies at the beginning of 1918 pointed to the imminence of a massive offensive by the German Army aimed either at the Channel ports, only 50 miles away from their forward elements, or at Paris, some 80 miles distant. British sources expected the attack to commence in March; the French, on the other hand, thought it would be delayed until May or June. At a meeting of the Supreme War Council at Versailles on 30 January, convened to devise a common strategy for the Allied High Commands, General Foch saw fit to criticize the war effort being made by Britain. Lloyd George retorted that since July 1916 the British casualties had exceeded those of any of her allies. He might well have pointed out that if the immediate German objective was to be the Channel ports the brunt of the onslaught was bound to fall on the BEF.

Whilst the opposing armies on the Western Front were completing their final preparations for the coming battle the government were being pressed continually in the House of Commons for more information regarding military executions. In reply to a question put to him by Philip Snowden in the middle of January, the Under-Secretary for War stated that Sir Douglas Haig personally examined the record of every court martial at which a sentence of death had been passed and invariably received the advice of the Deputy Judge Advocate General in France before he exercised his power of confirmation. The Minister added that a soldier was usually executed approximately 14 days after his court martial.[1]

The following month Mr Snowden enquired whether at trials for cowardice and desertion medical evidence that the accused men were not suffering from shell-shock was always given on oath and was subject to cross-examination. Mr Macpherson answered both questions in the affirmative and assured the House that every witness at a court martial was obliged to give his testimony on oath and could always be cross-examined; any departure from the rules of procedure, he said, would nullify the whole trial.[2] This was true, of course, but the Minister did not disclose that the medical examination frequently took place after the court martial was finished and that in such cases the findings of the Board were never shown to the prisoner or to his defending officer: they were, however, considered by the confirming authorities. In reply to supplementary questions from other Members, Mr Macpherson repeated the assurance he had given in the past that the greatest attention was paid to the mental condition of men accused of cowardice or desertion. Whenever there was the least suspicion of shell-shock, he said, 'every possible medical advice is obtained'. He 'deeply resented' a suggestion by Mr Whitehouse, a Labour back-bencher, that there had been occasions when men suffering from shell-shock were executed, and he demanded that the allegation should be withdrawn. Mr Whitehouse explained that he was referring to the specific case of a soldier who had been treated for shell-shock and subsequently had been shot by a firing squad. Although he withdrew any insinuation to which his previous remark had been open 'absolutely and unreservedly', the Minister declined to make any further comment on the matter.

On the evening of the same day, when the House was debating the Army Estimates, Mr Whitehouse proposed that the War Office should issue a regulation making it impossible for any soldier to be sentenced to death after he had been invalided home suffering from shell-shock.[3] The next speaker, Mr Morrell, said there was an impression in the country that at one time in the war death sentences had been carried out with frequency at the front. The Under-Secretary for War, he went on, had denied that any of the executed men had either been wounded or had suffered from shell-shock, but there were in fact numerous cases when this had occurred. He repeated Mr Whitehouse's plea that no soldier should be executed who had ever suffered from shell-shock and he also asked for an undertaking that every prisoner standing his trial at a capital court martial would have a friend to represent him. Another member informed the Minister:

There is no question among the people as a whole today upon which they feel more concerned and more strongly than the carrying out of death sentences, not because of anything said in the House, but because of the stories told by soldiers themselves, and because of statements made by the men who have to carry out these death sentences – the horror of them!

Mr Macpherson, replying to the debate, agreed that there was a great deal of public concern regarding military executions, but he said he felt very strongly that the officers who sat upon courts martial, the Judge Advocate General who dealt legally with the cases, 'the various doctors who may be summoned at any given moment when any plea of insanity or shell-shock is put forward', and the Field-Marshal Commanding-in-Chief and his advisers were all just as humanitarian as any Member of the House. He concluded by saying:

I have made, and shall continue to make, investigations with regard to the facts stated in the various questions, and I have not yet been able to come across a single case where a man who was proved in the past to have suffered from shell-shock, or was proved to have been wounded, has suffered the death penalty after being sentenced to death.

The subject of military executions was raised again on 20 February during the Committee stage of the Army Estimates.[4] Mr Morrell, who was later congratulated on the moderation of his speech by the Under-Secretary of State for War, said he did not question the need for the death penalty in time of war. But, he continued:

Of all the horrors of war, I think nothing is more horrible than that men are condemned to be shot, and are actually shot by their comrades, in many cases for failure of nerves, or it may be sleeping at their posts – something which does not necessarily show moral delinquency, but only grave neglect of duty.

The executions, he said, were clouded in obscurity; the House was not even allowed to know the number which had taken place because, they were told, it would be contrary to the public interest to reveal this figure. The relatives of the condemned men were kept in ignorance of the details of the courts martial at which the death sentence had been passed. In the interests of mercy and of justice, he pleaded for the capital court martial system to be re-examined, in particular to see that soldiers who had been wounded or shell-shocked might be treated as a special category, to ensure that men on trial for their lives should be properly defended, and to establish a right of appeal against a death sentence to the civil Court of Criminal Appeal.

The Under-Secretary for War then announced that the War Office was in the process of publishing a new order reiterating an accused soldier's right of representation at his court martial. The order would state that:

> If the accused desires to make his own selection of a friend subject to military law, whether of commissioned rank or not, the request should be granted. . . . The friend of the accused shall be notified and a copy of the evidence given to him in sufficient time to enable him to give due consideration to the case and to consult with the accused.

At Question Time a few weeks later Mr Macpherson said that the granting of a right of appeal from a court martial could only be brought about by an Act of Parliament and the government did not propose to introduce the necessary legislation for that purpose.[5]

The concern felt by a small group of Members remained unallayed. The execution of shell-shocked soldiers was raised again in a debate on the Consolidated Fund Bill on 14 March and drew from the Under-Secretary of State for War an unequivocal statement that shell-shock should not be associated with cowardice.[6] 'One has come across case after case of the most gallant fellows who ever drew breath,' he said, 'whose nerves are so badly shattered that only half of their whole bodily strength and mental vigour remains.' To show that the commanders of the British forces on the Western Front shared this view Mr Macpherson produced a letter he had received from Sir Douglas Haig and read a portion of it to the House. Haig had written:

> When a man has been sentenced to death if at any time any doubt has been raised as to his responsibility for his actions, or if the suggestion had been advanced that he has suffered from neurasthenia or shell-shock, orders are issued for him to be examined by a medical board which expresses an opinion as to his sanity, and as to whether he should be held responsible for his actions. One of the members of this board is always a medical officer of neurological experience. The sentence of death is not

carried out in the case of such a man unless the medical board expresses the positive opinion that he is to be held responsible for his actions.

Whether or not it was the result of public and parliamentary concern in England it is difficult to say, but the incidence of military executions in the BEF decreased significantly from the beginning of 1918. During the last three months of 1917, 39 of the death sentences passed at courts martial in France were confirmed by the Commander-in-Chief: in the first five months of 1918 he only confirmed 13. No executions took place of men who were tried on the Western Front in January; the figure for February was two, for March two, for April five and for May four. The trial of the last soldier to be shot during the war for any offence other than desertion or murder occurred in December 1917.

The two executed men who were sentenced to death in February were tried on the same day by different courts, one charged with murder and one with desertion. The former was a sergeant in a Rifle regiment aged 28 who had enlisted on a regular engagement in 1908 and had served with the BEF for exactly three years. He had picked up an unlicensed prostitute, described as a woman in her forties, at a café in Le Havre and she had taken him back to her home nearby. Soon after they entered a series of loud bangs and thuds were heard coming from the house. The police had forced their way into the prostitute's bedroom, which was locked on the inside; they had discovered her half-naked body lying across the bed and the room in a state of disorder. A post-mortem revealed that the woman had been strangled. The sergeant was seen at his camp on the evening of her death with severe scratch-marks on his face. The motive for the murder was never divulged at the trial as the sergeant, although he admitted going to the prostitute's house and having sexual intercourse with her, insisted that she had been alive and well when he left her. He explained the marks on his face by saying he had hung up his equipment and it had fallen down on this head.

The deserter was a French-Canadian who had enlisted in a Scottish regiment during the first month of the war and had served with the BEF for more than two years. His battalion had been in the forefront of the fighting throughout the Battle of the Somme and he had achieved the reputation of being a reliable and courageous soldier. He deserted in January 1917, but he was soon arrested and he received a suspended sentence of three years' penal servitude. The following August, within a month of his rejoining the battalion, he was admitted to hospital suffering from shell-shock. After two months' treatment he was returned to duty. He deserted again at the end of November when his battalion was finishing a rest period at Arras and was about to march up to the line. After 15 days he was apprehended and was placed under close arrest in the guard-room of his unit. He had escaped from there a week later and had remained at liberty until 15 January 1918, when he was detained at Abbeville dressed in civilian clothes. For these last two desertions he was sentenced to death. There is no indication that any medical opinion about his condition was supplied to the court martial or to the confirming authorities. However, when he had been discharged from hospital the previous October he was, presumably, considered to be completely cured of all the symptoms of shell-shock.

Both the men who were sentenced to death and executed in March had been convicted of desertion and both had committed a similar offence before. Private H, a 24-year-old married man from Lancaster, had joined the Army as a volunteer in September 1914. He was wounded in the foot in September 1915, three months after joining the BEF. He returned to France in March 1916 and served with his battalion until his first desertion at the end of 1917. For this offence he was condemned to death, a sentence which had been commuted to a suspended term of 15 years' penal servitude. H was then returned to his battalion but deserted again on the day of his arrival. He gave himself up to the Military Police five days later, telling them that he had been looking for an oculist as his battalion medical officer had refused to do anything about his bad eyesight. H was described by his commanding officer as a quiet and well-conducted man – but a coward. The other executed man came from Yorkshire. He was a conscript who had served with the BEF for six months and had already received a suspended sentence of ten years' penal servitude for deserting in December 1917.

The German offensive started on the morning of 21 March against the ill-prepared positions of the BEF. The forward British trenches, manned by a high proportion of inexperienced officers and untrained replacements, were pulverized by a five-hour bombardment of high explosive and gas shells. Then the German infantry, which was led by specially-trained storm troops, poured across no-man's-land through a thick ground mist. Although the defenders fought valiantly in every sector the front was broken to the south of the River Somme where General Gough's hard-pressed Fifth Army fell back in confusion, suffering heavy casualties and losing huge quantities of guns, ammunition and stores.

On 22 and 23 March the Germans pressed home the attack relentlessly on the shattered divisions of the Fifth Army and General Gough was forced to continue his retreat by day and by night. Haig implored him to hold the line of the Somme but this was virtually an impossible task for troops who had been in action without sleep for something like 72 hours. The Third Army on the left of the Fifth and the First Army holding the northernmost portion of the British positions also gave ground as Haig sought desperately to straighten and to stabilize his front. General Pétain, watching from the sidelines, refused to offer any help at the outset because he feared that the main German offensive would take place in Champagne and he wished to keep all his forces intact for the defence of Paris. General Pershing, however, realizing the gravity of the situation, placed all the American divisions in France at the disposal of his allies. On 23 March, as a modest contribution to the struggle, Pétain promised to strengthen the French forces on the immediate flank of the beleaguered Fifth Army.

With the whole of the BEF in retreat and disquieting rumours of crumbling morale, the War Cabinet decided to send to the Western Front every trained and semi-trained soldier then available. Plans were set in motion to recall divisions from Italy, Salonika and Palestine, and improvised drafts were hurried across the Channel from England. When conscription had been introduced in 1916 a regulation had been made that no man of under 19 would be sent to any theatre of war. Now the minimum age was reduced to eighteen and a half and the minimum period of training before troops were sent into action was set at three months. The French Army, in spite of its shortage of manpower, did not allow any soldier into the line who was aged less than 20.

The Official History comments that at this stage of the operations in France the behaviour of certain headquarter staffs was contributing to the despondency of the fighting formations and generally dislocating the machinery of command. This was brought about by their readiness to withdraw as far away as possible from the advancing Germans. 'Often on the slightest provocation,' says the war historian, 'a corps or divisional headquarters, with long processions of vehicles, plainly labelled, carrying their equipment and accumulated possessions', would be seen moving further and further to the rear. The adjutant of a Royal Artillery regiment watched in disgust as his corps headquarters performed one such hasty evacuation using transport which would have been more usefully employed in carrying ammunition or materials to the front. 'Lorry after lorry rolled up,' he wrote, 'to be loaded with such delightful etcetera as an electric lighting set, arm chairs, and a fine kitchen range which certainly had not been paid for by the present owners.'[7]

During the last few days in March the German advance seemed to be slowing down, although Ludendorff was striving desperately to maintain the momentum of the onslaught. Marshal Foch had now been placed in supreme control of all the Allied forces on the Western Front, and General Gough, who was most unfairly blamed for the initial débâcle, was relieved of the command of the Fifth Army.

By the beginning of April the British line was holding fast but was perilously positioned a mere 50 miles from the coast. In the 15 days from 21 March to 5 April the BEF had sustained losses amounting to a total of 178,000, of which more than 70,000 officers and men had been killed. A number of battalions were commanded by junior officers and drafts of reinforcements were being allocated where they were needed, irrespective of the soldiers' regiments. On 11 April Haig issued a Special Order of the Day:

> There is no other course open to us but to fight it out. Every position must be held to the last man: there must be no retirement. With our backs to the wall and believing in the justice of our cause each one of us must fight on to the end.

The German Army, still drawing reinforcements from the east, continued to batter the British line in the certain knowledge that it would require only one further breakthrough to destroy the whole of the BEF. Haig appealed repeatedly to Foch for assistance but was met with an adamant refusal on the ground that the French troops had not yet recovered from their efforts and their casualties in the first two years of the war. Eventually, on 17 April, Foch gave way to the pleas he was hearing not only from Haig but also from the British Cabinet, and he sent three French divisions to the aid of his allies.

Miraculously the British line still held but the losses were appalling and the troops were reaching the limits of their endurance. Some divisions had been reduced to a third of their proper strength; the only replacements they were receiving were youths of 18 and returning wounded. The Germans launched the last great drive of their spring offensive on 24 April. Again the British weathered the storm and the fighting only ebbed to a close because the German Army had exhausted itself and Ludendorff had reluctantly decided to reorganize and rest his wearied divisions before he could resume his attack. The BEF had suffered some 300,000 casualties since their retreat began. Mercifully for them they were given almost the whole of May to recover from the terrible mauling to which they had been subjected.

On 17 April, while the battle for the Channel ports was surging to a climax, the House of Commons held what was to be its last debate of the war on executions in the field. The discussion, which was notable for the restrained sincerity of the speakers, took place during the Committee stage of the Army (Annual) Bill.[8] The matter was first raised by the MP for Somerset, Mr King, who said that courts martial for desertion were causing a great deal of interest in the country and arousing a considerable amount of public disquiet. Thousands of anxious parents now had young sons who had been taken straight from civil life and after a very short period of training had been sent to France 'and put in circumstances of terror and horror and strain such as soldiers have never before undergone'. He admitted that he would have liked to press for the abolition of the death penalty for offences of cowardice and desertion, but he realized that this rectification would be very difficult to bring about at the present time. However, he urged the government to introduce a number of modifications to the court martial procedure which would alleviate unnecessary hardship, coupled with a suspicion of injustice, and would inspire greater confidence in the fairness of the trials. Mr King was followed by nine other members, five of whom were commissioned officers, all supporting his contentions and all stressing the fact that the established military law had not been fashioned for an army of citizen-soldiers. The principal reforms for which they called were that the accused should be informed of his sentence at the conclusion of the trial rather than being left in suspense until it had been confirmed, that an officer with legal training should be available to represent every soldier charged with a serious offence, and that the president of a court martial should whenever possible be a person with previous experience of evaluating evidence.

The Under-Secretary for War then intervened to say that he appreciated the anxiety which was being felt with regard to military executions 'not only in the Service, but in every family in the Kingdom'. He was quite satisfied that soldiers in France always received a meticulously fair trial, but there was one important modification he was prepared to introduce immediately. He had always regarded it as strange, he went on, that when a court martial had convicted a prisoner of a capital offence they should not be able to disclose their sentence to him. The regulations would be altered so that in future if the accused had been sentenced to death he would be informed of the fact there and then and he would also be told if he was being recommended to mercy. The oath taken by the members of a court martial, by which they swore not to divulge the sentence until it had been confirmed, would be amended accordingly.

The method in which this new procedure was operated was explained in the House of Commons in 1920 by Major Lowther, a Member with extensive experience of wartime courts martial in France.[9] The prisoner had been handed 'a secret envelope' by the president of the court, said Major Lowther, which informed him that he had been sentenced to death and reminded him that such sentence was liable to revision by higher authority.[10]

A total of nine soldiers were sentenced to death and shot on the

Western Front during the months of April and May; seven of them had been convicted of desertion and two of murder. It is noticeable that four of the deserters had been previously court-martialled for the same offence and another two were being tried for more than one desertion. Further, that there was now far more likelihood of a medical opinion being sought if the accused man had made any suggestion that he was suffering from mental instability. A 22-year-old Scottish private, who pleaded guilty to deserting four times between October 1917 and January 1918, told the court that his mother and his brother had died in lunatic asylums and he himself had been confined in one for nine years during his childhood. After his court martial he was examined by a medical board, and although they could find nothing wrong with him they declined to pronounce him responsible for his actions until they had received a report from the mental institution at which he claimed to have been a patient. Enquiries were made there but no trace of his name could be found among the records and he was shot at the end of May.

There was still a danger that if a deserter did not directly or indirectly affirm that he had been suffering from some neurasthenic disorder at the time of his offence such a possibility would never be investigated. A Londoner of 30, a married man with two young children, was a case in point. He had volunteered in August 1914 and had served at Gallipoli. He had joined the BEF in March 1916 and, according to two sergeants who gave evidence at his trial, he achieved a considerable reputation for his bravery in action. At the beginning of 1918, his character had seemed to change and one of them said he had appeared to be labouring under a perpetual sense of grievance. He deserted in April and again in May but on both occasions he was apprehended after only a few days' absence. He told the court he was unhappy in the battalion and hinted vaguely that he had troubles with his family. He was sentenced to death and shot without being medically or mentally examined. Another soldier on whom a neurological report might have been desirable was a regular corporal in a Scottish regiment, also aged 30. He had served in France since November 1914 and had been slightly wounded on two occasions during the first two years of the war. He deserted in August 1916 and received a suspended sentence of imprisonment. Having returned to his battalion he soon became an NCO. He deserted again in the spring of 1917 and lived behind the line until he was arrested by the French police the following September. While he was awaiting court martial in October he broke out of his regimental guardroom and remained at liberty for four months. The court's recommendation to mercy, because of his previous service, was ignored by the confirming authorities and he was executed on 11 May. It was never even considered that many months in the front line might have a deleterious effect on this man's nervous system.

Three of the men who were executed during April and May had been unable to put forward any mitigating circumstances for their offences. A Scottish private aged 25, who had enlisted as a volunteer early in 1915, had become a persistent deserter and was described as having a very bad army character. A man of 22 from Lancashire, a conscript in 1916, had deserted from the line in April 1918 because, as he told the court, he was 'fed up with the war'. And a regular in a Manchester regiment, who was also 22 and had absented himself from the front at much the same time, had already been sentenced to death for desertion the previous October.

In spite of Mr Macpherson's assurances to the House of Commons a private soldier who was court-martialled for desertion on 26 April 1918 and was executed the following month had not been represented at his trial. Probably he would have had no defence to the charge; nevertheless, a disturbing feature of the case was that the prisoner neither cross-examined the prosecution witnesses nor made any statement on his own behalf. It should perhaps be mentioned that every soldier who was put to death in this period had an experienced Court Martial Officer on the court which tried him. Also, that all the executed men seem to have been over the age of 22.

The two murders for which the death penalty was inflicted took place within a few days of each other. They are of interest not only because of their similarity, but because they were both so blatant and so pointless that a doubt must arise as to the mental balance of the soldiers who committed them. Private S was a Welshman of 38. Before the war he had served for 12 years in the Navy and he enlisted in an infantry regiment in October 1914. He had been in France continuously since the end of 1914, except for a couple of brief periods at home recovering from wounds which he had received at Loos and at Passchendaele. On the morning of 13 April, when his battalion was in the reserve line trenches, he slipped away on an illicit leave of absence. Immediately he returned he was placed under close arrest by his platoon sergeant. Private S, who was carrying a loaded rifle at the time, took aim at the sergeant and shot him in the neck, killing him instantly. He said in his defence that he was drunk at the time and had no recollection of the incident. He added that he and the sergeant had been as friendly as two brothers. The court had recommended S to mercy on account of his previous good character.

Sapper B was serving in a Field Company of the Royal Engineers. He was a man of 29 who had enlisted in January 1915 and had been with the BEF since December 1915. On 17 April the company was in a reserve position and B's section was paraded to have their rifles and emergency rations inspected by a lieutenant. The officer ordered B to fall out and put on his puttees. B went away but returned almost immediately and shot the officer through the body from a distance of a few feet. Death was instantaneous. B denied having fired deliberately and said he had no ill-feelings towards the lieutenant.

Notes

1. House of Commons, oral answers, 16 January 1918.
2. House of Commons, oral answers, 19 February 1918.
3. House of Commons, Army Estimates, 19 February 1918.
4. House of Commons, Army Estimates, Committee stage, 20 February 1918.
5. House of Commons, oral answers, 6 March 1918.
6. House of Commons, Consolidated Fund Bill, Third Reading, 14 March 1918.
7. Arthur Behrend, *As From Kemmel Hill.*
8. House of Commons, Army (Annual) Bill, Committee stage, 17 April 1918.
9. House of Commons, Army and Air Force (Annual) Bill, Committee stage, 13 April 1920.
10. This procedure was officially authorized by ACI 570, dated 22 May 1918.

17

THE FAR-FLUNG BATTLE LINE

THE ALLIED TASK force had landed at Salonika in October 1915 to prevent the Serbian Army, then retreating in disorder, from being surrounded and destroyed by the victorious Bulgarians. Though this objective was accomplished within a few months, French and British troops remained on the Macedonian Front until the end of the war. From Britain's point of view the campaign was very much a subsidiary operation and the size of her contingent there was never more than five divisions.

During the autumn of 1915 an ill-equipped British expedition struck northwards from Salonika into the barren rugged hills of Serbia. At first they encountered few Bulgarian soldiers but they suffered greatly from cold and exposure, nearly 2,000 officers and men having to be sent back with frostbite. Towards the end of November they came up against a Bulgarian army which outnumbered them by five to one, and owing to the odds and the worsening weather they were forced to withdraw and to take refuge across the frontier of neutral Greece. The French had fared no better, but at least the Allied operations had enabled the remnants of the Serbian Army to escape to the Adriatic coast. It was decided at this stage to concentrate all the available British, French, Italian and Serbian formations around the perimeter of Salonika, both to deny the port as a possible base for German submarines and to preserve a continuing threat against the soft underbelly of Europe.

The Allied defensive line was established in the middle of December, manned by a joint force of approximately 300,000 men. The winter passed quietly. In the spring of 1916 the French commanders wanted to attack but the British Staff preferred to hold the existing front and to prevent the bulk of the Bulgarian Army from taking part in operations elsewhere. Finally, the French view prevailed and it was decided to launch a combined offensive during the approaching summer.

The attack commenced in August and was mainly carried out by the French and Italians; the British Salonika Army, which was seriously afflicted with malaria, confining itself to small localized assaults and diversionary raids. During the fighting the Bulgarians attempted to outflank their opponents by invading the Eastern Macedonia province of Greece; in spite of this the Greek king was on the verge of entering the war on the side of the Central Powers.

The battle that summer and autumn, though conducted on a small scale, was considered to be entirely successful for the Allies. The British losses were small, their total casualties from August to December being a little in excess of 5,000. Indeed, the inroads on their strength made by sickness were vastly greater than those attributable to enemy action.

Throughout the winter of 1916–17 French Ministers were trying to persuade the British War Cabinet to send substantial reinforcements to Salonika for a new offensive during the following spring or summer. Their arguments fell on deaf ears. Lloyd George and his colleagues, who had just come to power, were opposed to committing any new troops other than drafts to keep up the existing establishment. In this they were supported by the General Staff.

The only main Allied attack during 1917 took place early in May and was repulsed without undue difficulty by the Bulgarians. The British Salonika Army was then considerably weakened by the removal to Egypt of a part of its infantry, cavalry and artillery formations. This finally relegated the campaign in Macedonia to a level of comparative unimportance in the overall Franco-British war strategy. The operations for the rest of the year were of a minor character and the armies took up their winter positions early in October.

By the beginning of 1918 the initiative had passed decidedly to the Bulgarians. During the great German offensive on the Western Front in March and April 12 battalions were withdrawn from the four British divisions remaining in Macedonia and sent to France. It was decided not to transfer the whole of the Salonika Army, partly because of French opposition and partly because it was known to be riddled with malaria.

The emasculated British formations played their part in the closing battles of the Macedonian campaign during August and September 1918, when the Bulgarian Armies were routed and driven back to their own frontier.

Three British soldiers were shot for desertion on the Macedonian front. The first, Private B, had enlisted as a volunteer in a well-known Scottish regiment in September 1914. After serving in France for 18 months he was sent with a draft to Salonika in the spring of 1917. He joined a division which was waiting to sail for Egypt, but on 6 May his battalion were suddenly warned for duty in the forward trenches in Macedonia. Before they moved out of Salonika B went absent and was arrested next day by a Military Policeman in a back street of the town. He was court-martialled on 20 May and it is not clear if he was represented; apparently he offered no defence to the charge and no plea in mitigation was made either by him or on his behalf. Although B does not seem to have been in any previous trouble during his entire army service his brigade commander, in recommending that the death penalty should be carried out, commented that he was plainly a shirker, a coward and a man of criminal character. B was executed on 1 June.

Sergeant A was charged with deserting two days later than Private B. He was another Scot but was serving in a different regiment and in a different division from B. A's battalion was going to take part in a dawn attack on the Bulgarian trenches on 9 May. They had assembled in a wood behind the British line during the previous night and most of the men had gone to sleep. A lance-corporal in Sergeant A's platoon had woken up to find that it was already morning and the rest of the battalion had moved off. Then he had noticed A sitting beside him, wide awake. He had suggested they should try to find the others but A had replied that it would be silly to do so. The lance-corporal had gone off by himself and A was not seen again until he reported back to his company the following evening at ten o'clock. He said at his court martial that he had been fast asleep when the battalion had left the wood and he had searched for them unsuccessfully for some time in the morning. Sergeant A was also a volunteer from September 1914. He had been wounded twice on the Western Front and had been transferred to Salonika in the summer of 1916. His court martial did not take place until 28 June and he was shot on 8 July.

The third capital desertion occurred during the final Allied offensive on the Macedonian front in 1918. Private Y, who came from Worcestershire, had been conscripted in May 1917 at the age of 20. After six months' training he was sent to Salonika, arriving there in January 1918. A month later he was court-martialled for stealing and absence without leave; his sentence of two years' imprisonment with hard labour had been suspended the following July and he had been posted to a battalion in the line. On 3 September, when his company was in a reserve position, they were heavily shelled by the Bulgarians. They suffered a number of casualties and Y, who had never been in action before, had his dugout completely destroyed. That evening he had turned up at a YMCA tent in the rear where he told another private that his platoon had almost been wiped out and the survivors had been sent back to rest. He was immediately offered accommodation by the YMCA staff. Two days later he was arrested as a deserter. Y's defence was that during the shelling he had carried back a badly wounded man to the regimental aid post and he had been so upset he had been unable to return to his company. In his plea in mitigation he said that he was the only child of a widowed mother whom he had not seen since 1915.

The brigadier had had no hesitation in recommending that the death sentence should be confirmed. As they were on the eve of active operations, he said, there was a danger that Y's behaviour might contaminate other soldiers. Y was executed on 16 September, 25 days before the Armistice.

Mesopotamia, the modern state of Iraq, had been part of the Ottoman Empire since the seventeenth century, and when Turkey entered the war on the side of the Central Powers it became imperative for Britain to safeguard her oil supplies from the area of the Persian Gulf. Consequently, in November 1914 a small force of British and Indian troops captured the Mesopotamian port of Basra, overcoming the garrison without difficulty, and settled down to await the arrival of reinforcements while the Turks took up a siege position around the outskirts of the town. There was little activity during the winter months apart from skirmishing and raids, but the following spring two columns set out from Basra to press separately into southern Mesopotamia, one of them following the line of the Euphrates and the other striking up the Tigris in the direction of Baghdad.

The south of Mesopotamia was a vast plain – arid, sandy and roadless. The terrain provided neither shade nor shelter and the temperatures in May, June and July ranged between 100° and 120°. Both columns were extremely short of transport and of medical facilities. As was to be expected, the ranks were soon decimated by sickness, the British formations suffering worst of all from sunstroke, fever, dysentery and para-typhoid. However, the advance continued, with the Turkish Army, despite the great superiority in numbers, choosing to withdraw rather than to engage in outright battle.

The Turks were supported by thousands of Arab irregulars for whom the impelling motives were killing and plunder. These men were merciless with the wounded. A historian of the Mesopotamian operations, A. J. Barker, has said:[1]

> Working like jackals the Arabs rapidly stripped the clothing from the bodies of the casualties lying in No Man's Land. Any sign of life was rewarded by a knock on the head, or a handful of sand thrust into the mouth and a tight grip to hold it shut until the individual concerned succumbed.

In September 1915 the Tigris column, under the command of General Townshend, captured the town of Kut al Amara, about 100 miles to the south-east of Baghdad and just under 200 miles from the main British strongpoint at Basra. Townshend was given permission to try to capture Baghdad, but in November he was heavily defeated by the Turks and was forced back to Kut where he was cut off with a garrison of 12,000 men, a high proportion of whom were either sick or wounded.

The siege of Kut is another of the small, heroic and agonizing incidents in British military history. Desperately short of food, water, ammunition and medical supplies the defenders held out for four months against overwhelming odds in the unfounded belief that they were going to be relieved. They were obliged to surrender on 29 April 1916. Although the Turkish commander had assured General Townshend that his men would be accorded the respect and humanity due to prisoners of war, in the event they were treated by their captors with scarcely-conceivable brutality.

After the fall of Kut the British War Cabinet decided that the Mesopotamian Expeditionary Force, then numbering 150,000 men, must confine itself to a purely defensive role for the remainder of the war. General Sir Stanley Maude, who had just taken over as Army Commander, had other ideas and immediately began to prepare for a winter offensive. Throughout the summer and autumn of 1916 supplies of equipment, guns and ammunition poured into Basra. At the same time Maude carried out a complete reorganization in the field, paying particular attention to the health and the wellbeing of his troops. The result inevitably was a considerable improvement in efficiency and morale. Then, in early December, the British offensive began just after the opening of the rainy season.

During the next three months Maude's army gained a complete mastery over their Turkish and Arab opponents who were gradually pushed back closer and closer to Baghdad. The War Cabinet viewed the success of these operations with unenthusiastic satisfaction, apprehensive that there would be another setback reminiscent of the surrender of Kut. At the end of February during a lull in the offensive Maude asked permission to make 'a further advance against a beaten enemy who could only reach Baghdad as a disorganized mob'. He was told, with some reluctance, that the future conduct of the campaign would be left to his own discretion. On 8 March 1917 the British forces resumed their attack and three days later they captured Baghdad.

The summer of 1917 in Mesopotamia was the hottest in living memory and very little fighting took place. General Maude died of cholera in November at a time when he was planning a new offensive against the demoralized remnants of the Turkish Army to the north of Baghdad. However, by that time the shortage of manpower on the Western Front was becoming acute and the general policy of the War Office was to withdraw as many formations as possible from the secondary theatres of operations. As a result of this the British Army in Mesopotamia was so reduced in size that it shrank to little more than a holding force; and so it remained until an armistice was concluded with Turkey on 1 November 1918.

The battles in Mesopotamia, says A. J. Barker, were an excellent illustration of the British ability to 'muddle through' to eventual victory.[2] In summarizing the campaign, Liddell Hart has written:[3]

> Although its origin was sound its development was another example of 'drift' due to the inherent faultiness of Britain's machinery for the conduct of war.

Four sentences of death were carried out, all in 1917, on British soldiers serving with the Mesopotamian Expeditionary Force. The first three of the executed men were all members of the same battalion of a North Country regiment.

Private J, who was 40 – normally about the top age for service in the front line – had volunteered for the infantry within a month of the outbreak of war. He was court-martialled for desertion on 30 January 1917. According to the prosecution evidence J had gone absent on 21 January, leaving his rifle, his equipment and his kit in a dugout. Then, without obtaining a sick-report from his regimental medical officer, he had presented himself at a field ambulance unit, complaining of sore feet. He was examined, but as he appeared to have nothing wrong with him he was ordered to return to duty on the following morning. He had failed to do so. The court, which consisted of a lieutenant-colonel, a major and a captain, had wrongly allowed the prosecuting officer to include in his case a written statement by the Post Commander at Imam, a small town on one of the few railway tracks in Mesopotamia, to the effect that J had reported to his office on the afternoon of 23 January and asked for a rail pass to Sheik Sa'ad, approximately 100 miles away towards the Persian border. A telegram had been sent to J's battalion and it was discovered that he was an absentee. These vital facts would have been perfectly admissible if they had been given under oath by a witness, but it was highly improper to accept them in documentary form. J had pleaded 'not guilty' to the charge. He denied that he had intended to desert and said he had been feeling unwell for several days before he went absent.

The record of the court martial proceedings was examined in due course by the judge-advocate attached to the Mesopotamian force who pointed out in a memorandum to the Commander-in-Chief that J had been convicted on certain inadmissible evidence. The court must have reached the conclusion that J had formed the necessary intention to desert, he wrote; but in doing so it was obvious that they had been strongly influenced by a document they never should have seen.

Somewhat surprisingly, the judge-advocate went on to say that there was sufficient legal evidence, quite apart from the wrongly-admitted statement, to support a finding of 'Guilty'.

The Commander-in-Chief had been faced with two possible alternatives. He could have overlooked the serious impropriety which had occurred at the trial, or he could have annulled the entire proceedings. He chose to adopt the former course and J was shot on 21 February.

The next two men to be put to death in the Mesopotamian Expeditionary Force were the only British soldiers in the war who were executed for sleeping on their posts. Private B and Private D belonged to the same platoon and both committed their offences on 6 February 1917. Their courts martial were held separately on successive days but the evidence against each of them was practically identical. A sergeant had taken them out in the early hours of the morning and posted them as sentries in a forward part of the firing line, their tour of duty being supposed to last for two hours. A short while later the sergeant and a lieutenant, on a routine visit to platoon positions, had found both men sitting side-by-side in their trench, sound asleep with the rifles lying beside them. They were immediately woken up and placed under close arrest.

No time was lost in convening the courts martial. In fact, Private B was tried later that same day. He stated in his defence that he had been tired and run down, but had made up his mind to stick it out rather than reporting sick. On the previous night he had also been suffering from severe indigestion. After the court had decided to convict, the adjutant told them that B, whose age was not mentioned, had a good character and had done excellent work with the battalion. Private D, at his trial on the following day, said that he had felt exhausted even before the commencement of his tour of sentry duty and he had done his best to keep awake. According to the adjutant he too was a man with a clean record who had served the battalion well. He had joined up as a volunteer in August 1914 when he was 19 years old and had been wounded in Gallipoli.

B and D were sentenced to death without being recommended to mercy. Their commanding officer, in his comments, spoke very highly of their soldierly qualities, but the brigadier considered that despite their excellent characters there were no mitigating circumstances for their conduct. For his part, the divisional commander suggested that the sentences should be commuted to terms of five years' penal servitude which should then be suspended. At this stage both men must have had a reasonable chance of escaping with their lives. However, the corps commander recommended forcibly that no clemency should be shown to either of them. Their behaviour, he said, had shown an utter lack of appreciation of their duty as sentries and of their responsibility for the lives of their comrades. This opinion was apparently shared by the Commander-in-Chief as he confirmed the sentences on 16 February, exactly ten days after the two men had been discovered asleep at their posts.

The last soldier to be executed in Mesopotamia was a Scot who had deserted on 5 February 1917 and had managed to remain at large for four months. He explained to the court that he had won some money playing cards and had only intended to stay absent until he had spent it. He was shot on 25 July.

It was revealed in 1922 that apart from the death sentences carried out by the Army in the principal theatres of British ground operations – the Western Front, Gallipoli, Salonika and Mesopotamia – executions of military personnel 'including camp followers, Native labourers and Chinese coolies, subject to the Army Act', took place between August 1914 and March 1920, in such places as East Africa, Constantinople, Egypt, Italy and Palestine.[4]

Private C, the only British soldier to be executed in Egypt during the war years, was tried by court martial in August 1917, on two charges of striking a superior officer. At the time he committed these offences C was a prisoner in a military detention camp at Kantara, a town some 20 miles south of Port Said on the Suez Canal, where he was serving a sentence of one year's hard labour for 'persistently marching improperly'.

In the late afternoon on 26 July a captain had been riding his horse past the detention camp when C and five other prisoners standing in the compound started to call out jeering remarks and to bang on biscuit tins. The captain dismounted, found a sergeant-major on the staff of the camp, and ordered him to bring the men under control. Taking a sergeant and a corporal with him the sergeant-major entered the compound. The prisoners were aggressive at first and refused to hand over their tins, but they were eventually persuaded to do so. Just as the sergeant-major was preparing to march them to the punishment cells C picked up a large piece of wood and hit the sergeant in the face with it, knocking him to the ground. The corporal closed with C who drew a razor from his pocket and started to lash out with it. After a brief fight the corporal, now bleeding profusely, managed to over-power C and to sit on him until help arrived. C was then tied up and locked in a punishment cell, while the corporal was taken to a hospital where he was found to have two deep cuts, one in his stomach and the other in his left forearm.

Private C neither denied the evidence given by the prosecution witnesses nor offered any defence to the charges. He was a man who had numerous entries on his conduct sheet, including a finding earlier that year that he had used insolent language to an NCO. He was sentenced to death and was shot on 11 August 1917.

The third and the last person in the British Army to be executed for mutiny during the war was a member of the Egyptian Labour Corps. During 1917, to offset the shortage of manpower, large numbers of Chinese and Egyptians were brought to France for employment on unskilled manual work behind the lines. These men came under the overall control of the Commander-in-Chief and were subject to military law.

The Egyptian Labour Corps were stationed in a large camp at Marseilles where they were commanded by British officers and by their own NCOs, who held ordinary army ranks. In the summer of 1917 there was serious unrest in the camp because a number of the Egyptians believed they had only come to France for seven months, whereas, in reality, they had signed on for the duration of the war. Their discontent was magnified in September by the circulation of a rumour that when one of their leaders had laid their grievances before the Commandant he had been told that they were all going to be kept in France permanently, and that they would be severely beaten if they refused to work.

On 16 September 500 of the Egyptians broke away without permission from an evening parade and returned to their tents. It was noticed that Y, a man with a reputation for disobedience, was urging on the others and he was heard to shout that they intended 'to get the officers'. A short while later a party of about 150 mutineers marched through the camp brandishing sticks, with Y at their head. A young second-lieutenant who went forward to remonstrate with them was set upon by Y and knocked down unconscious. He was rescued by members of the camp staff and removed to hospital.

As the mutineers became more menacing the officers and NCOs armed themselves and concentrated in one area of the camp. Y, now holding a rifle with bayonet fixed, challenged them repeatedly to come out and fight and threatened them that they were all going to be killed. The mutiny ended when three Egyptian NCOs attacked Y and disarmed him.

Y was court-martialled for mutiny at Marseilles on 28 September. Although he pleaded 'Not Guilty' to the charge he did not deny his part in the disorders. His record did not assist him as he had received 15 lashes for insubordination the previous April, and 10 lashes for causing a riot in the camp the previous May. The sentence of death which was passed upon him was carried out at dawn on 10 October.

There are soldiers in every army who, when they are stationed in a distant land, are tempted to behave in a manner which is entirely different from their behaviour nearer home. Due, perhaps, to the remoteness of things familiar and to the shielding anonymity of uniform the conventional restraints are suddenly lifted from them.

Private M, a youth of 18 who had borne an excellent character during the eleven months he had served with his regiment, was executed in Palestine on 22 December 1917 for murdering an Arab. M had happened to pass a well as the Arab and his young wife were drawing water from it. The girl's movements had awakened M's desires and he had asked her bluntly to have sex with him. When she angrily refused he had thrown her to the ground intending to rape her, but her husband had come to her assistance. M had shot the man twice with his rifle and had run off leaving him dying from his injuries.

The girl described her assailant to the military police and the next day the whole of M's battalion took part in a massive identification parade. She was led down the ranks, looking carefully at all the men. When she came to M, and before she had identified him, he panicked and warned her not to say anything. He was promptly arrested and taken to the guardroom where he made a written confession to the murder, attributing his conduct to the fact that he had had too much to drink.

Notes

1. A. J. Barker, *The Neglected War, Mesopotamia, 1914–1918*.
2. A. J. Barker, op. cit.
3. B. H. Liddell Hart, *History of the First World War*.
4. Statistics of the Military Effort of the British Empire During the Great War, Part XXIII – Discipline.

18

THE LAST OFFENSIVE

D URING THE LULL in the fighting on the Western Front neither the French nor the British General Staffs knew where the next German blow would fall. They only knew that a massive new onslaught was pending.

On 27 May the Germans opened their attack along a 24-mile front against the French Sixth Army, which had four British divisions attached to it. Everywhere the defenders gave ground and by the end of the day a large and dangerous salient had been driven into the Allied line. The French were now convinced that the German High Command had turned its attention from the Channel ports and that the main objective was Paris; actually Ludendorff's plan was to draw off the Allied reserves from Flanders before delivering the *coup de grâce* to the BEF.

Georges Clemenceau, the French Prime Minister, visited the Sixth Army front the following morning and he was given the dispiriting information by the commanders in the field that the German advance, methodical and relentless, was still sweeping forward in spite of all their efforts to bring it to a halt. By 30 May the French forces had fallen back to the line of the Marne. With the enemy nearing Paris the morale of the people in the capital sank to a low ebb and increasing demands were made for Pétain to be replaced.

General Pershing consented to a proposal from Foch that five of the American divisions in training under the British should be sent immediately to the threatened French sector, but Haig resisted all suggestions that additional formations from the BEF should be temporarily transferred to Pétain's command. The British Minister for War explained to Clemenceau that the Germans had concentrated substantial reserves opposite to BEF positions and they were already within striking distance of the Channel ports.

Once again the Allies were saved by the exhaustion of the German Army. At a moment when the French were on the verge of collapse the fury of the assault suddenly abated. On 6 June the immediate crisis ended abruptly when the Germans paused to rest and reorganize.

During the rest of June the fighting was only of a minor character. In accordance with the directions issued by Foch both the French and British Armies were adopting an increasingly offensive attitude,

engaging in continual raids and localized attacks. Haig was sure that
the next German offensive would be directed at the Channel ports.
Pétain felt equally certain it would be aimed at Paris; he appealed to
Foch for 'a more complete participation of the British Army in the
burdens which have been weighing on my Armies for three and a half
months', and requested that more British divisions should be attached
to his left flank. This proposal was opposed by Haig as being premature until the intentions of the German High Command had become
more clear.

In the event the Germans launched a further attack on the French on
15 July. Pétain renewed his pleas for British support but Haig was not
yet convinced that the main onslaught was not going to fall upon the
BEF. This time the French line held. On 17 July, aided by the
Americans, they made a surprise and successful counter-attack and the
Germans, unexpectedly finding themselves on the defensive, were
driven back from their advance positions on the Marne.

The sudden reversal in the fortunes of battle had not been foreseen
by the Allied commanders; indeed, Foch had recently asked Pershing
if it would be possible for 80 American divisions to be ready for a big
offensive in the spring of 1919. Foch, however, was too adept a general not to seize the initiative which had been so fortuitously passed
into his hands and he instantly prepared for a vigorous thrust by the
Allied armies along the entire front. In making this decision he was
encouraged by intelligence reports that the latest batches of German
prisoners were showing signs of warweariness and were admitting to
a disinclination to continue the struggle any longer. They had been
told, they said, that their most recent attack was the last they would be
called upon to make, and would culminate in a victorious peace.

Foch started his counter-offensive an hour before dawn on 8 August
with British, French, American, Australian and Canadian infantry
pouring across no-man's-land, supported by tanks and enshrouded by
a thick ground mist. The Germans were taken completely unawares.
Their front line yielded nearly everywhere and the attacking troops
pushed forward to capture their second and third objectives. It was a
day of unmitigated success for the Allies. 'As the sun set on the 8th
August on the battlefield,' says the German Official Monograph,[1] 'the
greatest defeat which the German Army had suffered since the beginning of the war was an accomplished fact.'

The attack was continued for four more days against mounting
German opposition. Foch, sensing that victory was at hand, kept on
urging his subordinate commanders to greater efforts. Even though
the advance came to a temporary halt on 12 August there was a general
realization that the tide of battle had turned. According to the Official
History:

For the first time both the German High Command and the men in the ranks admitted a defeat, and that the greatest defeat of the war. And they never in the coming days were able to shake off the impressions of the inevitableness of the final collapse.

About this time the Kaiser remarked to General Ludendorff, 'We have nearly reached the limit of our powers of resistance. The war must be ended.'[2]

One of the more pleasing aspects of the closing battles on the Western Front was the ever-strengthening bond of comradeship between the French and British soldiers in the line. The liaison between the staff officers of the two nations was not so satisfactory; each of their armies knew so little about the organization and methods of the other that the planning or the conduct of co-ordinated operations was difficult. The ranks of the BEF were now filled with half-trained boys and inexperienced NCOs. The German Army, too, ravaged by four years of attrition, was forced to find its replacements from the very young, the unfit and the middle-aged. It was as though an unobtrusive host of understudies had taken up position and was silently awaiting the final scene.

Towards the end of August the Allied attack was resumed. The Germans, although increasingly demoralized and surrendering in large numbers, were still fighting back and still inflicting heavy casualties as they retired from position to position across the war-scarred plains of Flanders. Throughout September the slow retreat continued with the BEF advancing an average distance of 25 miles a day on a frontage of about 40 miles until, at the end of the month, their way was barred by the heavily-fortified Hindenburg Line. From 8 August until 26 September they had suffered over 180,000 casualties.

The Hindenburg Line was broken by the Allies at the beginning of October and the wearied German Army commenced another withdrawal. One of their generals reported in a confidential letter that the power of resistance of his men was diminishing daily. 'They surrender in hordes, whenever the enemy attacks,' he wrote, 'and thousands of plunderers infest the districts round the bases. We have no prepared lines, and no more can be dug.'

After Hindenburg had informed the Kaiser that Germany's military resources were at an end and that the situation of his army left no alternative but to seek an immediate armistice, the German High Command only prolonged the struggle in order to obtain the most favourable peace terms possible from the Allies.

With the portents of victory becoming more and more evident the discipline of the BEF was in no way relaxed. Between 1 July 1918 and the day of the Armistice 25 executions were carried out on the Western Front, 19 for desertion and six for murder. Five of the condemned murderers were Chinese coolies, three of whom had killed other coolies in the course of private quarrels, and the remaining two had killed a French woman whilst committing a robbery at an estaminet.

The first of the condemned coolies was executed on 23 July. A few days previously the Second Army had issued detailed instructions to his company commander in the Chinese Labour Corps. Four of his friends would be allowed to visit him on the evening before his death and the same four would form the burial-party after he was shot. At 7 p.m. he would be removed by ambulance to the place of his execution where arrangements would be made for his accommodation for the night. 'The question of any extra rations for the condemned man on the evening of the 22nd instant," the order concluded, 'will be arranged by his own unit.' This final injunction would seem to be in accordance with the British Army's practice in bygone generations. Francis Grose has said that a prisoner was entitled to a special meal before his execution, and he cited the contingency bill of a provost-marshal in 1691 which included an item for expenses incurred in providing 'extraordinary treats after the sentence of death' for two soldiers about to be hanged for rape.[3]

A number of senior officers felt apprehensive about the quality of the most recent reinforcements to the BEF, and they were convinced it was only by exercising the most rigorous control that some of these recruits would be coerced into doing their duty. In recommending the execution of a 21-year-old Irish private, who had been in action for the past three years, his brigade commander said, 'An example is needed as there are many men in the battalion who have never wished to be soldiers, but who were conscripted and who do not understand the seriousness of desertion.' Sir Henry Horne, Commander of the First Army, expressed the same view in July when upholding the death sentence passed on a 23-year-old deserter from Middlesex. 'I am of opinion', he wrote, 'that in the interests of the service, in view of the number of young soldiers now serving in the battalion, the sentence should be put into execution.'

The deserters from the BEF, however, were not always the newest recruits. During the later stages of the war an increasing number of soldiers with considerable experience of active service were failing to return to their units at the end of periods of home leave. It was especially distressing for a man who had an unsolved domestic problem to go back to duty in the front-line trenches and to the prospect of being killed or wounded in the none-too-distant future. On 12 July 1918 General Horne drew the attention of the Commander-in-Chief to the fact that 'the offence of desertion whilst on leave is a common one at the present time'.

Private B, whose age was not given at his court martial but who would seem to have been in his early twenties, had lived in Sunderland with his parents and his younger brother until January 1915, when he enlisted as a volunteer in an infantry regiment. His brother had also joined the Army for the duration of the war. B had been sent to Gallipoli towards the end of 1915, and was returned to England suffering from dysentery after only three months in action. He was posted to the BEF in December 1916, leaving his 18-year-old girl-friend eight months' pregnant with his child. After the birth of their baby, and in the face of resolute opposition from B's parents, the couple agreed to get married at the first possible opportunity.

B had had to wait until January 1918 before he was granted leave. As soon as he arrived back in Sunderland he had an emotional scene with his mother during which she warned him that if he persisted in defying the wishes of his parents he would be cutting himself off from both of them irrevocably. In spite of this the marriage took place as arranged. B had then embarked on a desperate and unsuccessful attempt to find a job for his wife and a place for her to live with the child when he went back to France. He had failed to obtain either. He said at his trial that he had applied for an extension of his leave on compassionate grounds but had received no reply. This was neither confirmed nor denied by the prosecution.

According to B, his wife was friendless and had no close relations except a brother who was serving on the Western Front. Rather than leaving her homeless and alone, he said, he had taken her with their child to Scotland where he had obtained work on a farm. The following June he had received a letter from his mother pleading for his help as his father had died and his younger brother had just been killed in action. A few days later he was arrested as a deserter by the Scottish police and was taken back to France. At his court martial on 5 July he was condemned to death and although the mitigating factors were fully disclosed he was not recommended to mercy. He had been in no trouble since joining the Army but he was described as a bad soldier, his commanding officer adding the damning comment, 'His NCOs describe him as a coward.' B was shot at dawn on 19 July.

Private G had deserted when he should have returned to France at the end of his leave in February 1918. He was a 27-year-old married man from Glasgow who had enlisted as a volunteer in a Scottish regiment in 1915 and had been in France since January 1917. When he returned home after serving for a year on the Western Front he had had a violent quarrel with his wife who had admitted to him that during his absence she had been going out habitually with another man. For the remainder of his leave, he said at his trial, he had been drinking heavily and there had been constant scenes. He had been too upset to return to France so he had decided to become an absentee, originally intending to give himself up as soon as he had sorted out his matrimonial problems. The longer he stayed away the more apprehensive he became of what would happen to him if he returned. Eventually he was arrested by the Glasgow police on 18 June, still living at his home and still dressed in uniform.

G was taken back to his battalion in France to await his court martial. In the middle of August they were in the front line preparing to attack and G, who was serving with his old company, was told that if he acquitted himself well it would probably result in a more lenient sentence. On the eve of the attack he again went absent and was detained by the Military Police two days later on the outskirts of a town in the rear. He was tried on two charges of desertion on 10 September. In his plea in mitigation he said he was worried to distraction about the preservation of his marriage, especially as his only two children had both died in their infancy. He was condemned to death on each of the charges. The sentences were confirmed and he was executed on 24 September.

One can imagine that when Haig was deciding whether or not to confirm a death sentence he was considerably influenced by the opinions regarding the condemned man's capabilities as a soldier which had been put forward by his colonel and his brigadier, the two reporting officers in the best position to ascertain the true facts. These comments were sometimes dispassionate and sometimes they were immoderate: sometimes they were even savage. In June 1918 the commanding officer of a Home Counties battalion wrote about a 23-year-old deserter, a volunteer from 1915, 'He is devoid of any soldierly qualities. . . . He is absolutely undependable and unreliable. In the face of any danger he could always be relied upon to run away.' The following month a brigadier reported on a 46-year-old American deserter, who had enlisted voluntarily in an Irish regiment during the summer of 1917, 'This is one of the worst characters in the army. He openly defies all authority and deliberately commits crime.' Also in July, a commanding officer in another Home Counties regiment described a private, convicted of desertion, in the following terms:

He is a useless soldier and a bad example to the battalion. No one can speak a good word for him as to his character from a fighting point of view and his conduct in action. His record shows him to be an incorrigible waster and the worst possible example to young soldiers.

A commanding officer in a Midland regiment was equally damnatory in his observations about a 26-year-old deserter, one of the earliest of the Kitchener volunteers. He wrote in August:

This man's company commander considers that he had a disturbing and very bad influence on the other men in his company. I am of the opinion that it is distinctly bad for discipline to have a man of such little value as a soldier and with such a disgraceful record moving about with men who are doing their duty.

All four of the soldiers upon whom these strictures were passed had their sentences confirmed and were executed. Although it is understandable that an officer in the line of battle should wish to rid himself of a man whose effect on those around him might be unsettling, or otherwise detrimental, the writers of such comments must have realized that they were virtually inscribing warrants of death. Admittedly, a number of the men who were shot for desertion during the last year of the war had very bad records, but their previous convictions were usually for military offences. The touchstone which decided whether they should live or die seemed very often to be the likelihood of their redeeming themselves as soldiers in the future; peacetime values, as such, were almost entirely disregarded.

In spite of the concern which had been voiced in the House of Commons, and the assurances given by the Under-Secretary of State for War, men who had previously been wounded in action were still being sentenced to death and shot, even during the closing phases of the campaign. It had happened once in September and twice in October. In none of these cases were the condemned soldiers examined by medical boards before they were executed.

Private B, a 28-year-old North Countryman, had enlisted within three months of the outbreak of war. He was wounded in 1916 after serving for a year on the Western Front. In 1917 for some reason he went to pieces. He was found guilty of absence without leave and desertion; finally he was sent home to England suffering from a self-inflicted wound. He deserted again when he was ordered back to France in 1918, but he was apprehended and posted to a battalion in the line. At the end of July he deserted from the support trenches and walked back to Calais where he was arrested. B was executed on 10 September.

Private K, a Londoner, had had a history somewhat similar to B's, but he was more explicit about the roots of his trouble. He had been an early volunteer and had been wounded in the leg on the Western Front during the spring of 1915. He returned to France in 1916 and during that year he was court-martialled three times, twice for disobedience and once for desertion. He deserted for a second time in April 1918 and stayed absent until the following August. At his trial in September he told the court that he had completely lost his nerve and could not stand the strain any longer; also, that he had not been home on leave for two and a half years and he was very worried about his widowed mother. K was executed on 6 October.

Private E, aged 28, was a married Scotsman who had enlisted as a volunteer in the autumn of 1915 and had served with the BEF since the beginning of 1916. He had had a bad record during his time in France, being convicted by court martial of desertion and of striking a superior officer, for both of which offences he had received suspended sentences of imprisonment. In February 1918 he was slightly wounded but was soon back to duty again. At the beginning of May E heard that his wife had been admitted to hospital to await an operation. Shortly afterwards he was placed in his battalion guardroom for some matter which was never carried any further. While he was being detained there his sister had sent him a registered letter, but he was told he could not receive it while he was a prisoner. Suspecting that the letter might contain information about his wife, E broke out of the guardroom, intending to make his way back to Scotland. He was arrested at Boulogne by the Military Police in the middle of June and admitted being an absentee. He was court-martialled on 20 September and was shot on 11 October.

The third and last British Army officer to be executed in the First World War was 2nd Lieutenant P who was tried by General Court Martial at Boulogne on 11 and 12 September 1918. In retrospect there is something puzzling about this case – something unexplained. The facts emerge in misty sequence, orderly and precise, but at the end the enigmatic quality still remains.

P was 28 at the time. Before the war he had been working as a trader in West Africa. He came back to England and volunteered for the infantry in the spring of 1915. Towards the end of the year he was sent to France as a private soldier and he was wounded twice on the Somme in 1916. In March 1917 he was sent home to attend an officer-training course. He was commissioned in a southern counties regiment in September 1917 and he returned to the Western Front as a platoon commander two months later. Nothing was said at his trial either in praise or in detriment of his capabilities as an officer.

On 26 March 1918, when P's battalion was in reserve near Ypres, he was sent forward in charge of a night working-party to repair a section of a front-line trench. As his detail was moving into position P told his sergeant that he had to return urgently to collect some papers. He had then gone off and had completely disappeared.

On five occasions during April and May a British Army officer answering the description of P had visited various banks in the neighbourhood of Calais and cashed cheques which were later found to be forged. By that time, of course, P's particulars had been circulated to the Military Police and the search for him was concentrated around the Channel ports.

Early in the evening on 3 July a sergeant and a corporal in the Military Foot Police were on patrol duty in Port de Boulogne, a small village near Calais, when they saw P coming down the street with a French girl. They approached him and told him he resembled an officer who was wanted for questioning. P gave them a false name but said that he had no papers on him to prove his identity. When P and the girl walked off the NCOs, who were far from satisfied, followed a short distance behind them. Outside a house on the fringe of the village P stopped and admitted to the police that he was, in fact, the officer for whom they were looking. He asked them if he might go into the house to have a cup of tea with the girl before he was arrested. The sergeant agreed and said that he and the corporal would wait outside until P was ready.

After about an hour and a quarter P came out of the house and told the NCOs that he would like a little more time to complete his arrangements. He then went back again. As it was growing dark the police separated, the sergeant taking up position in a yard at the back of the house and the corporal staying in the road beside the front gate. The French girl, who remains a shadowy figure throughout, gave evidence for the prosecution at P's court martial. She said that P was watching the movements of the police from a window and after telling her that if they did not leave he would fire at them he went out into the yard.

The corporal was the only prosecution witness who saw what happened next. He had heard a shot from the back of the house followed by the sergeant's voice calling out 'What's that?' He rushed round to the yard and saw P standing in front of the sergeant, pointing a revolver at him. P fired three times before the corporal could reach him and the sergeant collapsed on the ground with blood pouring from his mouth and nose. The corporal then turned and ran back to the road to summon assistance. The French girl had heard the shooting and had hurried out. She found the sergeant dying from wounds in the chest and P, who was bleeding in the area of the groin, still standing beside him with his revolver in his hand. He told her that he had not intended to kill the man. Before the corporal returned with other soldiers P and the girl had left the house and gone into hiding. After two days they had parted company and P had travelled from place to place until he was arrested by the French police at St Omer on 22 July.

At his court martial P pleaded 'Not Guilty' to desertion and 'Not

Guilty' to murder, but 'Guilty' to four charges relating to the forgery of cheques. The defending officer, a qualified barrister, made a successful application for the contested charges to be dealt with separately, and the trial for murder took place first. P did not dispute any of the prosecution evidence. He told the court that he had only meant to scare the sergeant as he had not wanted to be arrested on that particular evening. He had been holding the revolver in his pocket and it had gone off accidentally and shot him in the groin. He had then taken it out and it had gone off again. He did not account for the third and fourth bullets he had fired.

After P had been convicted of murder and sentenced to death the prosecution had not proceeded with the charge of desertion. He was executed at the end of September.

For most of October the German Army continued its slow, dispirited retreat along the whole of the Western Front. Short of men, guns, ammunition and supplies, and reaching the limits of human endurance, it was still managing to fight a desperate rearguard action. Bulgaria had already capitulated and in an Order of the Day on 5 October the Kaiser revealed to his armed forces that other of Germany's allies were negotiating for a cessation of hostilities.

On 25 October Foch paused to rest and regroup his weary armies which had been in action almost continuously since their victories during the previous August. During that time the BEF had suffered severely. The casualty returns of the British, Canadian, Australian and New Zealand divisions had reached a combined total of just under 300,000 officers and men.

The alliance of the Central Powers was fast disintegrating. An armistice was signed with Turkey on 30 October. The Austrians were withdrawing in disorder on the Italian front. Vienna and Budapest were in a state of revolution. At such a moment Ludendorff announced that military surrender was unacceptable to the German Army.

But the end was near. On 1 November the Allies resumed their offensive: the Germans their retreat. The advancing troops were now encountering less and less opposition. One German division refused to take up position in the line. Reinforcements from the Eastern Front staged a mutiny and had to be disarmed. Desertion and ill-discipline were rife. The German Navy was affected too. Ships were refusing to put to sea and the chief naval ports were adorned with a profusion of red flags.

General Gröner, who had replaced Ludendorff, urged the German government to seek an immediate armistice. 'We can hold out long enough for negotiations,' he said. 'If we are lucky the time might be longer; if we are unlucky, shorter.'

The last two British soldiers to be executed during the war were shot at dawn in different parts of France on 7 November, five days before hostilities were ended.

Private H was a single man aged 23. He had enlisted voluntarily in March 1915, but was discharged soon afterwards when he was found to be medically unfit. He was called up as a conscript in April 1916 and posted to a Yorkshire regiment. Probably H had not been a very satisfactory soldier as his conduct sheet showed numerous entries for offences of a minor character. He had deserted at the beginning of September 1918 when his battalion was preparing to carry out a night attack against an enemy-occupied village and was arrested the following morning in his regimental transport lines. He offered no defence and nothing was said on his behalf by way of mitigation of sentence.

Private J, also a single man, was nine years older than H, being 32 at the time of his death. He was a Londoner and claimed not only that his mother and father had both died in lunatic asylums, but that he himself had been afflicted with mental trouble in the past. J had been called up in July 1916 and was sent to France after four months' training. During the summer of 1917 he had received a two-year suspended prison sentence for absence without leave. He had then been out of trouble until he deserted at the end of September 1918. After a few days he was caught and was placed in his battalion guardroom to await court martial. He had escaped and again had only been at liberty for a few days before being recaptured. On 16 October he was tried on two charges of desertion. The reason he gave for committing the offences was that he had been habitually bullied by his sergeant-major and he felt himself to be despised by the other men in his company. The time had come, he said, when he could stand it no longer and his one thought had been to get away from everything. It had not been considered necessary to have H seen by a doctor before he was shot, as his brigadier had reported, without giving any details, that on a previous occasion he had been medically examined and found to be sane.

On 9 November Foch sent a message to Haig telling him that the Germans were still yielding ground along the whole front and urging that the Allied advance should be accelerated. Rumours of an impending armistice had spread amongst the troops but no official announcement was made on the progress of the negotiations, and the scale of operations continued undiminished. Early in the morning on 11 November orders were issued to all formations in the field that hostilities would cease at 11 a.m. The Official History describes the final scene:

> When 11 a.m. came the troops took the occasion in their usual matter-of fact way: there was no outburst of cheering, no wild scene of rejoicing. Those who could lay down to sleep. The others went quietly about their duties with a strange feeling that all danger was absent.

Private Fred Dixon's recollection was similar. On the previous day there had been talk in his battalion about an armistice but no one had really believed it. At dawn on 11 November they were marching up to the line and they met some gunners who told them the war was over. Presently they halted in a farmyard where their officer confirmed the news. Dixon says:[4] 'We showed no emotion whatsoever. We simply went into billets and lay down. I don't think we quite got it.'

Even from a distance in time of nearly three-quarters of a century the immensity of the carnage of the First World War is very difficult to conceive. The countries which comprised the British Empire alone suffered a total of 2,289,860 casualties, of whom no less than 996,230 officers and men were listed as killed in action, died of wounds, missing presumed dead, or died as prisoners of war. It was estimated that 704,803 of the dead had been serving in the British Army, 560,000 of them having perished on the Western Front.[5]

Notes

1. Quoted in the Official History.
2. Major Niemann, *Kaiser und Revolution*, quoted in the Official History of the campaign.
3. Francis Grose, *Military Antiquities*.
4. Imperial War Museum, oral history recordings, Western Front, 1914–1918, Private Fred Dixon.
5. All the figures quoted in his paragraph are taken from the Official History.

19

THE TRANSITION TO PEACE

A STATISTICAL RETURN of the sentences of death passed by courts martial from the outbreak of the First World War until the end of March 1920 was published by the War Office for the first time in 1922.[1] It showed that during the period covered 3,080 men had been condemned to death and 346 of them, 11.23 per cent, had been executed.[2]

The numbers shot for various offences were as follows:

Desertion	266 (including 2 officers)
Murder	37 (including 1 officer)
Cowardice	18
Quitting Post	7
Striking or Violence	6
Disobedience	5
Mutiny	3
Sleeping on Post	2
Casting away Arms	2

The theatres in which the executed men were serving when they had committed these offences were:[3]

France and Belgium	322
East Africa	5
Mesopotamia	4
Constantinople	4
Gallipoli	3
Salonika	3
Egypt	2
Italy	1
Palestine	1
Serbia	1

Those executed had been members of the following branches of the services:

Imperial Troops	291 (including 3 officers)
Overseas Contingents	31
Colonial Forces	5
Chinese and Coloured Labour Corps	14
Followers	5

Something must now be said of the policies of the other principal powers engaged in the fighting on the Western Front with regard to capital punishment for offences in the field.

Shooting by a firing squad was an authorized penalty in the French Army, but the exact details of military executions during the First World War are not available because under the present French regulations they cannot be disclosed until 100 years after they occurred. The figures which have now been released, however, show that 83 soldiers were condemned to death and executed between the outbreak of war and 3 March 1916, and that there were 50 executions between 16 April 1916 and 31 January 1918. These sentences were passed for the offences of abandonment of post before the enemy; refusal to obey an order; desertion in the face of the enemy; and insurrection.[4]

Capital punishment was also permitted by the military law of the United States of America. The death sentence could be passed for various offences including desertion, disobedience, misbehaviour before the enemy, sleeping on post, murder and rape. Ten executions were carried out in the American Expeditionary Force in France, all for murder or rape and none for a purely military offence.[5]

The German land forces during the First World War consisted of four separate armies serving under a unified command: the Royal Prussian Army, the Royal Bavarian Army, the Royal Wurtemberg Army and the Royal Saxon Army. Although they were all subject to a common military penal code each was responsible for the maintenance of its own discipline and the preservation of its own records. All the Prussian Army records were destroyed by fire during air raids on Berlin in 1943 and no information is at present available with regard to the whereabouts of the court martial records of the other armies.[6]

The Official Historian of the Australian Imperial Force in France has stated that the death penalty was applied more rarely in the German than in the British Army.[7] He has quoted Prince Rupprecht of Bavaria who wrote in his diary on 21 December 1917:

The administration of discipline by the English is very rigid. Whilst on our side there is known to me only a single case in which a soldier on account of aggravated refusal of duty in the face of the enemy was shot, I gather from a compilation of the British orders which have been found, that at least 67 English soldiers have been shot under martial law in the period between 27 October 1916 and 30 August 1917.

There can be little doubt of the opinion of the British military commanders that the existence of the death penalty was indispensable to the fighting efficiency of the Army. This was borne out by the repeated attempts which were made to persuade the Australian government to authorize the execution of deserters from the Australian Expeditionary Force in France.[8] Under the Australian Defence Act a sentence of death could only be passed by a court martial for the offences of mutiny, desertion to the enemy and certain forms of treachery. Even then the sentence could not be carried out unless it had been confirmed by the Governor-General. In July 1916 the Australian government declined a proposal from the War Office in London that its forces overseas should be subjected to the disciplinary provisions of the British Army Act.[9] The following December Haig reported to the War Office that the desertion rate in Australian divisions in France was 'assuming alarming proportions' and urged that the introduction by Australia of the death penalty for desertion was 'a matter of grave urgency'.

The Army Council informed the Australian government in February 1917 that the application of the Army Act to the Australian forces in France had now become a necessity for the discipline of the BEF as a whole. The request was again refused. In the summer of 1917 Haig complained that the increasing ill-discipline of the Australians might well infect the other troops under his command. If that occurred, he said, he could not accept responsibility for the serious consequences which might ensue. He undertook, however, that if the death penalty was sanctioned by the Australian government it would be used 'very sparingly' and only in cases of the most deliberate desertion where an example was badly needed.

According to the Australian Official War History the government in Sydney was well aware that the imposition of the death penalty upon men 'who had gone out voluntarily to fight at the other end of the world in a cause not primarily their own' would have been incompatible with the sense of justice of the Australian people. Also, it would have been bitterly resented in the lower ranks of the Australian forces in France, whose attitude was strengthened, says the Official History:

By the constant reading out, on parade, by an order throughout the British Army of reports of the infliction of the death penalty upon British soldiers – a ceremony which aroused in the Australians, officers and men, only a sullen sympathy and a fierce pride that their own people was strong enough to refuse this instrument to its rulers.

In the event, no Australian soldier was executed during the whole of the war. The death penalty was carried out on two occasions on men serving overseas in New Zealand divisions, one of whom had been convicted of desertion and one of mutiny.

It would be an oversimplification to attribute the draconian penal code of the British Army during the First World War simply to a lack of humanity on the part of its higher commanders. For many generations a tradition of brutal punishment had been considered a vital adjunct to the enforcement of military discipline and there had seemed no reason for a change of policy just because the Army now comprised a heterogeneous mass of non-professional soldiers. Indeed, many senior officers believed that this immense infusion of civilians had intensified the need for rigorous control. The lack of martial inclination of the British had been well known for generations. Wellington had commented in 1809: 'We are not naturally a military people; the whole business of an army upon service is foreign to our habits, and is a constraint upon them.'[10]

Whether the BEF had any proper leadership from Haig is a question for military historians. His biographer, Duff Cooper, has come to the restrained, but somewhat flattering, conclusion that he was 'as good a general as it is possible for a man without genius to ever become'.[11] It could be said that Haig's dismissal of the machine gun as 'a much overrated weapon',[12] of tank warfare as 'a minor factor',[13] and of the aerial bombing of munitions factories as 'unsound in theory',[14] derived not so much from a strategic myopia as from his utter isolation from the realities of the battlefield. Duff Cooper goes out of his way to emphasize Haig's kindness, his compassion and his abounding dedication to the service of his country.[15]

It must be remembered, too, that these wartime executions took place in an age when capital punishment was accepted in Britain as a necessary component of the penal structure.

During the early 1970s Dr Esler, who had witnessed the execution of a deserter in France,[16] was asked if at the time he had considered this penalty to be a reasonable one. He replied:

I think it was absolutely essential. It was setting a bad example to the men. They would have begun to feel that you only had to walk off during a battle and then come back afterwards and you escaped death or mutilation. . . . I think it was a necessary punishment.

Another medical officer in the war, Lord Moran, whose study of morale in action was published in 1945,[18] considered that some of the men who had been accused of cowardice on the Western Front should not have been treated as cowards at all, but others were 'plainly worthless fellows'. Moran neither specifically condoned nor condemned capital punishment for military offences. He suggested, however, that soldiers without the temperament for battle should have been weeded out before they ever reached the front line and been transferred into labour battalions, though he admitted that there was no satisfactory solution as to what should have been done with them.

In the aftermath of the Armistice there was a great deal of public concern regarding the standard of justice of some of the Army courts martial which had taken place during the war years, and there were grave doubts about the competency of ordinary military officers to exercise powers of punishment as great as those possessed by High Court judges. It was partly to alleviate this anxiety that in April 1919 the Army Council set up a committee 'to enquire into the law and rules of procedure regulating military courts martial, both in peace and war, and to make recommendations'.

Ten members were appointed to the Committee: Sir Charles Darling as Chairman, the Judge Advocate General and his deputy, two serving generals, and five MPs, including Horatio Bottomley who had returned to the House of Commons in 1918. An ex-court martial officer regretted at the time that no single member of the Committee had had any real experience of a court martial in the field.[20]

Mr Justice Darling, aged 69, was then the senior puisne judge of the High Court. His elevation to the Bench in 1897 had been unpopular and controversial as it was universally considered to have been a reward for political services to the government of the day.[21] *The Times* had devoted a leading article to a condemnation of his appointment and the *Daily Chronicle* had denounced it as 'the grossest scandal of recent times'.[22] Perhaps Darling's closest connection with the Western Front had been that his son had served there as a cavalry officer and had won a DSO in 1916.[23] Horatio Bottomley, who had been one of Darling's few admirers during his early years as a judge, was destined to terminate his public career in 1922 when he was sentenced to seven years' penal servitude on his conviction for fraudulent conversion.

The Darling Committee sat on 22 days hearing oral evidence from witnesses and they also considered various submissions made to them in writing. They recommended that none of this evidence should be published and, in fact, it was never printed.[24] Their main report was signed by seven of the members, a separate report being presented by Bottomley and two of his fellow MPs.

The majority report drew attention to the fact that during the four years of war 252,773 courts martial had taken place in the British Army, an average of about 160 a day; according to the statistics which were published in 1920, over 89 per cent of them had resulted in convictions. The report went on:

> The results of our investigations into a limited number of cases put before us as typical lead us to the conclusion that, having regard to all the circumstances, the work of courts martial during the war has been well done. We are satisfied not only that the members of courts martial intend to be absolutely fair to those who come before them, but also that the rank and file have confidence in their fairness.

Nevertheless, the Committee was of the opinion that there were certain respects in which the system could be improved. They felt that greater reliance should be placed upon officers with legal training and that there should be a better scheme for teaching regimental officers the principles of military law and procedure. However, they rejected a proposal that Other Ranks should be entitled to appear as defending counsel at courts martial in addition to barristers, solicitors and serving officers, as amateur lawyers had defects of their own and frequently did damage to the case for the defence.

The Committee expressed concern regarding an idea which seemed to exist 'in certain quarters' that courts-martial were secret tribunals. 'This is a complete mistake', they said. 'Even upon active service, every Court-Martial is a public Court open to all members of the public for whom there is accommodation – subject only to the exception, that a Court-Martial, like other English Courts may sit in camera.' They also criticized the senior officers who had issued circulars setting the scales of punishment which they considered to be appropriate to various offences, since it was 'of the utmost importance that members of Courts-Martial should feel that they are absolutely free to exercise their judicial discretion in cases which come before them'.

The Committee considered that the members of courts martial were often too young and recommended the adoption of the rule which applied in the French Army that no officer should be eligible for membership unless he was at least 25 years old. They did not agree with the suggestion that a prisoner should never be convicted unless the members of the court martial had reached their decision unanimously, but thought that if the finding was not unanimous the confirming authority should be informed of the voting figures and of the chief points of difference between the members.

When a court martial had decided to convict, said the Darling Committee, it was both unfair and unnecessary to keep the accused in doubt about the nature of his sentence until after it had been confirmed. They recommended that the conviction should be disclosed immediately and:

> (1) That where the sentence is one which does not entail dismissal from the service or restraint of liberty, it should be at once announced in open Court, the accused being released, and informed that the sentence requires confirmation but cannot be increased;
> (2) That the sentence, in other cases, should at once be privately communicated to the accused in writing together with the information mentioned above.

The Committee were adamant that there should be no right of appeal from the decision of a court martial, even when a sentence of death had been passed on the accused. The Judge Advocate General's staff, they said, ensured that there had been no legal error in the conviction and the military authorities alone were in a position to assess the propriety of the sentence. They added:

> In our opinion a Commander-in-Chief, who is entrusted with the safety of his Army, must not be fettered in his decision as to a point which so vitally affects the discipline of that Army. . . . An exemplary punishment speedily carried out may prevent a mutiny from spreading or save an Army from defeat.

The signatories of the minority report stated that although they agreed with the findings and recommendations of the majority in many respects they differed from them in others. They complained that their Chairman had prevented them from inquiring into the facts and merits of any particular court martial trials, 'except in so far as they threw light upon the present law and procedure of Courts-Martial'. Consequently, they had been unable fully to investigate any cases of alleged miscarriage of justice. In spite of this, however, it had been abundantly proved to them that irregularities had occurred in the proceedings of courts martial.

The minority thought that there had been far too many courts martial during the war and they suggested that commanding officers should be given wider powers of punishment so that they would deal with more cases themselves. They also considered that too many offences were punishable with death. In their opinion courts martial should be entirely composed of officers with legal training and they favoured the complete abolition of the system of confirmation. If courts were thoroughly competent, they said, the finding and the sentence could be pronounced at the conclusion of every trial without the necessity of submitting the record to higher authority.

One of their most interesting proposals was that any person who was sentenced to death by court martial, either in peace or in war, should have a right of appeal to the civil Court of Criminal Appeal, possibly sitting with special military assessors. Apart from courts martial in the field, any accused who had not received a death sentence would be entitled to appeal to a military Court of Appeal, 'composed of three officers, who should be officers of long service and experience at Courts-Martial'.

In April 1920, soon after the publication of the Report of the Darling Committee, Major C. Lowther proposed in the House of Commons that a new clause should be inserted in the Army Act to the effect that: 'In all cases of death sentences there shall be a right of appeal to the Court of Criminal Appeal.'[25] Major Lowther, who had been a member of the Darling Committee and one of the signatories of the minority report, said that wartime courts martial had been 'renowned for fairness and impartiality', but none the less it was open to question whether the officers serving upon them had had a sufficient knowledge of military law to arrive at perfectly proper decisions. He contrasted with the lot of the duration-soldier the position of a civilian temporarily employed in a munitions factory. If the latter ran foul of the law, Major Lowther commented, he could have the legal implications of his case considered in the Court of Criminal Appeal by the finest legal brains in the country. It was only right that the soldier under sentence of death should be in no worse a position.

Major Lowther's proposed clause did not differentiate between appeals against conviction and appeals against sentence, so presumably it was intended that it should apply to both. An appeal against conviction would normally be taken on a point of law, for instance on the ground that some highly prejudicial but inadmissible evidence had been adduced at the trial, or that the prosecution have failed to establish one of the vital components of the charge. An appeal against sentence would be based on the submission that the punishment was excessive in view of all the facts of the case or of the personal circumstances of the condemned man. It would seem to be logical for an appeal against conviction, which might entail a complex legal argument, to be decided by a bench of experienced judges, whereas an appeal against sentence, probably involving considerations of discipline and morale, could most suitably be settled by higher army officers.

In a short debate on the proposed new clause it was vehemently opposed by three army officers, two colonels and a major. Besides the utter impracticability of referring the proceedings of courts martial in distant fields of operations to a Court of Appeal in London, they said, the clause would seriously diminish the condemned man's chances of escaping with his life. They reiterated all the old arguments about the compassion and care of the existing procedure. The record of the trial was checked and re-checked during the process of confirmation; it was meticulously examined for legal errors by a member of the Judge Advocate General's staff; and the propriety of the sentence was personally endorsed by the Commander-in-Chief. After all that, the accused still had a right to petition against his conviction or his punishment.

One of the colonels contrasted the excellence of the military system with the inadequacy of the appeals procedure in the civil courts, which was solely concerned with 'the pure legal aspect of the case' and resolved all matters in issue by 'dry-as-dust' methods. He quite accepted that convictions by courts martial should be perfectly legal, but he contended that whether they were so or not was best decided according to 'the human element' rather than by 'the pure logic of legality'.[26] Another colonel emphasized the interconnection between punishment and discipline. He said:

The whole point of the death sentence, like that of many other punishments, is that it should act as a deterrent. If the sentence is imposed and six months elapse while the case goes to the other side of the world, and the comrades of the man have no idea of what happens to him, then how can it act as a deterrent as it should be?[27]

An Under-Secretary of State, winding up the debate, said:[28]

The view that the Government take on this matter is that the present system ensures on the whole a fair trial to the man, and, in the second place, it is in its results more favourable to the man from the point of view of leniency and clemency than any system which depended solely or mainly upon the advice or recommendations or decisions of a civil court of appeal.

He stressed that military punishment needed to be exemplary and speedy, otherwise there might be a total breakdown in discipline. The Army Council had considered the proposed new clause but had rejected it.

Major Lowther's motion was lost by 124 votes to 42.

From the day of the Armistice until the end of April 1920 there were 13 capital courts martial in the Army, all for the offence of murder, as a result of which a total of 18 men were sentenced to death and shot. Only three of the condemned were British soldiers, the remainder being members of Chinese, Egyptian, Cape Coloured or Black Sea Labour Companies and muleteers from the Macedonian Mule Corps.

Ten of these courts martial were in France, one was in Italy, one in Turkey, and one in Egypt. Most of the trials were by Field General Court Martial with neither a judge-advocate nor a qualified CMO being present to give advice, so that any difficulties which arose at the hearings over matters of law or procedure must have been determined without any legal guidance.

One of the executed British soldiers was tried by General Court Martial in Italy at the beginning of December 1918. Three months previously he had killed another private in his company by running him with a bayonet during a drunken brawl. In this case the death sentence was promulgated on a formal parade exactly a week before the condemned man was shot.

A 20-year-old gunner who was court-martialled in the spring of 1919 had deserted from his battery in France three weeks after the signing of the Armistice. He had gone into hiding in Paris and early in March he had been stopped in the street by two corporals of the Military Police carrying out an examination of leave passes. The gunner told them that all his documents were at a nearby hotel where he was staying. They had insisted on accompanying him there and while one of them remained downstairs in the hall the other had gone into his bedroom with him. Once inside the gunner had produced a revolver and had shot the corporal in the stomach and chest. He had then escaped from the hotel, shooting the second corporal in the arm as he was passing through the hall. The gunner was chased and detained by a crowd of gendarmes and civilians. He was convicted of the murder of one of the corporals and the attempted murder of the other and was exected on 27 May 1919.

The third British soldier to be condemned to death and shot after the war had ended was Private C, an infantryman from Lincolnshire. During the summer of 1918 he and three other members of his battalion had carried out a series of burglaries in the neighbourhood of Calais. One night at the end of August, after they had broken into a house, Private C became suspicious that one of his fellow-thieves had not shared out with the rest of them all the money he had stolen. A fight ensued, in the course of which C throttled the suspect and the other two men hit him repeatedly with revolver-butts causing multiple injuries and breaking his neck. The body was discovered next day and the hunt for the murderers had begun. Private C was arrested on 10 September and although he made a full confession he feigned mental illness so successfully that his court martial was delayed until 13 June 1919. The day after he was sentenced to death he made an application that he be allowed to see his wife before the date fixed for his execution. Arrangements were made for his wife to visit him at a military prison in France at public expense a week before he was shot.

The practice of appealing from the findings of a court martial by petition was used so rarely it had almost fallen into abeyance. Most convicted soldiers, even if they knew the procedure existed, probably felt that it was destined to certain failure. As far as can be ascertained, out of all the men condemned to death and shot during the period from the beginning of the war until the end of April 1920, only one had exercised the right to petition. He was a private in the Cape Coloured Labour Corps who was court-martialled in France in August 1919 for a particularly brutal murder committed during the previous June. He had had a quarrel with another private in his unit concerning a French girl to whom they were both paying their attentions and he had killed his rival by hitting him on the head with a hammer. Afterwards he had stolen money from the dead man's pocket and had thrown the body into a river, weighted with a large piece of stone. He appealed against the death sentence on the ground that he was an only son and was the sole support of his widowed mother. The petition was rejected.

There was a further military execution in 1920, outside the period covered by the War Office statistical return, resulting from the tragic mutiny of the Connaught Rangers in India. Private James Daly was shot by a firing squad on 2 November 1920. In a book published in 1969[29] the author, Sam Pollock, states incorrectly that Daly was 'the last soldier of the British Army to suffer death in peace or war for a military offence'.[30]

During January 1919 the reconstituted Irish Republican Army, commanded by Michael Collins and largely financed by American sympathizers, began a campaign of guerrilla warfare against both the British Army units stationed in Ireland and the Royal Irish Constabulary. During the following year, the British government recruited a special auxiliary force, known from their uniform as the 'Black and Tans', which was sent into Ireland specifically to combat terror with terror. The whole country was soon plunged into a ferment of atrocities, arson and killing. The Black and Tans achieved lasting infamy for their oppression and brutality; amongst the many voices raised in protest against their methods was that of Herbert Asquith, the former Liberal Prime Minister, who said 'Things are being done in Ireland which would disgrace the blackest annals of the lowest despotism in Europe.'[31]

In June 1920 the 1st Connaught Rangers was on garrison duty in the Punjab with two companies in barracks at Jullundur and one company on detachment about 20 miles away at the hill-station of Solon. Most of the men in the battalion came from the south or the west of Ireland and there was naturally a great deal of distress and anger about the news coming through from their homeland. Sam Pollock has described how on 28 June a large group of NCOs and men voluntarily placed themselves in the battalion guardroom at Jullundur in protest against the behaviour of the Black and Tans.[32] They were eventually disarmed by members of other regiments and 48 of them were taken to Dagshai Military Prison to await court martial.

The happenings at Solon were far more serious. When the garrison paraded on the morning of 30 June Private Daly, acting as spokesman, informed the captain in charge of the station that they intended to do no more work until all British troops were removed from Ireland. Daly then marched the others to the canteen where they spent the day singing Irish nationalist songs. In the evening Daly was seen breaking into the arms racks and later, holding a bayonet in his hand, he led an attack on the magazine. The guard, who were drawn from another regiment, fired warning shots into the air and when some of the attackers still came on opened fire on them killing two men and seriously wounding a third. Eventually the mutineers were over-powered and 27 of them were sent to Dagshai to join the prisoners from Jullundur.

The 75 mutineers from the Connaught Rangers were tried in groups at three General Courts Martial held successively over a period of a few weeks. Sam Pollock, who derived much of his information from interviews in the 1960s with survivors of the participants, has asserted that Private Daly at his trial declined to acknowledge the jurisdiction of the court.[33] This was not so. Daly pleaded 'Not Guilty' to the charge and at the close of the prosecution case elected to give evidence on his own behalf. He denied on oath that he had taken part in the mutiny and said that during the attack on the armoury he had been trying to persuade the others to desist.

Fourteen of the accused were acquitted. Nine, including Daly, were sentenced to death, and the rest received prison sentences ranging from one year to 20 years. All the death sentences except Daly's were commuted to imprisonment for life.

At the time of his execution James Daly was just 21 years old. According to Sam Pollock he was tied to a weighted chair and was shot by a firing party from the Royal Fusiliers.[34]

The rest of the convicted mutineers were sent back to serve their sentences at prisons in England. They were released in 1923 under the terms of an amnesty arranged between the British and the Irish Free State governments.

Notes

1. Statistics of the Military Effort of the British Empire During the Great War, Part XXIII – Discipline. Some of the figures slightly exceed the total numbers of executions for the period set out in the Appendix. The reason for this discrepancy

is that the author has only included in the Appendix the cases of which he has been able to find out the details.

2. These figures do not include executions in the Indian Army.
3. No executions took place in the United Kingdom.
4. Information supplied by the Service Historique at Vincennes.
5. War Department Annual Reports 1919, Washington, Volume 1, Part 1, Report of the Judge Advocate General.
6. Information supplied by Military History Research, Freiburg im Breisgau.
7. C. E. W. Bean, *Official History of Australia in the War of 1914–1918*, Volume V.
8. Twenty-five soldiers in the Canadian Expeditionary Force were executed in France, 22 for desertion, 2 for murder, and 1 for cowardice. Information from Desmond Morton, 'Canadian Deaths by Firing Squad in the First World War', *Queen's Quarterly*, Vol. 29, 1972, Kingston, Ontario.
9. C. E. W. Bean, op. cit. All the information which follows is taken from the same source.
10. Wellington to the British Minister in Portugal, quoted in Elizabeth Longford in *Wellington. The Years of the Sword*.
11. Duff Cooper, *Haig*, Vol. II.
12. B. H. Liddell Hart, *History of the First World War*.
13. Ib.
14. Ib.
15. Op. cit.
16. See pp. 52, 53.
17. Imperial War Museum, oral history recordings, Western Front 1914–1918, Dr M. S. Esler.
18. Lord Moran, *The Anatomy of Courage*.
19. Ib.
20. Arthur Page, 'Courts-Martial in France', *Blackwood's Magazine*, June 1919.
21. Derek Walker-Smith, *The Life of Lord Darling*.
22. Ib.
23. Ib.
24. Report of the Committee Constituted by the Army Council to Enquire into the Law and Rules of Procedure regulating Military Courts-Martial, 1919.
25. House of Commons, Army and Air Force (Annual) Bill, Committee stage, 13 April 1920.
26. Ib., Lieutenant-Colonel Ward.
27. Ib., Lieutenant-Colonel Hurst.
28. Ib., Sir A. Williamson.
29. Sam Pollock, *Mutiny For The Cause*.
30. See p. 212.
31. Quoted in A. J. P. Taylor, *English History 1914–1945*.
32. Op. cit.
33. Op. cit.
34. Op. cit.

20

AFTERTHOUGHTS AND
REFORMS

I N THE HOUSE of Lords on 28 April 1920 Lord Southborough[1] asked
the government to set up an inquiry into the different types of
hysteria, commonly called 'shell-shock', which had affected so many
soldiers during the Great War, with particular attention 'to the death
penalty inflicted upon men by Courts-Martial on the charge of
"cowardice" (without inviting any re-opening of the evidence in such
painful cases)'.[2]

Throughout the war, said Lord Southborough, the British people
had been confronted at all times with 'the sinister and terrible disorder
of shell-shock'. When they had first become aware of its existence they
had been assured that it was specifically associated with the particular
conditions under which the Army had been fighting. Now, however,
the consensus of opinion in Britain, France and America was that
soldiers said to be shell-shocked were, in reality, suffering from
varying types of hysteria or traumatic neurosis which were common
and well known in civil life. He went on:

> If it is the fact that a true identification of the disorder was wanting in the
> early months of the war, then I fear that, through inadvertence and want
> of knowledge, dreadful things may have happened to the men who had
> in fact become irresponsible for their actions.

It was easy to understand, said Lord Southborough, the anxiety of
the generals and the perplexity of courts martial when confronted by
these cases. They were principally concerned with the interests of
discipline and fighting efficiency. On the other hand:

> One might expect that boys taken from the plough, the factory, or office
> stool would in some cases crack on the sudden exposure to the inferno of
> fire, noise, blood and death to which they were exposed. The ever-
> present and glorious wonder is that the vast majority of them stood firm
> and sound in mind and body to the end.

Lord Southborough suggested that a soldier suffering from acute
hysteria might temporarily undergo a complete loss of willpower and

have no control over his actions. He wondered whether wartime courts martial had been empowered to consider the condition of the accused man's mind at the moment when he had committed his offence.

Lord Southborough's motion was supported by Lord Horne,[3] who admitted that in the early days of the war 'there may have been cases where injustice led to the extreme penalty being enforced', but added that, in practice:

> If there was the shadow of a doubt, if there was any suspicion that the crime committed might have been caused by any of the forms of hysteria which are included under the term 'shell-shock', I may confidently state that the sentence was not confirmed until the accused had been under the observation of medical authorities.

At the close of the debate Viscount Peel, the Under-Secretary of State for War, said that the government took the view that great advantages might be obtained by such an inquiry as had been proposed, with the proviso that it would be very wrong and detrimental to discipline if there were to be an investigation of cases which had already been settled.

The War Office Committee of Inquiry into 'Shell-Shock' was appointed in August 1920 under the Chairmanship of Lord Southborough. Out of the 15 members eleven were medically qualified. They examined 59 witnesses, most of whom had had experience either of active service or of the treatment of servicemen suffering from hysteria and traumatic neurosis. Unlike the Darling Committee they published in their Report a synopsis of the evidence of all the principal witnesses who had appeared before them.[4]

The Report stated that the term 'shell-shock' had been 'a gross and costly misnomer'. The war had produced no new nervous disorders and those which had occurred had all been previously recognized in civil medical practice. The cases had been divisible into three classes: genuine concussion caused by an explosion, emotional shock and nervous exhaustion. Although the Committee had been able to discover no recorded instances of shell-shock in earlier wars it was probable, they said, that any soldier who had lost control of himself had been court-martialled and punished. They had consulted John Fortescue, the eminent military historian, on this point and he had told them:

> No doubt there were men who, from one cause or another, broke down in every campaign; and I have little doubt that this was one of the causes which led to desertion. But such breaks-down, when they are recorded, are not very sympathetically treated, and unless a man had proved

himself of good courage earlier in action, are dismissed as not differing greatly from cowardice. Of course, numbers of men went out of their minds in the old campaigns, as they still do.

Fortescue had also expressed the opinion that the bravest man could not endure to be under fire for more than a certain number of consecutive days, even if the fire was not very heavy.

The Committee were extremely critical of the medical examination of the men who had enlisted for service in the early stages of the war. 'Many recruits were passed into the Army', they said, 'who were quite unfit to withstand the rigours of a campaign or even, in many cases, preliminary training'. The general attitude of the public had been that every man who appeared to be physically fit should be sent to the front, and this was the policy which had been applied at the recruitment centres. With the vast surge of new recruits the conditions had been chaotic. During the first 18 months of the war, when enlistment had been on a voluntary basis, no real effort had been made to weed out the men who might be unsuitable for military service because of their mental or nervous instability. The civilian doctors who had carried out the preliminary medical checks were seeing an average of 200 to 300 men a day. Colonel Clay, the Chief Recruiting Officer for London District at the time, had told the Committee that he knew of one doctor who had examined 400 men a day for ten days. According to Clay's evidence, between 20 and 30 per cent of the recruits were given no medical examination at all.

The medical board system had been introduced at the end of 1915, but even then preliminary examinations had remained very cursory, each board being expected to examine 200 recruits every day. Throughout the first three years of the war, said the Committee:

> A great number of men who were ill-suited to stand the strain of military service, whether by temperament or their past or present mental or nervous health, were admitted into the Army; there is no doubt that such men contributed a very high proportion of the cases of hysteria and traumatic neurosis commonly called 'shell-shock'.

From 1 November 1917 the medical examination and classification of recruits had been taken over by the Ministry of National Service. In the opinion of the Committee the new medical boards, which consisted of four doctors and examined 60 men a day, were more thorough and more satisfactory.

The consensus of opinion amongst the medical and military witnesses had been that any type of individual might suffer from one or other form of neurosis if exposed for a sufficient time to the conditions of modern warfare, and that it was extremely difficult to predict beforehand what sort of man was most likely to break down. No reliable statistics were available, said the Committee, but it seemed that the most vulnerable age-group were soldiers between 18 and 25. A London consultant, who had been in charge of a special neurological hospital during the war, stated in evidence that emotional, highly-strung men were the principal sufferers from war neurosis, especially those who possessed an artistic temperament. Another neurologist had found that feeble-minded persons were peculiarly susceptible to the incidence of emotional shell-shock. A doctor with considerable experience on the Western Front said:

> The most likely type of man for 'shell-shock' is the brooding, introspective, self-analysing man; the type who was constantly estimating his chance of survival, whose imagination added the terrors of the future to those of the present.

The Committee had no doubt that soldiers in the immediate vicinity of a bursting shell or mine might suffer concussion of their central nervous systems. However, a senior neurologist with extensive experience of the fighting in France expressed the view that less than ten per cent of the cases of so-called shell-shock were the direct result of an explosion. The remainder had been caused, or partially caused, by emotional factors.

Loss of sleep was the most potent element in the production of shell-shock, said one witness. Others mentioned the influence of exhaustion, the terror of life in the trenches, and the prolonged exposure both to the elements and to danger. A doctor who had served as medical officer with a battalion of the Black Watch told the Committee that his division had been in the Ypres Salient for a continuous period of 14 months. During the bitter winter of 1917 they had been holding a portion of the line in which there were no proper trenches and sometimes the men had had to remain for as long as three days and three nights, under constant fire, in shell-holes up to their thighs in water. Eventually he had written to army headquarters saying that he could not answer for the wellbeing of his battalion unless it was immediately withdrawn from the zone. 'Humanity', he commented, 'has only a certain limit of endurance.'

The Consultant Physician for Gas Cases with the BEF spoke of the soldier's dread of being gassed. He said:

> The unknown has greater terrors than the known. Gas mainly acts on the respiratory tract, and the fear of suffocation causes great emotional disturbance. It is rather akin to the fear of being buried alive.

Several doctors believed that a man suffering from disease or illness was predisposed to war neurosis, and one thought that a letter from home containing bad news, such as the death of a parent, might so upset the control of a soldier that he would no longer be able to stand the conditions of the front line.

The Committee considered that inactivity might be yet another contributory factor to the psycho-neuroses of war. 'As may well be imagined', they said:

> a state of inaction under fire acted perniciously on the nerves of men in the trenches or troops massed together awaiting orders to attack.

In view of the number of soldiers who pleaded loss of memory as a reason for deserting, it is significant that several neurologists informed the Committee that both amnesia and mental confusion can be caused by either commotional or emotional shell-shock. They give examples of cases, apparently genuine, when men had been found wandering about a few miles from their own units, without the least idea how they had come to be there.

Describing the clinical appearance of a soldier who had broken down in the line, a witness said:

> The man looked obviously out of control; he gave involuntary move-ments, wringing his hands, his eyes became staring, and he had the look of a hunted animal – you cannot mistake it. When the crash does come he loses all shame and cringes.[5]

Sometimes men suffered from more serious hysterical symptoms such as paralysis or loss of speech. A bursting shell or the stress of war could also cause insanity, either of a temporary or a permanent nature.[6] A medical officer said in evidence:

> I saw a man, a regular officer, who went out to Gallipoli and went mad on the beach. He saw the whole beach covered with jewelled spiders of enormous size. They did not know what to do with the man so put him on one of the boats, and as the barges came up with the wounded he saw his wife and child on a barge, cut in pieces.

Witnesses with experience as regimental medical officers were agreed that it was a practical impossibility in the most forward areas to distinguish between the soldiers who were suffering from acute emotional disturbance due to fear and those who were exaggerating their symptoms or were even feigning them. Cases had occurred in which men had simulated loss of memory or paralysis, but one doctor thought this sort of malingering was extremely rare and happened mainly with raw recruits. A medical officer who had been decorated with the DSO discussed the handling of shell-shock cases in the field. 'I must confess,' he said, 'that when I went to France, for the first two or three months I was inclined to look upon the men far too much as malingerers, and I very quickly changed my mind.'

The neurologist to the Fourth Army in BEF was asked by the Committee whether he had any experience of shell-shock being put forward as a defence in a court martial for desertion. He replied that he had frequently been called upon to examine accused men and to report upon them in such cases. He had found it an exceptionally difficult and distasteful task. He went on:

> I very soon came to the conclusion that it was almost impossible for the Medical Officer to make a decisive statement that the man had been responsible for his action when he ran away.

The Committee remarked that in spite of the abundance of informed medical opinion on the subject many army officers still refused to believe in the existence of the condition known as 'shell-shock'. This obstinacy might have derived from the past. A regimental medical officer said in evidence:

> The old Regular Army had a much fiercer way of looking upon anything approaching cowardice, because their standards were based upon wars previous to this war in which the calls made upon a man's courage were as nothing compared to this war. It was a much fiercer standard.

The third reading of the Annual Army and Air Force Bill for 1920 took place in April of that year, some time before the shell-shock Committee had issued their Report. A Labour Member, Mr Palmer, took the opportunity of urging once again that there should be a right of appeal from a sentence of death imposed by a court martial.[7] Serving soldiers should be treated as human beings, he said, and they should not be compelled to forfeit the constitutional rights which belonged to them as citizens. The next speaker, a Conservative who had been a regular soldier, contended that a capital sentence in the Army was already subject to 'an automatic series of appeals' during the process of confirmation. The greatest safeguard possessed by every condemned man, he went on, was that it would ultimately depend upon the decision of one officer, the Commander-in-Chief, whether he would live or die. This seemingly illogical observation was amplified by another Member who explained that the Commander-in-Chief assessed a capital case not 'by cold law and cold facts', but under 'a code of sympathy' which was always weighted in favour of the accused. A ministerial spokesman winding up the debate said that this matter had been very carefully examined by the Darling Committee and the government accepted their view that an appeal procedure from courts martial was neither necessary nor desirable.

The principal support in the 1920s for the curtailment or the complete abolition of capital punishment in the Army always came from the Labour Party, and was prompted by a philosophical belief which was partly pacifistic, partly humanitarian and partly reformative. When the first Labour administration took office in January 1924 it might have been expected that the melioration of the military penal code would have featured in their legislative programme. However, their position was extremely precarious as they were a minority government and were, in fact, only the second largest party in the House. For the time being they went no further than referring to an Interdepartmental Committee a list of proposed disciplinary amendments to the Army and Air Force Act. The Committee was to be chaired by the Financial Secretary to the War Office and was to consist of an admiral, a lieutenant-general, and an air vice-marshal, together with the legal advisers to their respective branches of the armed forces. The Labour government lost office in November 1924, to be replaced by a Conservative administration under Stanley Baldwin, and the Chairman of the Interdepartmental Committee was replaced by a Conservative Minister who was himself a retired naval captain.

The Report of the Interdepartmental Committee was published on 1 April 1925.[8] They could find no foundation, they said, for the suggestion that there had been any miscarriages of justice at wartime courts martial owing to a failure to distinguish between real cowardice and physical breakdown, or due to the harsh or unfair conduct of the trials. High-ranking officers who had had to confirm death sentences during the war had told them that it was essential to retain the death penalty 'as a power in reserve', but that it was only required as a last resort in extreme cases. The Committee recommended that the death penalty in time of peace should be abolished for all military offences other than mutiny. They also recommended that four of the offences punishable with death when committed on active service should become non-capital. This would have had little practical effect as the four offences they mentioned were very seldom tried by court martial and no soldiers had been executed for any of them within living memory. The Committee stated that they fully agreed with the recommendation of the Darling Committee that there should be no appeal to a civil court against a death sentence imposed by a court martial.

The modifications proposed by the Interdepartmental Committee were not sufficiently extensive to satisfy the Labour opposition in the House of Commons. Immediately after the publication of the Report,

Ernest Thurtle[9] endeavoured to get a number of other offences, including cowardice, sleeping on post and shamefully casting away arms, removed from the death penalty.[10] A soldier was in reality a citizen in uniform, he said. During a war an army was subjected to a very terrible ordeal and if any man was unable to stand up to it – a fault beyond his control – he was liable to be court-martialled and shot. 'If you have got to keep the men fighting,' he went on, 'by saying to them "If you do not fight we will shoot you in cold blood", then I say you have no right to keep them fighting at all.'

Many of the arguments which were put forward in the debate that followed were to be repeated during the next few years whenever the subject of military executions was discussed in Parliament. The retentionists placed their principal reliance on an assertion that the death penalty was indispensable for the maintenance of discipline. The abolitionists replied that an exactly similar contention had always been advanced against the termination of flogging and of field punishment.[11] Labour Members insisted that the rank and file of the British Army were bitterly resentful about the execution of their comrades. This was vigorously denied by Conservative speakers, some of whom predicted that if cowards and deserters were no longer liable to the death penalty there would be a danger of their fellow soldiers taking the matter into their own hands and carrying out an execution themselves. The abolitionists often cited the Australian Army as an example of the valour and tenacity with which troops could fight, though free of the shadow of the firing squad. The retentionists, whilst acknowledging the bravery of the Australians, were critical of their standards of discipline.

At the conclusion of the April 1925 debate the Secretary of State for War had told the House that the government were unable to accept Mr Thurtle's motion. The Darling Committee and the Interdepartmental Committee had carefully considered whether or not the death penalty for military offences should be abolished, he said, and both had reported against abolition. In fact the Minister's recollection on this point was faulty. The Darling Committee had made no pronouncement on the subject which was, in any case, outside their terms of reference. As has been seen, their minority report included a recommendation that less military offences should be capital.[12]

In April 1926 Ernest Thurtle, with the full support of the Parliamentary Labour Party, proposed an amendment to the Army Act which would have removed the death penalty from all military offences except treachery and desertion to the enemy.[13] He appealed emotively for 'elementary human justice' for the troops and suggested that the War Office policy was to keep men fighting by the 'discipline of fear'. A retired regular colonel asked the House to study the example of the

Zulus, 'probably the bravest fighting nation in the whole world'. It was a matter of honour with them, he said, 'to go forward and die'. The colonel seemed to attribute this courage of the Zulu warriors to the fact that cowardice and sleeping on post were punished summarily in their armies by running the culprit through with a spear. Replying for the government, the Financial Secretary to the War Office stated that nothing had altered since the debate a year before. Penal servitude or imprisonment, he said, would never be an adequate substitute for death in the case of a soldier who had given way to his fear. Mr Thurtle's proposed amendment was defeated by a majority of a little over two to one.

The Army and Air Force Bill which was introduced into Parliament in the spring in 1928 contained an important modification inasmuch as eight offences, including sleeping on post, disobedience and striking a superior officer, were no longer punishable with death. The only capital charges now remaining were mutiny, treachery, cowardice, desertion and leaving a guard or a post without orders. 1928 was the last full year of Stanley Baldwin's government and this alteration indicated a considerable adaptation in ministerial thinking on the matter of army discipline. The Financial Secretary to the War Office revealed in the House of Commons that the Army Council had been consulted and had unanimously approved of the curtailment of the death penalty as embodied in the Bill.[14]

During the Committee stage of the Bill the Labour Party attempted to bring about the abolition of capital punishment for all military offences other than mutiny, treachery and desertion, but the government refused to extend the provision any further. The Financial Secretary to the War Office, in his reply, said it was the wish of the men in the ranks that those who had deliberately let them down in battle should still be liable to execution rather than being punished with a term of penal servitude in the sheltered safety of a prison remote from the battlefront. The motion was once more defeated, but this time by a slightly smaller margin than before.

The result of the general election in June 1929 was that no party was left with an absolute majority. The number of seats won by the three main parties in the House of Commons were: Labour 288, Conservative 260, Liberal 59. Ramsay Macdonald then formed his second Labour administration, again having to rely upon Liberal support in order to remain in power.

The following spring the new government introduced its first Army and Air Force Bill. This restricted capital punishment still further by removing the death penalty for the offences of cowardice and leaving a post or guard without orders. During the Committee Stage Thomas Shaw, the Secretary of State for War, said that he had consulted the Army Council about the proposed changes. He continued:[15]

> The military members of the Army Council were of the opinion that the death penalty for cowardice was a deterrent which prevented many a man from being a coward, and possibly saved many lives through the deterrent effect being powerful enough to prevent the occurrence of cowardice. That was also their opinion, very strongly felt, with regard to what has been called the crime of desertion.

Although the government had ignored the Army Council's advice regarding the offences of cowardice and leaving a post without orders, Mr Shaw said he agreed that desertion should still remain a capital offence and he would be opposed to any attempt to make it otherwise. Undeterred by his own party's official policy on the matter, Ernest Thurtle moved an amendment to the Bill substituting penal servitude for death as the maximum penalty for desertion on active service. Most of the men who were executed for cowardice during the last war, he said, might equally well have been charged with desertion, because it was frequently quite impossible to draw any real line of demarcation between the two offences. The government allowed a free vote on the amendment and it was carried by 219 votes to 135.

This was not the end of the matter, however, for when the Bill was considered in Committee by the House of Lords they decided by 45 votes to 12 to restore the death penalty for all three offences.[16] No doubt they were influenced in taking this course by the speeches of two distinguished wartime generals, Viscount Allenby[17] and Viscount Plumer.[18] Lord Allenby said the gravity of all three offences resulted from the fact that they might prejudice the success of military operations or endanger other soldiers' lives. He went on:

> I say most emphatically that in my opinion penal servitude is not a deterrent. It means safety. The only deterrent for the man who will wilfully behave in such a way as to endanger the lives of his own comrades in order to avoid the risk to his own life is the knowledge that, while his comrades may possibly incur death at the hands of the enemy, which will be a glorious and honourable death, he, if convicted of one of these offences by a Court-Martial and executed, will die a death which is dishonourable and shameful.

Next day the Bill was returned to the House of Commons for reconsideration.[19] A Conservative back-bencher proposed that, as a form of compromise, the government should revert to their original intention of abolishing the death penalty for cowardice and for leaving a post without orders, but should agree to its retention for the offence of desertion. This proposal was supported by Winston Churchill who deplored the prospect of a confrontation between the two legislative chambers. The government's position was stated by the Secretary for War. Mr Thurtle's amendment had been passed by a free vote, he said, and the will of the House of Commons must prevail.

The House of Lords decided not to pursue their objections any further and the Bill became law.

And so it came about that less than 12 years after the Armistice the only remaining military offences punishable with death in the British Army were treachery and mutiny.

Two important reforms in court martial procedure were brought about some years later. In 1947 the practice by which a finding of 'Guilty' and the consequent sentence were not disclosed until after they had been confirmed was ended. Thereafter, both the conviction and the penalty were announced in open court at the end of a trial, but the accused was told that they were subject to confirmation. Since 1951 it has been possible for a person convicted by court martial to appeal against conviction, though not against sentence, to a new appellate tribunal, the Courts-Martial Appeals Court, which is manned by ordinary civil judges.[20] This has placed trial by court martial in a similar position to any other form of criminal trial in Britain with regard to the judicial supervision of the superior courts.

During the six years of the 1939–1945 war there were only four executions for military offences in the British Army.[21] Three soldiers, all members of a colonial regiment, were hanged in August 1942 in the Cocos-Keeling Islands after their conviction for mutiny. The fourth man, a private in the RASC, was convicted of wartime treachery at a court martial in London in July 1946. He, too, suffered death by hanging.

The apprehensions of those who had predicted the dire consequences of alleviating the military death penalty proved to be unfounded. Throughout the Second World War the spirit and the pride of the British Army remained inviolate. One reason for this might have been that most of the higher commanders had learnt the lessons of leadership whilst serving as junior officers on the brutal and blood-sodden wastes of the Western Front. Perhaps they realized that there are better ways of controlling men in action than by resorting to a discipline of fear.

Notes

1. Francis Hopwood, First Baron Southborough (1860–1947), a distinguished civil servant who held many important offices. He was raised to the peerage in 1917. Although he never took part in political controversies he spoke in the House of Lords from time to time about matters which had aroused his particular concern.
2. House of Lords, 28 April 1920.
3. Henry Horne (1861–1929). Commanded the First Army on the Western Front from September 1916 until the end of the war. In 1919 he was promoted to the rank of general, raised to the peerage, received the thanks of both Houses of Parliament, and was presented with a grant of £30,000.
4. Report of the War Office Committee of Inquiry into Shell-Shock, 1922.
5. Those who took part in military battles during the Second World War will recognize the characteristics of the condition then known as 'bomb-happy'.
6. Edwin Vaughan once visited a platoon outpost in the Ypres Salient which had just been blown up. He found a sergeant and a private 'gibbering like monkeys' and had to send them back for treatment. Edwin Vaughan, *Some Desperate Glory*.
7. House of Commons, Army and Air Force (Annual) Bill, third reading, 15 April 1920. Mr Palmer, then the editor of *John Bull*, had been largely responsible for the Press campaign which led to the setting-up of the Darling Committee. A point not infrequently made against him was that he had not served in the forces during the war.
8. Report of the Interdepartmental Committee on Proposed Disciplinary Amendments of the Army and Air Force Acts, 1925.
9. Ernest Thurtle had published the booklet *Shooting at Dawn* during the previous year (see p. 49).
10. House of Commons, Army and Air Force (Annual) Bill, Committee Stage, 1 April 1925.
11. Field punishment had been abolished in 1923, against the wishes of most of the senior Army officers. Haig and Robertson in particular had wanted it to be retained.
12. See p. 195.
13. House of Commons, Army and Air Force (Annual) Bill, Committee Stage, 21 April 1926.
14. House of Commons, Army and Air Force (Annual) Bill, Committee Stage, 17 April 1928.
15. House of Commons, Army and Air Force (Annual) Bill, Committee Stage, 3 April 1930.
16. House of Lords, Army and Air Force (Annual) Bill, Committee Stage, 15 April 1930.
17. Viscount Allenby (1861–1936). Appointed a Field-Marshal, raised to the peerage and awarded a grant of £50,000 in 1919.
18. Viscount Plumer (1857–1932). Appointed a Field-Marshal, raised to the peerage and awarded a grant of £30,000 in 1919.
19. House of Commons, Army and Air Force (Annual) Bill, 16 April 1930.
20. Courts-Martial (Appeals) Act, 1951.
21. Details revealed in a written answer by the Parliamentary Under-Secretary of State to the Ministry of Defence in the House of Commons on 20 November 1970. There were 36 military executions for murder in the same period.

POSTSCRIPT

by
Frank Richardson

I T MUST SURELY be impossible for anyone with a deep affection for
that wonderful, if sometimes exasperating, character 'the British
Soldier' to read this book without powerful feelings of sadness, even
depression. An experienced battalion commander, the late Sir Martin
Lindsay, told me that his eyes were opened to the nature of his own
reactions and those of others to the stress of prolonged arduous
campaigning by reading Press reviews of Lord Moran's book *The
Anatomy of Courage*, published in 1945. One of Lord Moran's valuable
observations was that everyone, however brave, has what may be
called his 'bank balance' of courage, and when this is getting low, or
becomes overdrawn, he is in danger of the kind of nervous breakdown
being considered here. Another good analogy by which to explain this
problem to soldiers, who know that a vehicle cannot be run constantly
without periods of rest for maintenance or servicing, is a comparison
with the battery which recharges properly, but as it ages in use stays at
full charge for a shorter period each time it is charged up, and finally
will take full charge but will not hold it. A man's self-control is like
this. He responds to rest and goes back to battle apparently normal,
but each time his resistance is lowered, and finally, if not rested, may
break. Judge Babington cites cases of men who 'had reached the limit
of their endurance'.

Here let me confess that, as a retired Army doctor, the feelings of
sadness to which I have referred were accompanied by a sense of
shame engendered by the many instances in which doctors, who
should have spoken up for their patients, fell into line behind the
upholders of the disciplinary process. I cannot entirely endorse the
condoning of their conduct which is implicit in Judge Babington's
observation that knowledge of psychiatry was then in its infancy. C.
G. Jung said, 'Modern psychology is the testimony of a few individuals here and there regarding what they have found within them-

selves.'* In the light of that pronouncement by perhaps the greatest of the triumvirate – Freud, Jung and Adler – who pioneered the fascinating territory of man's unconscious mind, it is not excessive to feel that doctors, privileged to care for our soldiers, should have been capable of understanding something of their reactions to stress, without recourse to text-books. But if they had endeavoured to make a stand against the rigours of military law could they have achieved very much? Probably not, for a peculiarly painful aspect of this sad story is that strong recommendations to mercy by officers who had tried the victims, by brigade commanders and commanding officers who knew just what they had been called upon to endure, even by divisional and corps commanders, seldom seem to have moved inflexible army commanders or the Commander-in-Chief himself. Testimonials about previous good conduct and bravery in action; strong compassionate grounds, as we call them today; extreme youth; doubts as to whether the man should ever have been exposed to battle, or even allowed to enlist in the Army; suggestions of unsoundness of mind before he did so – all these were ruthlessly set aside. Yet one must assume that these stern higher commanders were not so much ruthless as convinced that the death penalty was essential; indeed members of courts-martial well knew that they were expected to convict and to exact the supreme penalty. All this 'for the sake of example' – *pour encourager les autres*, as Voltaire had written after the shooting of Admiral Byng. Perhaps it did have that effect; and, as Judge Babington writes, the deserter 'left a gap in the ranks to the prejudice of his more dutiful comrades'. Cowards jeopardized the safety of others, and panic can be catching. The generals who had to decide 'whether the prisoners were going to live or die' were in fact sentencing men to death 'each time they ordered an offensive operation'. The author very properly cautions us against judging these men by the standards of today; but it is not very long since General George Patton, advocating the prompt execution of men who go absent during combat, or shirk in battle, wrote that Army and Corps Commanders whose orders can result in 'thousands of gallant men being killed' are capable of 'knowing how to remove the life of one miserable poltroon'.† While the death penalty may have achieved its intended deterrent effect, there are indications that it could be, in the horrid jargon of today, 'counter-productive'. In one case cited by the author the shooting of a young Guardsman was resented as a slur on regimental pride. Regimental Spirit, for centuries the peculiar pride of the British Army, is for us an indispensable support of high morale and anything which might shake it must be deplored. Although in some of the cases described by Judge

* *Modern Man in Search of a Soul*, C. G. Jung, 1933.
† *War as I Knew It*, G. S. Patton, 1949.

Babington the accused men were of bad character (some were murderers) there remain far too many which must surely have aroused the pity of their comrades and distaste for such apparently undiscriminating punishment. I was reminded of a pathetic tale told by Sergeant Donaldson of the 94th Foot. A soldier had been caught taking flour from a miller who had refused to sell it to him. Tried and sentenced to death he was 'marched a prisoner with the provost guard' for such a long time that he hoped for a pardon. But the morning after Wellington's victory at Orthes:

> While he was sitting at the fire with some of his fellow prisoners, the provost came and ordered him to rise, when placing a rope round his neck he marched him forward on the road a short distance and hung him from the branch of a tree. Examples, perhaps, were necessary, but we were inclined to think that the time was often unfortunately chosen; and it was rather an awkward spectacle to greet the eyes of an army after a hard fought and successful battle; and the poor wretch's fate excited more compassion than detestation of his crime.★

Donaldson went on to say that the distress and revulsion led to strong criticism even of Wellington himself; which supports an important point made by Judge Babington when he shows how such cases could lead to impairment of good relations between officers and their men. Again, anything which could do that and thus weaken good leadership, another vital prop to high morale, must be deplored.

I was interested to read the words of that percipient peer, Lord Southborough, calling for an inquiry into 'the sinister and terrible disorder of shell-shock', which, he pointed out, was probably identical with the 'varying types of hysteria or traumatic neurosis which are common and well-known in civil life'. Interested indeed, but not surprised. I have the impression that soldiers experienced in battle have often led the doctors towards a proper understanding of this 'sinister and terrible disorder'. A famous officer of the Royal Artillery accurately diagnosed the condition a hundred years before the doctors gave it an inaccurate and, in the event, expensive name.

Captain Mercer at Waterloo disobeyed Wellington's order that the troops of the Royal Horse Artillery stationed in front of the infantry squares were to withdraw inside the square on the approach of the French cavalry, taking a wheel from each gun with them. Why did Mercer disobey the Duke, in itself a bold act? He was posted in front of the Brunswick square, manned for the most part by raw, young, scared soldiers. Mercer had seen them run at the sound of his horses' hooves during the withdrawal from Quatre Bras, where their Grand

---

★ *The Eventful Life of a Soldier*, J. Donaldson, 1827.

Duke was killed, to the Waterloo position, and he knew that if they saw British soldiers' backs turned to the French they would be off. Later he wrote, 'They fled, not bodily to be sure, but spiritually for their senses seemed to have left them.'★ 'Spiritual flight' is a more accurate diagnosis for many of these cases than 'shell shock', though we must not forget that, as Judge Babington rightly shows, men can be dazed, stunned, temporarily disorientated, even physically concussed, especially by a 'near miss'. Actual flight was virtually impossible at Waterloo, for the British infantry at any rate. Some of the foreign components of what Wellington called his 'Infamous Army' found no difficulty in adopting that solution to their problem – a problem which we should never underestimate, since they were expected to oppose the most formidable troops known to them, under leaders already legendary, while themselves under the command of a stern, undemonstrative general whose name meant little to them. But the British soldier in line or square stood shoulder-to-shoulder with comrades who, as we know from their journals and memoirs, prized courage as the chief aim in life and despised cowardice or lack of endurance. Among such men shooting might have been preferable to what befell a corporal in the 68th Foot, as related by Bugler John Green.

> He was led by the colonel in front of each company at the morning parade, the colonel saying as he passed 'Soldiers, behold a coward.' The corporal was then taken in front of the whole regiment his stripes taken off and he was sent ignominiously to his company as a private.†

Conspicuous among the rest, leaders were expected to lead and their men did not hesitate to tell them so. Ned Costello's comrade in the 95th Rifles, Tom Plunkett, once 'observed' to an officer in action, 'The words "go on" do not befit a leader Sir.'‡ John Shipp of the 87th wrote of a young officer who, in order to be inconspicuous in action, took off 'his epaulettes from his shoulder and his plate and feather off his cap'. Being ostracized, 'he never re-established his former character; in consequence of which he some time after left the regiment'.§ During his first battle, at Vimeiro, the splendid anonymous soldier of the 71st, sometimes referred to as 'T.S.', felt his 'mind waver'; but 'I looked alongst the line; it was enough to assure me. The steady determined scowl of my companions assured my heart and gave me determination.'★★ Compared to the fields of Vimeiro and Waterloo, from which

★ *Journal of the Waterloo Campaign*, C. Mercer, 1870.
† *Vicissitudes of a Soldier's Life*, J. Green, 1827.
‡ *Adventures of a Soldier*, E. Costello, 1841.
§ *Memoirs*, J. Shipp, 1830.
★★ *The Journal of a Soldier in the 71st Regiment*, Anon, 1819. [Republished as *A Soldier of the 71st*, Ed. C. Hibbert, Leo Cooper, 1975.]

it would have taken courage to run away, the modern battlefield is a lonely place on which wide dispersal and concealment can make the exercise of direct personal leadership very difficult. A young soldier facing his first battle may not have that scowling reassurance which young 'T.S.' found so heartening. He must develop his own resources of courage and determination and have within himself the seeds of leadership. How can we help him?

The answer must lie in the study of military morale; a study which has been one of the most important duties of every leader since Montgomery said, 'The morale of the soldier is the greatest single factor in war.' The morale of his men is an officer's most sacred responsibility. It is one in which doctors should be peculiarly well-qualified to advise, since it is they who must deal with what I call 'the last stage in the failure of a man's personal morale', the so-called psychiatric casualty. This term replaced the unsatisfactory one, shell shock, referred to in this book. My book *Fighting Spirit*, a doctor's contribution to the study of morale, was based upon what I had learned from experience of these cases in battle: and, as a doctor should, I described what I called the anatomy and physiology of morale, before dealing with its pathology – its breakdown – followed by ideas about treatment and prevention. Here, of course, we are concerned only with the pathology, treatment and prevention, because this book deals with the sad subject of the breakdown of a man's morale; and with the crude treatment which the generals believed should help to prevent further cases.

The psychiatric casualty was officially defined as 'the man who becomes ineffective in battle as a direct result of his personality being unable to stand up to the stresses of combat'. Our understanding of men's personalities can be helped by turning to the teachings of the triumvirate to whom I have referred; and of the three I believe Alfred Adler to be the most helpful. All human beings, Adler taught, have a deeply rooted desire for dominance or superiority. We all want to be thought well of, admired, respected and loved. Daydreams and castles in the air are evidence of our striving, partly conscious but, more importantly, unconscious towards what he called 'The Goal of Superiority'. Progress towards this goal is impeded by feelings of inferiority or inadequacy. Adler, though he did not use the term, can be called the father of the inferiority complex, that condition which we are all so ready to diagnose in our associates, and even in ourselves! Feelings of inferiority have been called 'perhaps the most common evil of our times', and Adler and others have asserted that few of us escape them entirely. The fortunate majority grow out of them but far too many men (and it is among them that our potential psychiatric casualty may be found) seize upon any evidence, real or imaginary, of their inferiority, and build up these feelings into a barrier across the path to the unconscious Goal of Superiority. Unwilling to admit true inferiority, the unconscious mind may invent excuses to account for the apparent failure. Such 'excuses' are often in the form of illness. The individual is, as it were, saying, 'I would have done as well as the others but for my poor digestion, my weak heart, my chronic headaches and so on.' The 'excuse' may be more positive, such as paralysis of a limb, blindness, deafness, loss of memory, when it is called Conversion Hysteria. This is one way in which psychogenic or emotional illness may be caused. These terms are nowadays preferable to 'neurotic' and 'hysterical', or even the older distinction between organic and functional illness – the latter conveying the impression of something to be slightly ashamed of, because not 'real'. But although such conditions may exist only in the mind and have no physical basis they are very real to the sufferer. Conversion hysteria, very common in the First World War, was quite rare in the Second. As Lord Southborough believed, the cases of shell shock, the psychiatric casualties, are indeed identical with the psychogenic illness of civilian life; but because the stress of battle is even more severe than the stresses of modern life, they may be more dramatic and intense – panic states, for example, may occur. I found that the barrack room in peacetime was a fertile breeding ground for feelings of inferiority, for reasons I need not define here, as we are considering a problem of wartime, and in war servicemen have an added factor of great importance. When a man puts on a uniform he is expected to put on also the personality of a brave soldier. Field-Marshal Slim defined what I call, '*The Soldier's Goal of Superiority*' when he said, 'I do not believe there is any man who, in his heart of hearts, would not rather be called brave than have any other virtue attributed to him.'*

Men who have deep-seated doubts of their courage, or who fear that their comrades doubt their fighting spirit, may save their faces by developing some form of psychogenic illness, a device of the unconscious mind to provide escape from the intolerable situation without the disgrace of running away. Of course, it has to be admitted that this is difficult territory in which it may be hard to decide if it is a case for the doctor or for discipline. But, reading between the lines in many of the cases described briefly by Judge Babington, malingering or shamming seem less likely than genuinely hysterical states, such as amnesia or fugues.†

During the Second World War many thousands of soldiers did not

* *Courage and Other Broadcasts*, W. Slim, 1957.

† The musical term 'fugue' has been adopted in psychiatry to describe states of disturbed consciousness, during which, for example, patients may wander about and have no subsequent memory of what they have been doing.

await the acid test of battle before taking 'spiritual flight'. Thousands of men were discharged from the Services on medical grounds, predominantly for three types of condition: a) Digestive disorders; b) Disordered Action of the Heart ('D.A.H.') or Effort Syndrome; c) Intractable Skin Diseases. No doubt these men were directed into useful work in industry and many might not have made good soldiers, but it is, I think, inescapable that a considerable wastage of manpower for the Services was, and could be again, attributable to psychogenic conditions. In Freudian terms many, probably most, of these men had no heart, no stomach for the fight – 'D.A.H.' was actually, and absurdly, called 'Soldier's Heart'. And what of the third category? Growing realization that the skin, like other organs of the body, can be greatly affected by emotional influences, is implicit in the comment on these cases by a leading dermatologist: 'They scratched their way out of the common liability *with a good conscience.*' Those last four words deserve emphasis. These men have nothing on their conscience. Blame for such wastage of manpower can be laid squarely upon the doctors. An article by the distinguished civilian Consulting Physician to the British Army showed a failure to comprehend the nature of the problem.★ The well-known physician Lord Moran told me that, after the First World War when he lectured to the Army Staff College about what he had learned in the trenches as Captain Charles Wilson RAMC, some deeply impressed Army officers urged him to write a book, which unfortunately he did not do until 1945. He greatly regretted this and urged me to go ahead with my own book. As I have indicated, doctors can and should proffer advice about morale, but the prime responsibility rests with officers and NCOs. It was often said that the morale of a unit was in the hands of the Commanding Officer, the Medical Officer and the Chaplain. Many great commanders have stressed the importance of sound religious faith. 'There are no atheists in foxholes,' though cynical, is an accurate statement. Men who have received any Christian teaching at their mothers' knees, and even those who have not, do tend to call upon God when afraid in battle.

When lecturing about psychological factors in war I have always defined the essential steps in the maintenance of high morale and the prevention of psychiatric casualties under two headings: a) Regimental Measures and b) Medical Measures. The most important regimental factor in promoting and preserving high morale is, of course, good leadership, which, in fact, ensures that all the other measures are taken care of, such as the wise use of *rest*, and sound *discipline*. Although I am thinking here particularly of leadership at battalion or regimental level

---

★ *Dyspepsia in the Forces*, Sir H. Letheby Tidy, *Journal of the Royal Army Medical Corps*, Vol. 77, 1941.

it also applies right up to the highest level – even perhaps as high as the Government which must convince the modern thinking soldier that he is called upon to risk his life in a just and a necessary war. Judge Babington paints no very warm picture of Haig as a leader. A sound military historian, Major-General E. K. G. Sixsmith, in his biography *Haig* (1976), believes, and cites Lord Trenchard and others in support of his belief, that the Army trusted Haig. Perhaps this is a tribute to the wonderful trusting nature of the good old British soldier, for his soldiers seldom saw him when in action. His Chief of Staff wept when he saw, *after* the battle, what the soldiers had been called upon to endure at Passchendaele. What a contrast to some of our really great leaders. Nelson on his quarterdeck at Trafalgar, his uniform ablaze with orders and decorations, was in full view of his sailors, and, alas, of the French sniper who killed him. Marlborough, old and ill, tramped the trenches in all weathers, to see that too much was not being asked of his men. 'The Duke of Marlborough's attention and care was over us all,' wrote Corporal Matthew Bishop.* Wellington was equally careful of the lives of his men, who were confident when they could see him, anxious when they could not. Montgomery made a cult of being well-known to his soldiers and before any major battle insisted that his intentions should be explained to every single man at appropriate times. Slim was so confident of his men's trust in him that, when a sergeant cried out after one of his talks, 'When the time comes we'll all be behind you,' his general could genially reply, 'Don't you believe it, sergeant; when the day comes you'll all be a long way in front of me.'

The importance of adequate rest and sleep needs no emphasis. Physical and mental exhaustion help to produce the pathological states which we are considering. Not only individuals but units and formations must be rested when possible. When this is impossible leaders must be on the lookout for signs that their men are not wearing well. I always stress that the signs which they must watch for are small changes in men's normal temperament and so on; signs, in fact, which men's most intimate friends are best able to notice. My reason for insisting that such signs are the only ones which should be taken as indications of threatening breakdown will emerge later.

The last regimental factor to which I will refer is discipline. Military authorities insist that discipline on the battlefield of the future may have to be as firm as ever before, if not more so. But good discipline must move with the times, must be an evolving process, and, above all, it must be *acceptable* to those subject to it. The pleasure of reading the memoirs of Wellington's men is often marred by descriptions of

---

* *The Life and Adventures of Mathew Bishop*, 1744.

the terrible floggings. How could our countrymen treat their men like that, we ask; for, although many officers hated it, most of them thought that flogging was indispensable to good discipline. Even the humane Sir John Moore thought so, and so did the men themselves. Sergeant Donaldson of the 94th was almost alone in condemning the practice in words such as we might use today. Some excellent soldiers even attributed their success to a flogging received early in their service, rather in the vein of autobiographers who describe school beatings with almost masochistic relish. Well may French and German writers on psychology call flagellation 'The English Vice'! There were many instances of men approving such punishments; in one case the commanding officer offered to remit the sentence on a man about to be flogged if only one of his comrades would speak up for him. None did; their attitude being presumably one which Bugler Green of the 68th Foot expressed, that flogging was 'absolutely necessary to punish such conduct or no man could live in the army or navy'. Flogging, then, was in its day an *acceptable* form of discipline to all ranks. Some Continental armies were more brutal than ours, but not the French. It would have been unthinkable to flog a soldier of the Revolutionary Army. Wellington, as usual, hit the nail on the head. Telling Lord Stanhope that the French did, in fact 'bang them about very much with ramrods and things, and then they shoot them', he explained that the French Army was completely different to our own because, on account of conscription, men of every social class served together.*
This is a nail which Anthony Babington hits squarely on the head when he writes of the wide social gap which existed between the leaders and most of those whom they led. Haig, like Wellington, was an aristocrat, a friend of his sovereign, accustomed to move in Court circles. Today the gap is much narrower and becomes still narrower when on active service. General Maximilien Sebastien Foy, one of Napoleon's best generals, analysed the differences between the various European armies. He tempered his high praise of the British Army (which his master Napoleon had admired so extravagantly that he said, 'If I had had an English army I would have conquered the Universe') with this criticism:

> In the British army will not be found either the strong sympathy between the leaders and the soldiers, the paternal care of the captains, the simple manners of the subalterns, nor the affectionate fellow-feeling in danger and suffering which constituted the strength of the revolutionary armies of France.†

---

* *Notes of Conversations with the Duke of Wellington*, P. H. Stanhope, 5th Earl, 1888.
† *The Victories of the British Army*, Appendix III, Anon, 1847.

Our army today would surely satisfy General Foy on this score and his noble words 'affectionate fellow-feeling in danger and suffering' beautifully define the surest foundation upon which high morale and good discipline may be built. Now, I am well aware that there will always be military leaders who hold that discipline is the one answer to the problem. Good leaders by firm discipline must prevent the weaker men from yielding to their weakness. Comparisons of the records of certain units with those of others lend support to this view. But I am convinced that discipline by itself is not enough. Discipline is control from without; high morale demands control from within. Good training and the best of regimental measures may be ineffective unless men's minds are prepared for the stress of battle, which is the objective of what I call 'Medical Measures'. It is, of course, regimental officers and NCOs who must carry them out, and must understand the reasoning which underlies them. This reasoning is based upon understanding the psychiatric casualty and how such cases should be handled. Psychogenic disorders, the psychiatric casualties of war and peace, are cured principally by giving the sufferer insight into the nature of his condition, laying bare and explaining the mechanism by which his mind has produced a physical state. The sooner this insight can be given the better the hope of a satisfactory outcome. With every step a soldier takes towards the relative safety of some rearward area the harder it becomes to cure the disability. It is as if the unconscious mind is saying, 'This is working; keep it up if you don't want to be sent back to danger.' Once admit him to hospital or an 'Exhaustion Centre' and you may be sure it will be weeks or months before the psychiatrists find him fit for duty, if they ever do. Having observed during my first major battle, at Keren in Eritrea, how surprisingly easy it was for an ordinary doctor, untrained in psychiatry, to effect what seemed like miracle cures of cases of conversion hysteria and men who were taking their first tentative steps into 'spiritual flight', when one could catch them in the very heat of battle, at the first medical post (the Regimental Aid Post) or even before they reached it, I felt convinced that these conditions could be prevented by giving men the necessary insight before they were exposed to the causal conditions. I put this belief to the test in three subsequent campaigns, including such testing major battles as El Alamein, the invasion of Normandy, the Reichswald and breach of the Siegfried Line, and the assault crossings of the Rhine and Elbe. Of course cynics may say that doctors can always manipulate figures to 'prove' their theories; but I have published statistics to support what follows here.*

---

* *Fighting Spirit. Psychological Factors in War*, Leo Cooper, 1978, pp. 175–176.

Briefly then, a wartime campaign to prevent Combat or Battle Exhaustion should consist of three essential features. Firstly every officer and NCO, and, if time and circumstances allow, every single man in the formation, must know all about the nature and the causes of Battle Exhaustion, and how to spot the warning signs of threatening breakdown. Of course I was told that such widespread knowledge could lead to more cases. Men's reactions could be – if this is just ordinary illness, nothing to be ashamed of, why not 'report sick', join the cosy group discussions at the Exhaustion Centre? Well, of course, there is nothing to be ashamed of, but for all that it was part of my teaching that we must insist that it is a disgrace for a unit to have many such cases *evacuated outside the divisional area*. The disgrace must fall upon the leaders not upon the led; and there must be no stigma whatever upon men who are spotted in time and sent for a good rest at some suitable place within the battalion area or even the brigade area. The value of a sound plan for giving men a good rest in a fairly safe place not too far from the Forward Defended Localities is consider-able. Any such plans should cover guidance to leaders on how to spot signs of threatening breakdown and how to handle such cases. They should be treated sympathetically but firmly and must understand that they are not suffering from any sort of nervous or medical condition, but from the natural result of prolonged strain and danger, a state which a good rest and sleep will soon put right. Realization of the value of such treatment opened my eyes to the wisdom of the American term for these cases – 'Combat Exhaustion', which at first I had rejected. The diagnosis of shell shock had, I knew, conferred upon many cases, unworthy of it, the dignity of a war wound and conse-quent pensions. 'Exhaustion', I insisted, was nearly as bad, since it conveyed the impression of a weary warrior who had fought until he could fight no longer. By that time I had seen plenty of frank cowardice and I could not accept that this American term covered many cases of which I had experience. Always disinclined in any case to adopt 'Americanisms', I resolutely marked the field medical cards of appropriate cases 'Fear Neurosis'. But experience taught me that, for once, 'They' were right and I was wrong. I believe that the preferred term today is 'Battleshock', shorter and simpler perhaps, though arguably a step back to the outmoded shell shock. However, terminology is less important than methods of dealing with cases, which is, of course, much more enlightened than in 1914–1918.

My second recommendation is the inculcation of a competitive spirit among units in the elimination of such cases. Not only should units compete to have the fewest cases, but they should be shown to be disgraced if they have many. This I eventually achieved by the publication in divisional orders of what I called the 'Weekly Health

Ladder', on which was tabulated the incidence by units of preventable sickness, including Exhaustion. All this may sound harsh, but training and preparing for battle cannot be a soft process. Toes may have to be trodden on if lives are not to be lost. Clearly there can be no question of blame or disgrace unless and until the problem has been properly explained and is understood by *all ranks*.

Happily there is nothing harsh or unreasonable about my third requirement. It is by far the most important one because it concerns the emotional factor. Hence it is at the very heart of the problem; and I will pause for a last brief comparison of soldiers today with their 19th Century forbears. Compared with the modern soldier Wellington's men were ill-educated, often illiterate. They read no newspapers; no sensation-seeking journalists played upon their imagination by speculations about alarming new weapons. Simple straightforward peasants most of them; and the journals and memoirs of those with 'book learning' sound simple and straightforward too, though there are exceptions. Less imaginative than is usual today, they were more emotional; or rather they displayed their emotions more openly. They boasted of their courage and successes, shouted 'Hurrah for Old England', and spoke of themselves in the words used by the recruiting posters, as stout lads, bold sons of John Bull who could lick any six of the French. They wept when they felt like it. Wellington, often seen in tears about his casualties and the death of friends, was called 'The Iron Duke'. 'The stiff upper lip' had yet to be invented; public schools had not yet got around to explaining how un-English all that sort of thing is, that emotions must be suppressed. It is generally accepted that the suppression of a natural instinctive emotion may harm the personality. The most important emotion in battle is fear; and I am convinced that a very valuable measure is deliberately to foster a sane attitude to fear. Fear should be openly discussed, perhaps in one of the customary 'Current Affairs' sessions. Everyone must understand that fear is the normal reaction of a normal man to danger. The physical signs of fear should be explained. Rapid action of the heart, trembling, desire to empty the bowel or bladder, are all normal bodily processes when any animals in danger, designed to prepare the body for flight or fight. The trembling, for example, is caused by involuntary muscle activity, warming up the body just as an athlete warms up before a race, helping to speed up the dissociation of oxygen from the blood to generate energy. In the case of the tiger all this activity is in preparation for aggression, the pursuit of his prey; whilst with the seagull, startled on the beach, emptying of the bowel helps to lighten the body for flight. The soldier is expected to cast his lot with the tiger. These normal signs of fear must not be taken as an indication for steps to be taken to avert a threatened 'nervous breakdown', which is why I stressed the kind of thing which one should look out for. A former Director of Army Psychiatry told me that thousands of men were sent out of battle simply because they were showing the signs of fear. Of course one gets over fear; indeed the exhilaration of knowing that one can conquer it may lead to a tendency to 'show off' a bit, deliberately displaying fearlessness in order to encourage others by example. This is sometimes useful, even necessary, but it should not be overdone. A measure of well-judged caution, even some low cunning, are also useful attributes on the battlefield. I am convinced that nothing is lost by openly discussing fear but, while one must insist that there is no disgrace in feeling fear, one can never condone giving way to it. Every man must realize that fear is a normal hazard of the battlefield to be faced up to and overcome in the interests of the unit, his comrades and above all his own self-esteem. When fear is freely discussed, even joked about, it can lose its terror. It is particularly helpful to young soldiers, untried in battle, to know that they are not alone in feeling fear. This is especially valuable in the reception into a battle-hardened unit of young reinforcements before they have had time to absorb regimental tradition and comradeship, a process which demands great care, which was conspicuously lacking in some instances referred to by Judge Babington. Vague references to men being 'bomb-happy', surely one of the stupidest expressions coined in War, must be replaced by widespread understanding of the nervous strain of war, the causes, nature and prevention of the psychiatric casualty.

I know from experience that the kind of preventive campaign which I have outlined here could be valuable in a lengthy war but it is perhaps doubtful if we are likely ever to have to engage in such a war again. However, I believe that Army training could do a lot, by what I have long been advocating under the name of 'Mental Training' to prepare soldiers for a war whether long or short. I was disgusted by a War Office pronunciamento in 1957 that '*Mental Endurance, though vital in War, cannot be properly catered for in peacetime training.*' After retiring from the Army I was given the opportunity for many years to urge, at an annual lecture at the Army Staff College in Camberley, that Mental Training should be accorded as prominent and valued a place as Physical Training. Although those who have heard and approved my views have included Lord Alanbrooke and many very senior general officers, I doubt whether the Army will ever go as far in this direction as I recommend in my book (*Fighting Spirit* pp. 124–139), though I have recently heard that things have been moving satisfactorily. But I must not use Judge Babington's most interesting book to 'trail my coat'. Readers with any knowledge of the British Army, even those avowedly hostile to all it stands for, will know that nothing like the heart-rending events related here could ever happen again.

In conclusion I will re-emphasize two points. Lord Moran's analogy of the 'bank balance' serves to remind us that every soldier, however brave and resolute, has his breaking point. Of two broad groups of men especially liable to succumb I have concentrated on 'the immature, scared, young soldier'. The second group is at the other end of the military spectrum: the seasoned old soldier, often an NCO, who has served through many campaigns, supporting others but at the cost of drawing too heavily on his own resources. He is just worn out. In the Armed Services it is the RAF who have studied this subject most exhaustively, because the exceptionally demanding experience of aerial combat must surely accelerate the wearing-out process; and they know that it is unwise to drive a man, or more usually to allow him to drive himself, beyond the limit of endurance. American military writers have attempted to quantify the period of involvement in the combat zone which should make it advisable to withdraw a soldier, temporarily or permanently, to other duties. I am a little doubtful about whether mathematical rules can apply in this field, since human nature is so variable. Such decisions are probably best left to experienced commanding officers; which brings me to the second point which I want to make again. My 'doctor's contribution to the study of military morale' led to the prescription of 'medical measures'. These can have no value unless they are put into effect by officers and NCOs. The opinions of soldiers with experience of men in battle may often carry more weight than those of some psychiatrists who know men in the consulting room, where they usually deal with those who have problems (though I could name a few who combined experience at 'the sharp end' with specialist knowledge of psychiatry). I would not go so far as Winston Churchill, who openly expressed distrust of 'these gentlemen, who are capable of doing an immense amount of harm with what may very easily degenerate into charlatanry',* but I adhere to the opinion expressed in *Fighting Spirit*, which I like to think enshrines an aphorism:

The saying '*War is much too serious a thing to be left to military men*' has been attributed to both Talleyrand and Clemenceau. At the risk of being thought a traitor to my profession, I am content that the opinion that '*The problem of the psychiatric casualty is much too serious to be left to the doctors*' should be attributed to me.

---

* Quoted in full in *The Second World War*, Vol. IV, pp. 814–815.

APPENDIX: TRACEABLE EXECUTIONS IN THE BRITISH ARMY – 1914–1920

Table 1: Traceable Executions in the British Army – from the outbreak of war until the end of 1914 (France and Belgium)

Desertion	...	...	...	3
Cowardice	...	...	...	1
Total	...	...	...	4

Table 2: Traceable Executions in the British Army – 1915

	Desertion	Cowardice	Quitting Post	Disobedience	Murder	Total
France & Belgium	45	3	1		2	51
Gallipoli	1		1			2
Salonika				1		1
Cameroons		1				1
Total	46	4	2	1	2	55

Table 3: Traceable Executions in the British Army – 1916

	Desertion	Cowardice	Quitting Post	Disobedience	Striking a Superior Officer	Casting Away Arms	Mutiny	Murder	Total
France & Belgium	71	10	2	2	3		1	4	93
Gallipoli				1					1
German East Africa						1			1
Total	71	10	2	3	3	1	1	4	95

Table 4: Traceable Executions in the British Army – 1917

	Desertion	Cowardice	Quitting Post	Disobedience	Striking Superior Officer	Casting Away Arms	Mutiny	Sleeping on Post	Murder	Total
France & Belgium	86	1	2	1		1	2		1	94
Salonika	2	1							1	4
Mesopotamia	2							2		4
Palestine									1	1
Egypt					1					1
Total	90	2	2	1	1	1	2	2	3	104

Table 5: Traceable Executions in the British Army – 1918

	Desertion	Quitting Post	Murder	Total
France & Belgium	34	1	9	44
Salonika	1			1
Portuguese East Africa	—	—	1	1
Total	35	1	10	46

Table 6: Traceable Executions in the British Army – 1919

	Murder
France & Belgium	9
Turkey	4
Total	13

Table 7: Traceable Executions in the British Army – 1 January to 31 May 1920

	Murder
France & Belgium	2
Egypt	2
Turkey	1
Total	5

BIBLIOGRAPHY

The following is a list of the published sources to which reference has been made.

Reports etc.

Report from His Majesty's Commissioners for Inquiring into the System of Military Punishments in the Army, 1836.

War Office Return of Courts-Martial, 1853–1856.

War Office Return of Courts-Martial, 1899–1902.

Report of the Committee appointed to Consider the Education and Training of the Officers of the Army, 1902.

Manual of Military Law, 1914.

Directorate of Graves Registration and Enquiries, Instructions for the Burial of the Dead, June, 1917.

Report of the Committee Constituted by the Army Council to Enquire into the Law and Rules of Procedure Regulating Military Courts-Martial, 1919.

Report of the War Office Committee of Enquiry into Shell-Shock, 1922.

Statistics of the Military Effort of the British Empire During the Great War, 1922 (part XXIII – Discipline).

Report of the Interdepartmental Committee on Proposed Disciplinary Amendments to the Army and Air Force Acts, 1925.

Imperial War Museum, Department of Sound Records, Oral History Recordings, Western Front 1914–1918, (Interviews recorded between 1973 and 1975).

Hansard, Reports of Proceedings in Parliament.

Journals and magazines

Blackwood's Magazine
John Bull
Contemporary Review
Law Quarterly Review
Past and Present
Queen's Quarterly

Pamphlet

Shootings at Dawn. The Army Death Penalty at Work, by Ernest Thurtle MP, 1924.

Official histories

The History of the Great War, Military Operations, France and Belgium.
The History of the Great War, Military Operations, Gallipoli.
The History of the Great War, Military Operations, Salonika and Macedonia.
The Official History of Australia in the War of 1914 to 1918, Vol. 5.

Books

Ascoli, David, *The Mons Star, The British Expeditionary Force 5th Aug–22nd Nov. 1914* (London, Harrap, 1981)

Allison, William and John Fairly, *The Monocled Mutineer* (London, Quartet Books, 1978)

Asquith, Raymond, *Life and Letters*, edited by John Joliffe (London, Collins, 1980)

Bancroft, George Pleydell, *Stage and Bar* (London, Faber & Faber, 1939)

Barker, A. J., *The Neglected War, Mesopotamia* (London, Faber & Faber, 1967)

Baynes, John, *Morale, A Study of Men and Courage* (London, Cassell, 1967)

Behrend, Arthur, *As From Kemmel Hill* (London, Eyre & Spottiswoode, 1963)

Bloem, Walter, *The Advance from Mons 1914* (London, Peter Davies, 1930. Published in Germany in 1916)

Blunden, Edmund, *Undertones of War* (London, Collins, 1928)

Brittain, Vera, *Chronicle of Youth, War Diary 1913–1917* (London, Gollancz, 1981)

Clode, Charles M., *Military Forces of the Crown* (London, John Murray, 1869)

Connell, John, *Wavell, Scholar and Soldier* (London, Collins, 1964)

Cooper, Duff, *Haig* (London, Faber & Faber, 1936)

Dearden, Harold, *Medicine & Duty* (London, Heinemann, 1928)

Dictionary of National Biography (Oxford, Oxford University Press)

Dunham, Frank, *The Long Carry* (Oxford, Pergamon, 1970)

Farrar-Hockley, Anthony, *Goughie* (London, Hart-Davis, 1975)

Gordon, Huntley, *The Unreturning Army* (London, Dent, 1967)

Gladden, Norman, *The Somme 1916* (London, William Kimber, 1974)

Gladden, Norman, *Ypres 1917* (London, William Kimber, 1967)

Glubb, John, *Into Battle* (London, Cassell, 1978)

Graham, Stephen, *A Private in the Guards* (London, Macmillan, 1919)

Graves, Robert, *Goodbye to All That* (London, Jonathan Cape, 1929)

Grose, Francis, *Military Antiquities* (London, 1801)

Hart, B. H. Liddell, *The Memoirs of Captain Liddell Hart* (London, Cassell, 1965)

Hart, B. H. Liddell, *History of the First World War* (London, Cassell, 1970)

Herbert, A. P., *The Secret Battle* (London, Methuen, 1919)

Lambert, Arthur, *Over the Top* (London, John Long, 1930)

Longford, Elizabeth, *Wellington. The Years of the Sword* (London, Weidenfeld & Nicolson, 1969)

Magnus, Philip, *Kitchener, Portrait of an Imperialist* (London, John Murray, 1958)

Moore, William, *The Thin Yellow Line* (London, Leo Cooper, 1974)

Moran, Lord, *The Anatomy of Courage* (London, Constable, 1945)

Pollock, Sam, *Mutiny For The Cause* (London, Leo Cooper, 1969)

Pound, Reginald, *A. P. Herbert* (London, Michael Joseph, 1976)

Remarque, Erich Maria, *All Quiet on the Western Front* (London, Putnam, 1929)

Sassoon, Siegfried, *Memoirs of an Infantry Officer* (London, Faber & Faber, 1930)

Sassoon, Siegfried, *Sherston's Progress* (London, Faber & Faber, 1936)

Taylor, A. J. P., *English History 1914–1945* (Oxford, Clarendon Press, 1965)

Vaughan, Edwin Campion, *Some Desperate Glory, The Diary of a Young Officer, 1917* (London, Frederick Warne, 1981)

Walker-Smith, Derek, *The Life of Lord Darling* (London, Cassell, 1938)

INDEX